Re-Creating America

Re-Creating America

The Ethics of U.S. Immigration and Refugee Policy in a Christian Perspective

Dana W. Wilbanks

ABINGDON PRESS / Nashville

in cooperation with
THE CHURCHES' CENTER
FOR THEOLOGY AND PUBLIC POLICY
Washington, D.C.

RE-CREATING AMERICA
THE ETHICS OF U.S. IMMIGRATION AND REFUGEE POLICY
IN A CHRISTIAN PERSPECTIVE

This book is printed on recycled, acid-free, elemental chlorine–free paper.

Library of Congress Cataloging-in-Publication Data

Wilbanks, Dana W.
    Re-creating America: the ethics of U.S. immigration and refugee
policy in a Christian perspective/Dana W. Wilbanks.
       p.   cm.—(The Churches' Center for Theology and Public
Policy)
    Includes bibliographical references and index.
    ISBN 0-687-00444-6 (pbk.: alk. paper)
    1. United States—Emigration and immigration—Government policy—
Moral and ethical aspects.   2. Refugees—Government policy—Moral
and ethical aspects—United States.   3. Emigration and immigration—
Religious aspects—Christianity.   I. Title.   II. Series: Churches'
Center for Theology and Public Policy (Series)
JV6483.W53   1996
241'.622—dc20   96-28840
                                                                  CIP

Scripture quotations are from the New Revised Standard Version Bible, copyright © 1989, by the Division of Christian Education of the National Council of the Churches of Christ in the United States of America.

96 97 98 99 00 01 02 03 04 05—10 9 8 7 6 5 4 3 2 1

MANUFACTURED IN THE UNITED STATES OF AMERICA

To Linda

CONTENTS

ACKNOWLEDGMENTS

I want to express appreciation first of all for a vibrant and supportive communal context at the Iliff School of Theology. The Board of Trustees, with the support of President Donald Messer, Dean Jane Smith, and faculty colleagues, granted me a sabbatical leave for the 1992–1993 academic year to undertake the research for this book.

We are blessed at Iliff with wonderful students and staff. I am grateful especially for research assistance from Jeanette Baust and Gail Murphy-Geiss, and for bibliographical help from Robert Miller, Kirk Van Gilder and Donna Patterson. Robert also carefully proofread the final copy. Tisa Anders, Brook Bollinger, and Gichan Nam read and commented on a nearly completed draft of this book in a special seminar that dealt with ethics and migration policies. In the early stages of the book Margaret Manion provided excellent assistance in revising and formatting the manuscript; and Shirley Kaaz skillfully aided me in preparing the completed manuscript, including the bibliography.

Faculty colleagues generously contributed their reflections on my work at two different faculty gatherings and in a number of instances responded to specific requests for information and counsel. I also received written and oral comments from faculty and students in a Ph.D. Colloquium in the Area of Religion and Social Change after a session in which I presented some of my work. It is hard to imagine how I could have completed this book without this rich context for research, reflection, and dialogue.

ACKNOWLEDGMENTS

I am also extremely grateful to Barbara Harrell-Bond, the director, as well as the very helpful staff, at the Refugee Studies Programme at Oxford University (U.K.) for an exceptionally valuable six-month sojourn as a visiting research fellow in 1993. I cannot imagine a better setting for research on migration policies. The documentation center, the quality of courses, the diversity and insights of students and research fellows, the range of scholars in migration studies who participated in lectures and discussions, the opportunity to present a lecture at a refugee studies programme seminar, and access to Oxford University itself, provided exactly what I needed. I am especially grateful to my office-mate Abbas Shiblak and to Charles Keely and Andrew Shacknove, who gave insightful comments on my work and generously shared their time and expertise with me during my time at Oxford.

Migration studies is a major arena of research in fields such as international law, political science, history, sociology, and anthropology. But there has been very little ethical reflection on the subject from philosophical and theological perspectives. I am grateful to the organizers of two recent international and interdisciplinary consultations on ethics and migration for the invitation to respond to several of the papers prepared for these occasions.

I am grateful to Philippe Van Parijs for an invitation to participate in a consultation on "The Ethics of Transnational Migration" at the Université Catholique de Louvain in Louvain-la-Nueve, Belgium, in April 1993. The consultation was constructed around a series of essays by Joseph Carens, and I was invited to respond to two of them in a session devoted to "Refugees and the Limits of Obligation." For the liveliness of the consultation, the intellectual significance of Joe Carens's contribution to ethical reflection on migration policy, and the overall hospitality of Philippe Van Parijs, I express my warmest appreciation.

I would also like to express my appreciation to Lydio Tomasi, Executive Director of the Center for Migration Studies, for an invitation to respond to two papers on religious traditions and migration in a conference on "Ethics, Migration and Global Stewardship: Towards International Consensus?" at Georgetown University in September, 1995. The leadership of this center in migration studies is extraordinary.

10

My first major exposure to migration issues was as a member of the Task Force of the General Assemblies of United Presbyterian Church U.S.A. and the Presbyterian Church U.S. on "Mexican Migration." I am especially grateful for the staff leadership of Dean Lewis, Director of the Advisory Council on Church and Society (UPUSA). This task force prepared a study and policy recommendations that were adopted by the assemblies in 1981. Not only did I learn a great deal about the issues, I was also struck by how little had been written on migration questions from a Christian ethical perspective. I also benefited from membership on a working group that prepared the draft of a Presbyterian response to the Immigration Reform and Control Act (1986), which was approved by the General Assembly in 1990.

My work with the Advisory Council on Church and Society in the 1980s also put me in touch with the courageous and imaginative Christians who were involved in the sanctuary movement to protect refugees from Central America. This powerful witness, more than anything else, has shaped my interest in and perspective about U.S. migration policies.

I am indebted as well to the encouragement and support of James Nash of the Churches' Center for Theology and Public Policy for including this book in its jointly sponsored series with Abingdon Press.

In conclusion, I have been helped by many friends too numerous to mention who have expressed interest in this project and generously passed along resources and ideas. I am tremendously grateful for my family. My son and daughter-in-love, David and Wendy Wilbanks, clipped newspaper articles and flagged books at the Tattered Cover book store, where both of them work. My daughter, Caren Wilbanks, helped me hone my thinking in conversations about the book. My mother, Elsie Pritchard, and her husband Francis Pritchard, who has been father to me for the past twenty years, have provided enthusiastic support, articles, and stimulating discussions. My wife, Linda, has a great eye for pertinent articles in the newspapers and publications that flood into our home, and she has encouraged me unceasingly without ever expressing the exasperation I was feeling myself about how long it was taking me to finish this project.

Soon after I sent the draft of this book to the editors at Abingdon, our beloved daughter Caren died at age twenty-five. Caren's vibrancy

11

ACKNOWLEDGMENTS

in times of health and her courage in the struggle with mental illness are gifts that help us live through the grief and face a future without her presence. I dedicate this book to my wife, Linda, with love and with gratitude for our life together, which nourishes joy and hope in the midst of sorrow.

INTRODUCTION

We've always managed, despite our worst, unbelievably nativist actions to rejuvenate ourselves, to bring in new people. Every new group comes in believing more firmly in the American Dream than the one that came a few years before. . . . They go to night school, they learn about America. We'd be lost without them. . . . The old dream is still dreamt.[1]

Immigration evokes a range of often conflicting impressions and feelings for U.S. citizens. While many profess pride in the immigrant heritage of the United States, they often also express deep anxiety about too many current immigrants. While there is a desire for cheap labor for "menial" jobs, there is worry that immigrants are taking jobs away from U.S. citizens. While many persons in the United States support humanitarian aid for refugees abroad, they may at the same time resist receiving them in the United States.

Almost everyone agrees that immigration historically has been a positive ingredient in the shaping of the United States. A major part of this country's identity is its immigrant character. All but Native Americans can claim immigrant ancestry. Often this is experienced in quite personal ways. Many people in the United States spend a great deal of time and money tracing their ancestry back to the "old country." Family stories are told with great gusto about grandmothers and great-grandfathers who courageously came to the New World and struggled against severe odds to fashion a new life. Some came for religious freedom, others for political freedom, while still others, very likely the largest number, came to escape economic hardship or stifling social constraints and to seek out a better life.

The Statue of Liberty continues to function as one of the most powerful symbols of the distinctive meaning of this nation. Members of this country like to think of ourselves as a people who welcome the persecuted and downtrodden of other lands. Former president Ronald Reagan invoked this national ideal in his farewell presidential address. He extolled the United States as "still a beacon, still a magnet

. . . for all the Pilgrims from all lost places who are hurtling through the darkness toward home."[2]

Our national self-image is bound up with our immigrant heritage—a diverse people united by common allegiance to the United States, its Constitution, and its promise of freedom and opportunity. *E pluribus unum*—"Out of many one." Central to the national narrative (the story we tell ourselves about our country) is the theme that the United States welcomes diversity among its peoples and represents a perhaps unique experiment in fashioning a heterogeneous society in which members can pull together and get along even as they maintain significant differences.

Increasingly, also, people in the United States appreciate the multicultural character of communities with new and interesting types of food, arts and crafts, festivals, and dress. For some, surely, multiculturalism provides release from the confinement of parochialisms and an opening toward a more adventurous and richly textured life. Quite apart from such quest for meaning, however, some persons become bored with sameness and respond favorably to differentness and novelty. Julian Simon, for example, states that his preference for more immigrants is partly a matter of taste. "I delight in looking at the variety of faces that I see on the subway when I visit New York, and I mark with pleasure the range of costumes and the languages of the newspapers the people are reading."[3] While of course some would not share his sentiment, many of us do.

Yet, even more than with some other policy questions, there are other points of view. Immigration often evokes negative feelings and impressions as well. Immigrants are frequently perceived as strangers. Not only do we not know them, they look and act different. They may speak a different language, have different skin hue and facial characteristics, use different gestures, and exhibit differences in lifestyle. Their "strangeness" may make others wary, or fearful, or even hostile. The cultural distance is often unsettling to resident Americans.

These feelings are especially acute around race, in which peoples are categorized by skin color. White citizens often continue to have negative images of peoples of color. Thus, when white Americans are positive about immigration, they are frequently selective. If we are talking about "my kind of people," then it may be a quite different matter from when we are considering "those people."

United States citizens often state their perception that immigrants are flooding large cities and contributing to, if not directly causing, major urban ills: crime, drugs, drain on publicly supported social services, poor public schools, and neighborhood conflicts. Many worry that the border between the United States and Mexico is "out of control," with the constant entry of large numbers of "illegal aliens" into an already immigrant-saturated society. Very recently, some Americans feared that with only the slightest encouragement Haitians were poised en masse to join the desperate boat people in an effort to get to Miami. Another commonly expressed anxiety is that U.S. society is becoming increasingly divided by language and culture, thereby threatening cohesion and unity in many local communities as well as in the nation as a whole.

The United States has a divided mind and heart about immigration. This, in fact, is not new. Much of American history exhibits similar tensions and conflicts. Debates between restrictionists and inclusionists, cultural monists and pluralists, nativists and cosmopolitanists, have been vigorous and frequently bitter. As the struggles continue, the United States will redefine itself over and over again. New circumstances will render certain arguments obsolete while other long-submerged views will reappear in new form. Immigration policy is one of the most important arenas in U.S. public life for shaping and reshaping the character of the national community.

Above all, immigration has been characterized from the first by the brutalities of racism. The United States is one of those countries in which immigrants became the dominant power elite in relation to existing peoples of the land. White immigrants came from Europe to seek freedom and opportunity of one sort or another, and they quickly sought to control, conquer, or expel the various Native American peoples. White immigrants claimed the land as a divinely granted entitlement over which they were given authority. While immigration may be celebrated in the lore of many current U.S. citizens, it can hardly be celebrated within Native American communities whose peoples and ways of life have suffered grievously under its impact.

Additionally, the primary non-European migrant group to the colonies and the United States in early years was a cruelly forced migration, that is, Africans brought as slaves to this land. They were ripped away from their homelands, forced into chains in the hellholes of slave ships, delivered to the shores of the New World where they were sold like cattle into chattel slavery, with members of still intact

15

families dispersed as leaves in the wind. The forced migration of Africans is a critical feature of the settling of what came to be the United States as a cruel contradiction to the promise of freedom that animated so much of European immigration.

This contradiction, vividly disclosed in the relation of Euro-Americans to both Native Americans and African Americans, reveals the racism that has profoundly shaped the U.S. story from the first. Indeed, as Vincent Harding has argued, there was in fact no contradiction because the Euro-American dream of freedom was white supremacist at its core, and it would not yield to a more inclusive vision of freedom without terribly costly struggles.[4]

The story of immigration to the United States has been intertwined with racism from the outset. White supremacy has been further exhibited in Asian exclusion laws, discrimination against "darker" whites from southern and central Europe, explicitly racist quotas, and exploitation (e.g., Mexican migrants). Throughout U.S. history, immigrants have experienced mild to vicious resistance from settled members. Even so, immigration has unquestionably contributed to the "coloring of America," a development of a more multiracial and multicultural country, celebrated by some and deplored by others. Race remains at the center of current debates about migration policies, even when it is not explicitly articulated.

As one begins to examine current views about U.S. immigration and refugee policy, an odd feature becomes particularly evident. There is no telling with which side "conservatives" or "liberals" may be aligned.[5] Some conservatives support more open borders; others want U.S. policy to be more restrictive. The same observation can be made about liberals. It is certainly unusual to find Christian activists influenced by liberation theology to be on the same side of a policy question as proponents of free market capitalism. One can find this in debates about immigration. And it is also unusual to find environmental and political liberals aligned with very right-wing conservatives. This too happens in the advocacy for more restrictive immigration policies.

Another odd feature of the migration policy landscape to an ethicist is that very little has been written on ethical perspectives about these matters. Given the controversial character of immigration and its impact on the character of the U.S. national community, it is surprising that it has received so little attention in philosophical, political, and religious ethics. Specifically in the field of Christian ethics, I cannot think of a comparable public policy question about which there are so few substantive books and essays. While churches have been involved in profoundly important ways in supporting ministries with immigrants and refugees, and while a number of Christian denominations have prepared studies and reports about migration, there has been little critical reflection about the public policy issues from a Christian perspective.

As we begin this study, we enter into the middle of the story. We have a legacy of the past about which there is considerable pain and pride, and even a fair amount of agreement about how the story should be told. However, even though this agreement is significant, and even though the conflicts were just as intense in the past as they are now, this appeal to the past does not help much in dealing with the current debate. For example, critics of liberal admission policies today seldom make their case on the basis of overtly racial arguments as many did who held restrictionist views in the past.[6] For the most part these contemporary critics reject such arguments. Often they agree that immigration in the past has been largely beneficial for the United States. But they contend that there are different circumstances now that require a more restrictive policy as the United States responds to a different historical situation.

It is not the interpretation of the past that is contested now as much as it is the present and the future. There are radically different views about what is happening and where we are or should be going in terms of societal membership. Policy will be the provisional response to questions and convictions about migration. Policy will set a course for inventing and reinventing the United States. What should be the primary features of U.S. immigration and refugee policy? Which ethical perspectives shall we bring to bear on this policy question? Should the United States become more or less restrictive in its admissions? Who should be given priority in relation to the available slots? Who will be admitted and who will be turned away?

In this book I am especially interested in developing a Christian perspective on migration policy questions. I do not presume that Christian ethics will lead directly to policy solutions. But I do believe Christians can bring an orientation to migration issues that is significant not only for the church's own service ministries, but also for shaping the policies of the national community.

I agree with the proponents of public theology that Christians need to participate in the public arena with their own distinctive voice. However, Christian involvement in the struggle over migration policy should not be simply that of another partisan voice on one side or another. We should also be contributors to the dynamic task of shaping the public moral ethos that undergirds and informs policy enactments. What, then, are the contributions of Christian communities to public discourse, activism, and decision making on immigration and refugee policy?

We can readily see that Christian ethical reflection about immigration and refugee policy involves addressing a number of perennial questions in Christian social ethics, though many of these questions are being raised in fresh ways. What is the relation of Christian ethics and "American" ethics? the ethics of church and of American society? the character of the church and the character of American nationality? What is the responsibility of Christians in public life? What is the responsibility of the United States to its own members and to other peoples in the world? In other words, Christian ethical reflection needs to deal with questions not only about just and humane national migration policies, but also about the relation of Christians to national communities of which they are part.

The historical situatedness of migration issues raises a further set of issues which are germane for my study. Questions are being raised about the adequacy of the paradigm of national sovereignty for dealing with international relations. Similarly, what is the meaning of national borders in an interdependent world? What are the problematics and opportunities of multiculturalism, ethnicity, race, and nationality in fashioning contemporary societies?

A post–Cold War world opens both new possibilities and new threats. The movement from modernity to postmodernity, or whatever it is we are moving toward or already in, places us in a historical period of unsettledness. We are in a time of tremendous groaning and struggling for a new historical creation of some sort, whose shape still eludes us. Glenn Gray, in the midst of World War II, wrote about seeing Italian refugees traveling in large covered wagons, reminding him for a moment of American pioneers. But everything else was different. "With an aching heart I reflected on this regression from pioneers to refugees and wondered if some future historian might not find these terms characteristic of the nineteenth and twentieth centuries."[7] Fifty years later, this is still the century of the refugee as masses of persons continue to move in search of a safe place to live.

In the chapters ahead I shall describe and analyze the recent developments in U.S. policy on immigration and refugees. I shall emphasize the primary features of U.S. policy, the issues around which there are the most serious debates, and the moral dimensions of migration policy questions. The next section will explore selected normative theories in Christian ethics that can provide perspectives on immigration and refugee policy. Then, in the final section, I shall present my own interpretations and conclusions regarding a Christian ethical perspective on U.S. policy. The concrete historical experience of the sanctuary movement is paradigmatic for my viewpoint.

In this book I intend to describe issues and arguments in a way that is fair to the proponents of widely differing views. However, I shall also argue explicitly for a migration policy that continues to welcome newcomers and favors those in greatest need for a place of safety and opportunity. In my interpretation of Christian ethics, I draw insights from liberation thought, narrative ethics, and public theology. From liberation thought, I draw the importance of social location and solidarity with the poor. From public theology, I draw the importance of contributing Christian perspectives to public discourse and decision making about policy questions. From narrative ethics, I draw the importance of the particularity of the Christian moral tradition and of the church as a community of witness as well as advocacy. I do not view my position as ideal ethical theory but as a description and elaboration of that which has recently been historically enacted in the sanctuary movement. In other words, I believe Christian reflection about immigration and refugee policies needs to emerge from the experience of solidarity with the poor.

Recent Developments

In the past fifteen years, the United States has enacted major legislation on immigration and refugee policy. In 1980 the United States adopted a landmark refugee policy that sought to bring our country into compliance with international law governing refugees. In 1986, after eight years of study and congressional debates, and in specific response to the continuing entrance of large numbers of undocumented workers into the United States, the Immigration

19

Reform and Control Act (IRCA) was passed. This act was further modified in rather surprising ways in 1990, leading the president of the National Council of La Raza, Raul Yzaguirre, to comment: "Votes in both the House and Senate shattered the myth that Congress is unwilling to adopt fair, humane, generous immigration policies."[8]

The upshot of these policy developments and the migration trends to which they responded is that the United States has admitted a greater number of newcomers than ever before in its history. It is remarkable that this happened during a time when presumably the public was becoming alarmed about too many illegal immigrants from Mexico and too many asylum seekers from the Caribbean.[9] Scholars are quick to point out that the percentage of newcomers to the settled population is still substantially smaller than the large-scale immigration around the turn of the century. Still the accomplishment of a largely successful movement of high numbers of newcomers into U.S. communities is cause for no little wonder. While the very serious problems should not be ignored, the societal achievements need to be proclaimed more resoundingly than the rhetoric of the alarmists.

But how rapidly the political winds can shift! The change was represented most dramatically by the approval of Proposition 187 by California voters. Here voters expressed resentments against undocumented workers in particular, perhaps all types of newcomers more generally, even though all were not specifically targeted. Political representatives tended to move toward more restrictionist positions, believing that this responds to the popular mood of the times. Early in the 1990s even, immigration was a back burner issue; but now in the mid-1990s it is at the center of public life.

So far I have not drawn a clear distinction between immigrant and refugee. I have frequently referred to both under the more general term of "migrant." I suspect for most persons in the United States there is only the vaguest impression about the distinction. Both immigrant and refugee tend to get lumped together as migrants attempting to enter the United States to seek a better life. Refugee advocates especially insist on the importance of the distinction. *Refugee* refers to those persons who are forced to flee their homeland and cross a national border in order to seek safety due to a "well-founded fear of persecution." Refugees are often called "forced migrants." If they were not vulnerable to the genuine possibility of death, torture, or other forms of dangerous victimization, then they would remain in their homeland.

Immigrants, on the other hand, are those who choose to leave their homeland in order to search for better or other life opportunities elsewhere. Although they may be experiencing severe hardship in their native country, they are not subject to explicit persecution that is directed personally at them. They are not compelled to leave, as the refugee is. Because of this distinction, the refugee can make a legal claim on national states and the international community whereas the immigrant cannot. Refugees are dealt with in terms of refugee law for which there are standards in international agreements; whereas immigrants are treated by policies that are at the discretion of nation-states. Although there are many problems with these operative definitions, we shall adopt them provisionally, and return to the questions raised by these definitions later in the analysis.

Using the conventional distinctions, the moral case for admitting the refugee seems on the face of it to be stronger than the case for admitting the immigrant. Yet both seek to enter the United States, both are newcomers and strangers to be incorporated in communities and the larger society. Both raise questions about what kinds of would-be migrants should be given priority within the finite constraints of emotional, financial, and social resources of the settled population. It is unavoidable to treat immigration and refugee policy together, even as it is essential to keep the distinctions clear and the policies governing each separable.

I shall use the term *migrant* when I am referring to both refugees and immigrants. I realize the term *migrant* can also be confusing because we may associate it with migrant farm workers who move from crop to crop inside the United States, and who may or may not be labor immigrants who come from outside the United States. Nonetheless I shall risk this ambiguity because of the need for one word to refer to all those who enter or seek to enter the United States from another country.

Viewpoints regarding the admission of migrants to the United States involve a complex tangle of both empirical and normative judgments. Some argue that there are "too many." But how many is too many? Data may be pointed to that support the case that the United States cannot continue to admit current numbers because it costs too much or causes too many problems. But other data can be used to support the case that migrants on the whole are benefiting the country. I do not want to say that careful assessment of data is unimportant. Still, how one reads the data or which data one draws on depends a great deal on one's values. Whether or not the admission of immigrants and refugees is viewed as a good thing, it is not simply a matter of data analysis but also of perspective.

Metaphors of Migrants and Migration

This complex interrelation of so-called fact and value is vividly represented in the metaphorical discourse about immigration and refugee policy. Some metaphors play on the lure of the United States and the relative openness or restrictiveness of U.S. policy. To gain admission one must get through a door or a gate. The image of "Golden Door"[10] suggests a coveted entryway into the United States, which opens into a life of prosperity. Or perhaps the gold in the door is now tarnished.[11] Maybe the door is no longer open or, if open, it no longer provides an entrance to a wonderful life. *Still the Golden Door*[12] conveys a sense that people from developing nations still regard the United States as a land of opportunity, perhaps their greatest hope. "Promised Land"[13] functions intentionally as a religious metaphor to depict the promise of a new and bounteous life for those who can cross over.

The "Guarded Gate"[14] suggests there is still an entryway into the land of promise, but the way inside is carefully controlled with even the threat of force to keep some people from coming in. These images depict immigrants and refugees as supplicants who come to the door to knock with a great desire to enter. The United States controls the door or gate and determines who gets in and who is kept out. Yet it is also true that migrants seek ways to bypass the door and get in another way. It may be the "back door," implying that there are still ways to get in even if the policy seeks to keep them out. Or there is the "executive window,"[15] which points to the power of the U.S. president to open the way for certain migrants. The door imagery suggests that many want in and the U.S. heritage supports a relatively open door especially for the persecuted, but in fact the door is only half-open or carefully guarded in order to restrict entrance. The reality is different from the mythology of the national narrative.

Other images focus on the movement of immigrant and refugee. Frequently they are water metaphors, evoking emotional responses and implying the necessity for certain actions. It may be "waves,"[16] suggesting a succession of large-scale movements followed by smaller-scale migrations, perhaps shifting from one part of the world to another. This image implies that the movements are likely to continue and must be accommodated but that current patterns are likely to change. Or the movement may be a trickle, stream, flood, or even a tidal wave. If indeed current migration into the United States is a flood, then the threat of catastrophe signals the need for effective barriers in order to prevent massive damage. If, however, migration is a stream, we see a more gentle picture of a steady and relatively benign flow that needs only to be channeled and appreciated. Or, depending on the context in discourse, one may get the sense of a constant and perhaps unending movement of many persons, which may swamp the United States unless something is done to control the flow.

Metaphors are also used to depict the migrants themselves. None is as heavily loaded as "alien," implying a being entirely different from "us" and perhaps even a frightening creature. Response to the presence of aliens is to seek protection as the overriding concern with no sense that we are somehow humanly related. Yet if migrants are not aliens but friends or neighbors,[17] then they are to be welcomed into our circle of relationships, not feared. If migrants are "huddled masses," as the poem by Emma Lazarus inscribed on the Statue of Liberty depicts them, then they are large numbers of nameless and faceless persons who cling together as victims of persecution or deprivation. The appropriate response to this perception is to take them in, yet perhaps in a paternalistic sense that does not take adequate account of their own agency as persons and communities.

How are migrants and the dynamics of migration to be viewed? If migration is a "time bomb,"[18] then it must be stopped quickly before it explodes in horrors of violence and destructiveness. If migrants are still to be regarded as the "tired," "poor," "huddled masses yearning to breathe free," whom the United States gladly welcomes as central to its national character, then the United States must continue to admit migrants even as it seeks justly and humanely to handle the pressures that large-scale migration brings to existing communities. Data and perspective are deeply interrelated in debates about migrant policy and are not easily separated. An ethical analysis of migration issues will need to focus especially on the value perspectives of different viewpoints.

1

U.S. REFUGEE POLICY: HAVEN FOR THE PERSECUTED OR PAWN OF FOREIGN POLICY PRIORITIES?

Callous indeed is the person who does not feel empathy and compassion for refugees. One can scarcely imagine a worse condition. Forced to leave home and all that is familiar because of dreadful fears about starvation, persecution, and death, refugees depart for other places in search of safety and livelihood. Still, it is difficult for many persons in the United States to imagine what it would be like to be a refugee. "Radical vulnerability" may be an accurate characterization as far as it goes, but words fail to depict the combinations of desperation, fear, dependency, courage, hope, and resourcefulness that make up the refugee experience.

"Everything is a burden" for the refugee, says Elie Wiesel, a refugee from the Holocaust and World War II.[1] All those elements that provide a sense of security and at-homeness in the world are gone: food, language, social and physical environment, familiar place to sleep, and artifacts of one's personal and communal life story. A refugee has no meaningful citizenship, no state membership on which she can rely. She does not belong anywhere. She cannot go back, but she may have no place to which she can go. She is utterly dependent on others for protection and provision, but she also must employ every bit of wit, stamina, and ingenuity she can muster to maneuver successfully the dangerous and uncertain waters of refugee existence.

Wiesel further states that "by definition a refugee is a victim."[2] Refugees do not want to leave their homes and homelands. Circumstances force them to leave. Some are persecuted for political activity, religious beliefs, or ethnic identity. Some have experienced imprisonment and torture, the death of family members and friends, direct and indirect threats. Drought and environmental degradation force others to leave the lands of their ancestors. Still others have to flee from the terror of warfare between neighboring peoples and countries that sweeps through their communities.

Yet refugees are not only victims; they are also moral agents. In the depths of their souls they may prefer to remain in their homeland, yet they feel compelled to leave by the gravity of their plight. Still, to become a refugee is a decision one makes. Refugees are not merely passive reactors to hostile circumstances. They make choices, fateful choices, with no guarantees about outcomes. Persons can decide to remain where they are, with all the risks that choice entails. Or persons can choose to become refugees, with all the risks this choice involves. And often they must make these choices under the most stressful conditions imaginable. In her study of Greek refugees in the former Soviet Union, Effie Voutira emphasizes the "incommensurability of choices" and the time pressure that these refugees faced.[3] Refugees are neither mindless hordes nor rational utilitarians, but moral agents responding to a complex and intense set of pressures.

Elie Wiesel not only writes and speaks eloquently about refugees; he also addresses the persons who live in places to which refugees come. For him, it is impossible, ethically, not to respond to the suffering of refugees. "Every human being is the dwelling of God."[4] Refugees should be welcomed as friends. They are deserving of our respect and gratitude, not merely pity or the apathy of compassion fatigue. Refugees should be appreciated for the depth of suffering they bear and the courage which their actions require. "If I see a person or persons suffer, and the distance between us does not shrink, oh, then, my place is not good, not enviable."[5]

Wiesel provides the appropriate beginning place for a consideration of refugee policy. Reflection needs to start with the faces and life stories of refugees, and the moral challenge that refugees bring to those of us who live in more settled communities. Refugee policy is a personal and interpersonal moral matter. As persons and communities how will we respond to the claims of refugees? What kind of community do we want to be? Wiesel will not permit refugee policy to be treated only in abstractions. Who is the refugee, and how shall we respond? William Fullbright's comments about U.S. policy in Vietnam has continuing pertinence for refugees as well:

Man's capacity for decent behavior seems to vary directly with his perceptions of others as individual humans with human motives and feelings, whereas his capacity for barbarous behavior seems to increase with his perception of an adversary in abstract terms. This is the only explanation I can think of for the fact that the very same good and decent citizens who would never fail to feed a hungry child or comfort a sick friend or drop a coin in the church basket can celebrate the number of Viet Cong killed in a particular week or battle, talking of "making a desert" of North Vietnam or of "bombing it back to the Stone Age" despite the fact that most, almost all, of the victims would be innocent peasants and workers.[6]

Refugee policy is concerned with human beings who bear the scars of persecution and deprivation and the hope for protection in a new home, a new community. Refugee policy is above all an interpersonal moral challenge, not merely a problem for governments, and it must be addressed at this level if broader systems and structures are to be humane. Wiesel sees refugee policy as rooted in the "ethics of character," the need to shape a citizenry whose human response is to act as the "righteous Gentiles" did during the Holocaust when they sheltered Jews at great risk to themselves yet with no consciousness of themselves as moral heroes.[7] Moral persons welcome and protect refugees. This should not be conceived as exceptional acts of love but as what we expect from each other as persons who want to live in a morally responsible community.

A Picture of the Current Situation

In 1994, the American people were confronted daily and weekly by stories of refugees. Haitians fleeing a brutal dictatorship took to boats and tried to navigate to southern Florida and seek asylum in the United States. President Clinton reversed a campaign promise and adopted President Bush's policy of interdicting Haitians at sea to keep them from getting to U.S. shores. Haitian soldiers sought to destroy boats that the desperate people might use to flee the country. Overcrowding, panic, and dangerous waters led to terror and even death. At its height, up to five thousand refugees a week sought to escape by sea. Eventually, U.S. intervention to restore Aristide to leadership largely stopped the movement of refugees. But this did not prevent

27

the tragedies or answer questions about how the United States should respond to such crises.

In 1994 more than two million Rwandans fled the slaughter in their country and swamped the refugee camps hastily constructed across the border in neighboring countries. People were crushed to death in the panicked flight. Vivid reports of starvation and disease among the refugees presented a horrifying picture of their precarious situation. Staggering numbers of refugees were dying; many others were going insane. Children were orphaned or separated from parents. One observer characterized the chaos in Rwanda as "the beginning of the final days. . . . This is the apocalypse."[8]

Also that year boatloads of Cubans again began to embark for the United States. They sailed the shark-infested Straits of Florida in rafts, makeshift crafts, and hijacked boats. Thousands were picked up by the U.S. Coast Guard, but many others died of dehydration, exposure, and drowning. Government officials, worried about a repetition of the massive Cuban migration in 1980, announced that Cuban arrivals would no longer be treated automatically as refugees and that Cubans would be interdicted and taken to the U.S. naval base at Guantánamo. After negotiations between the U.S. and Cuban governments, the boat traffic was largely stopped and more regularized channels for U.S. reception of migrants were established.

Meanwhile we read and heard reports of war and ethnic cleansing in the former Yugoslavia, the horrors of which seemed unending. Women were raped, towns were shelled, minorities in Bosnia were murdered or beaten or captured for forced labor. "Protected" sites inside the country did not provide adequate protection. While some refugees fled to outside countries to escape the violence, many others were uprooted within their country. By the middle of 1995 more than one million persons were displaced within Bosnia and Herzegovina.

While water and distance have shielded the United States from most of the massive refugee movements of the twentieth century, recent events show that the United States cannot just neatly manage refugee admission by massaging bureaucratic procedures in other countries. Refugees are arriving—or at least embarking—in large numbers from within our own hemisphere. Increasing numbers of refugees choose to arrive in the United States and then seek asylum rather than to apply for refugee status outside the United States. What happens to Americans' image of the United States as a haven for the world's persecuted when the number of those seeking protection seems too great? And what is the United States' responsibility regarding the protection of refugees abroad, such as the Rwandans, when provision of protection and basic necessities is more immediate than questions of resettlement?

The number of refugees in today's world is staggering. According to a recent estimate, approximately 23 million persons fit the narrow definition of refugee in international law and approximately 26 million additional persons are displaced within their own countries. Twenty years ago the number was 2.4 million; ten years ago it was 10.5 million.[9] The escalation in refugees in today's world is indeed frightening, above all to the refugees themselves. Most of the refugees are women and children. They are the most vulnerable in contexts of violence. National and international policies dealing with refugees were forged in an earlier period and are inadequate to deal with the immensity of the current crisis.

The current international "order" is grievously disordered in its generation of so many violently uprooted persons. For Christians, it is a vivid picture of the whirlwinds of human sinfulness. Within the appalling statistics are individual children, women, and men who hurt and hope. Each is somebody's daughter or son, mother or father, friend or neighbor. There are 49 million stories which convey the distinctiveness of each person's enfleshment of God's image. A Christian perspective on refugees needs constantly to resist the depersonalization of refugees and to emphasize the personal as well as the political challenges of such widespread and devastating suffering.

Historical Background:
International Refugee Crisis

The United States understands itself as a land where the persecuted are welcomed. Indeed many who came here prior to the twentieth century were religious or political refugees. Political exiles in the nineteenth century moved rather freely in Europe as well. The movement of refugees is not new. But clearly something has changed. Gone are the days of relatively free movement across borders. Gone also are the days when the numbers were small and composed primarily of the educated elite.

Michael Marrus provides a fascinating picture of nineteenth-century migration in Europe. Political exiles simply entered another country without reporting to authorities or having to abide by special requirements. Exiles from the Revolutions of 1848 generally did not even have to give up their revolutionary politics![10] According to Marrus, England did not prevent the entrance of or deport any refugee throughout the entire nineteenth century.[11] It is hard for us today to imagine such freedom to move across borders, to travel without passports, visas, and other documents. Such freedom was also observed in the United States during that period. Marrus quotes a European who immigrated to the United States in the 1890s: "I had no passport, no exit permit, no visa, no number on a quota, and none of those things was asked for on my arrival in the United States."[12]

Not only was there a strong commitment to a tradition of granting asylum to exiles, but the countries had not yet developed the kind of technologies and bureaucracies to control the entry of outsiders. "Without fingerprints, photographic identification, efficient filing systems, and modern police communications, the refugees could cross frontiers with little difficulty and live virtually unmolested once they had arrived."[13]

Still, toward the end of the nineteenth century, the situation was beginning to change. Larger numbers of persons were leaving their homelands, and many were poor. Empires were weakening, and nationalism was ascending as an ideology. It was World War I, however, that changed the situation from the relatively free movement of persons to a hardening of national boundaries. The Austro-Hungary, Ottoman, and Russian empires were swept away, and the nation-state system of international relations was solidified. National self-determination became the dominant principle of the emerging international order.

In World War I, everywhere "passports came into use as a way of certifying nationality, regulating the flows of much-needed people, and providing checks on suspicious persons deemed security threats to countries engulfed in war."[14] These kinds of controls, formulated in response to exigencies of warfare, were continued after the war was over. The state government apparatus was marshaled to control who came inside a national border and who left. Large numbers of people were uprooted by the war, and new states were being established, often on the basis of an ethnic notion of nationality. In the empires, various ethnic groups were mixed together, but the emergence of the nation-state system brought about the "unmixing" of ethnic groups. Ethnic homogeneity defined membership in new nation-states, and the status of ethnic minorities in these states became precarious.

People who did not fit within the emerging nation-state system were literally "stateless." They had no place to live where they would be regarded as members, where they could belong and make claims for security and livelihood. There were "citizens" and there were "others." And if only "nationals" could be citizens, then those who were not nationals could not expect the state to secure and protect their rights. Nationality became a way to sort out who belonged and who did not. But not only did the formation of states based on nationality create stateless people, it also created alienated minorities who fervently believed they had a right to form their own nation-state on the basis of their own ethnic identity.

Hannah Arendt provides a powerful critique of the consequences of this development. In her view, the notion of human rights became captive to a nation-state international order. Presumably in the post–World War I world, every person was a citizen of some state. This state alone had the obligation to provide order and protection for its citizens. There was no authority outside the state to require it to grant similar protection for persons who were not already citizens. But what about those who did not fit into the national community or who were thrown out of a territory because they did not qualify for full citizenship?

Arendt argues that what is unprecedented here "is not the loss of a home but the impossibility of finding a new one. Suddenly, there was no place on earth where migrants could go without the severest restrictions."[15] These persons were designated refugees. They were adrift not because of anything they had done but because of their ethnic, racial, or religious identity. They had not committed crimes, but they received the heaviest punishment of all: their "loss of home and political status become identical with expulsion from humanity altogether."[16] They not only had no state which would protect their rights, they were deprived of a community to which they belonged and in which they could express their individuality.

The number of refugees generated by World War I and its aftermath was too great to cope with as exceptional cases. The League of Nations, still in its infancy, had to struggle with what to do. What was to happen to stateless persons in an international order constructed on the basis of nation-state sovereignty? The system that was devised to deal with the refugee crisis is now frequently referred to as the "international refugee regime." With little authority or money, and with the aid of voluntary agencies, the League attempted to ensure that the refugees' basic needs were met and to negotiate with states about where refugees could be resettled, or to determine if they could be safely repatriated. Individual nation-states, which were unwilling or unable to handle the crisis, viewed refugees as a problem for the international community.

This system, a weak reed in any event, utterly collapsed in the face of Fascist and Nazi racism and anti-Semitism in the 1930s. The combination of Nazi genocide and tight entrance requirements in safe nation-states doomed millions of Jews to death, as well as many others labeled inferior or undesirable. In this event the horror of refugee vulnerability is indelibly written on the twentieth century. Following the end of World War II there was again a terrible refugee crisis, with millions of persons uprooted and without homes. The United Nations now had to reconstruct an international system to deal with these refugees, building on the notion developed earlier that the protection of refugees was the collective responsibility of nation-states.

Once again the strategies were developed in response to a postwar crisis in Europe. This fact has led many current refugee scholars to argue that the international refugee regime is a "European construct" and is inadequate to deal with the character of third-world refugee movements in more recent decades. These differences in sociohistorical contexts are important as we consider what is needed today. Furthermore, it is an instructive, though tragic, irony that the generation of refugees came about as an unintended and unforeseen consequence of the principle of national self-determination, which seemed morally compelling to many ethically sensitive persons in the early part of this century. Indeed the refugee may well be the most appropriate symbol for the twentieth century.

Historical Background: United States

Between the two wars, the United States government did not recognize refugees as a distinctive type of migrant. Moreover, its immigration policy was very restrictive, so it did not admit many immigrants or refugees. The restrictive mood was revealed most tragically in the egregious failure of the United States to open its doors more widely to Jews seeking to escape the Holocaust in Europe. For example, Loescher and Scanlon write that "Franklin Roosevelt [in 1939] implicitly acknowledging the strength of popular anti-Semitism, provided no support for a bill introduced in Congress which would have provided special immigration opportunities for up to 20,000 German refugee children."[17]

Following the end of World War II, Europe again faced a refugee crisis of immense proportion. Millions of persons were uprooted and displaced. For the first time in U.S. law, refugees were identified as a special type of migrant, displaced persons, who had a special claim to admission into the United States. Even this effort, however, shows the reluctance of Americans, including Protestants and Catholics, to confront the primary challenge of Jewish refugees. Religious as well as political parochialisms and interests haunted U.S. responses. Prominent Christian leaders couched support for admission "in intentionally general language which downplayed Jewish and Eastern European origins and emphasized Christian and anti-Communist characteristics."[18]

Indeed, Cold War politics entered the picture soon after the war and became the controlling perspective for U.S. refugee policy until the mid-1990s. Refugees increasingly came to be regarded as an important element of anti-Communist foreign policy. Those who were fleeing from Communist countries were by definition regarded as refugees. "Since 1945, well over 90 percent of those admitted to the United States have fled Communist countries."[19] It is not that the suffering of these refugees was greater than that of persons from other countries. Refugees were a part of the Cold War arsenal to dramatize Communist failures and U.S. virtues. For proponents of this policy, it was a happy marriage of humanitarian principle to aid the persecuted and national self-interest in the global struggle with Soviet power. That this policy aided many genuine refugees who needed protection is not at question. But what of those subjected to persecution in countries whose governments were allies of the United States? The doors to the United States were closed. This was precisely the issue raised by the sanctuary movement in the 1980s in the advocacy for refugees from Central America.

In the early 1950s the United Nations adopted a "Convention Relating to the Status of Refugees." Refugees were defined as persons who had "a well-founded fear of being persecuted for reasons of race, religion, nationality, membership of a particular social group or political opinion." This definition marked a very important development in international ethics. It named specifically the bases on which so much of twentieth-century persecution had occurred. The Convention further articulated the obligation of the international community to provide protection for refugees.

Reflecting its ideological orientation, the U.S. government appallingly did not sign the 1951 Convention because it did not specify Communist governments as the primary cause of refugees. Still the United Nations' definition has remained intact in international law up to the present. Critics maintain that the definition reflects the circumstances of postwar Europe and therefore is inadequate to encompass the quite different character of refugee movements today. While this criticism is valid, the definition, limited as it is, provides a strong basis for criticizing the almost exclusive focus of the United States on persons fleeing Communism. Contrary to the impressions of many Americans who believe that U.S. policy has generously responded to the worldwide suffering of refugees, the dominance of anti-Communist ideology is the primary characteristic of postwar U.S. refugee policy.

In the 1960s, the United States adopted a sweeping change in its immigration policy. But refugees did not receive much attention. Indeed they were treated as a category of immigrant that occupied a low priority. Yet they continued to be an unavoidable feature of the Cold War struggle. The migration of Cuban refugees began soon after Fidel Castro assumed power. Until 1980 most of the refugees from Cuba were from professional and middle classes whose economic interests were threatened by Castro's policies. Although some clearly were escaping from persecution, many others were not really Convention refugees (persons who fit the United Nations definition) but economic migrants.[20] The presumption that Cubans fleeing Castro's regime were refugees continued until President Clinton, faced with yet another wave of Cuban boats, declared that Cubans' claims for refugee status would be handled by a case-by-case review rather than automatically conferred.

In the 1970s also a large number of refugees came to the United States from the Soviet Union. The USSR had previously kept a tight control on persons' freedom of movement, generally not permitting anybody within its territory to leave. Yet in this period they permitted persons in certain groups to emigrate, and significant numbers of Armenians and Soviet Jews especially came as refugees to the United

States. The Soviet Union fluctuated between tightening or loosening controls, and U.S. policy was directed to pressure the USSR to permit more persons to emigrate.

Even though the Cold War has now ended, emigration from the former Soviet Union in recent years has provided one of the largest sources for refugee admission to the United States. In fiscal year 1994, there was an approval rate of 96.3 percent of applicants from countries in the former Soviet Union.[21] Moreover, the Clinton administration has proposed that half of the 90,000 refugees admitted in 1996 come from the former Soviet Union and Eastern Europe.[22] Again it is important to ask if this operative preference is primarily a residue of Cold War politics and how many of those admitted fit the Convention definition of refugee. This question is complicated because many of these refugees are Jews and members of other religious and ethnic minorities who historically have been subjected to waves of persecution so that even relatively "calm" periods may not mean that they have no reasonable fear of persecution.

Many refugees have also come to the United States from Indochina. These are likely the persons that Americans across the country most readily identify as refugees. They are also the ones who may be tied most directly to United States actions abroad. As the United States intensified its commitment to a war in Vietnam and expanded the conflict into neighboring countries, the suffering of internal refugees was part of the war's horror. With the end of the war, the United States hoped that the refugees could be resettled within their home country. But when the U.S.-supported Saigon government suddenly fell in 1975, the United States was faced with a dramatically different situation. Thousands of Vietnamese had worked for the U.S. government or cooperated with its policies and were desperate to leave before the Hanoi Communist government took control of the whole country. "Some clung to helicopters as they took off, while others fled the capital and escaped by sea."[23]

Initially public opinion in the United States was against bringing Vietnamese to the United States. Yet the Ford administration and Congress, supported by prominent public leaders, supported the resettlement of more than 100,000 Vietnamese and Laotian refugees. Just as this crisis began to ease, however, a new one erupted. In the late 1970s, Indo-Chinese refugees again tried to escape wars and persecutions in their countries. Vast numbers of people sought safety in Thailand or risked their lives by sailing away in boats. While there was an international outcry of horror about the plight of "boat people," nobody wanted them. Many were received in Southeast Asian countries, but many drowned, others were murdered by pirates, and still others were forced to go back. The situation in Cambodia was particularly brutal, a nightmare of violence and death. Loescher and Scanlon refer to the years of 1975 through 1978 in Cambodia as "possibly the worst to befall a people since the Nazi holocaust."[24]

Again, according to polls the majority of the American public was not eager to welcome the boat people and other Indo-Chinese refugees. Yet Reimers also points out that most of those polled "said they would personally welcome refugees if any settled nearby."[25] Whereas the American public tends to regard large-scale abstract numbers of refugees as threatening, when faced with the personhood of refugees they are inclined to respond more generously.

By the end of the 1980s the United States had received about 900,000 Indochinese refugees.[26] The U.S. government also provided a great deal of financial support for refugee assistance in Asian countries. Many Indochinese refugees remained in refugee camps, waiting for years for resettlement or return to their home country. A break began to occur in the late 1980s when a Comprehensive Plan of Action for refugees in Southeast Asia was formulated, which included the repatriation of Cambodians. While conditions in Indochina stabilized a great deal in the 1990s, the largest number of refugees admitted to the United States in fiscal year 1993 continued to come from Indochina, especially Vietnam. Refugee advocates expect this to change in the next several years as fewer now qualify as refugees. Indeed, the Clinton administration proposes that most of the reduction from 110,000 to 90,000 refugees in 1996 comes from this region.[27]

The major change in U.S. refugee policy occurred in 1980, at the beginning of a decade when refugees suddenly became a publicly volatile issue. The Refugee Act of 1980 was regarded as a breakthrough by refugee advocates. For the first time the United States adopted the United Nations definition of refugee in place of its previous anti-Communist criterion. This Act clearly established refugees as a separate class of migrants from immigrants, and it set an annual number of persons who could be admitted as refugees. Proponents now had reason to believe that refugee admission would be handled in a more generous, fair, and less ideologically oriented way.

But almost immediately after the passage of this bill, a large number of Cubans and Haitians began streaming into Florida. The Carter administration was caught off guard. Although American people had generally looked with favor on Cuban refugees in the past (i.e., fleeing Communist Cuba), they perceived the 1980 influx differently. Fidel Castro agreed to let Cubans go to the United States, so many Cuban Americans secured boats to pick up friends and relatives at the Cuban port of Mariel. These refugees became known as Marielitos. Not only were there many of them, but there were reports that Castro was "getting rid of" criminals and persons with mental illness. The United States placed many in detention centers. Efforts to settle them in the United States, keep them incarcerated, or repatriate them continued in confusing patterns for years afterward amid severe tensions and controversy.

At the same time large numbers of Haitians were also arriving in Florida. Haitians had been coming to Florida in flimsy boats for some years. Civil rights and church groups advocated fairness and humaneness in the treatment of Haitians. But the Immigration and Naturalization Service (INS) of the U.S. government sought to deport most of them and was deterred only by legal interventions by advocacy groups. When Haitians were joined with Marielitos from Cuba, the image of a "flood" of desperate people flowing into the United States became widespread. Some officials expressed fears that this movement was a harbinger of what would happen in even greater numbers if the United States did not effectively secure its borders from the poor of the third world.[28]

The Haitians were particularly vulnerable in two respects. First, the conditions in Haiti were far worse than those in Cuba, and the Haitians' escape was more dangerous. Second, the INS was considerably more hostile to Haitians than to Cubans. Not only were Haitians not fleeing from a Communist country, as were the Cubans, they were black. It is difficult to deny the contention of the congressional Black Caucus that racism was an important element in the INS treatment of Haitians.[29]

Instead of dealing with the Marielito and Haitian migrants under the 1980 Refugee Act, the Carter administration created a new "special entrant" status to accommodate the unexpectedly large numbers of newcomers. The opportunity to deal fairly and impartially with asylum claims as the new law provided was lost. In fairness to President Carter, the 1980 Act did not anticipate the sudden emergence of the United States as a country of first asylum. The asylum provision was utterly inadequate for

37

responding effectively to the situation of the 1980s. Whereas applications for refugee status are processed outside the United States in ways that fit better within bureacratic procedures, asylum claims are filed by foreigners who have entered the United States with or without documentation and who argue that they have a "well-founded fear of persecution" if they are returned to their home country.

The hopes of refugee advocates for a less ideologically oriented refugee policy were further frustrated in the 1980s by the Reagan administration's treatment of claimants from Central America. Church workers along the U.S. border with Mexico were horrified by stories of murder and torture in El Salvador and Guatemala, often carried out by government or quasi-government forces supported heavily by the U.S. government. As the violence in Central America intensified and the numbers of Central Americans trying to cross the border into the United States increased, these church workers acted. Initially they tried to help the asylees apply for asylum, believing the U.S. government was legally and morally obligated to protect them under the terms of the 1980 Refugee Act.

Yet when Central American asylees were spirited away by the INS to detention centers and often deported without being given an opportunity to make a legal claim for asylum, the church workers initiated the sanctuary movement. This grassroots response sought to protect the asylees from deportation and to protest the failure of the U.S. government to implement its own law. The struggle between refugee advocates and the Reagan administration persisted throughout most of the eighties. In his acceptance speech at the Republican Convention in 1980, Reagan said: "Can we doubt that only a divine Providence placed this land, this land of freedom, here as refuge for all those people in the world who yearn to breathe free? Jews and Christians enduring persecution behind the Iron Curtain, the boat people of Southeast Asia, Cuba, and Haiti."[30]

While Divine Providence may have established the United States as a refuge, the Reagan administration did not. It rewrote the creed in a highly restrictive way. This administration required an ideological standard that was not contained in the 1980 Refugee Act. The U.S. government continued as before to admit almost exclusively persons who were leaving Communist countries. The anti-Communist ideological orientation remained dominant.[31] As Ann Crittenden bluntly stated: "Asylum applications from Salvadorans and

Guatemalans were almost invariably rejected, regardless of the merits of the case, while Poles, in contrast, were often welcomed regardless of their circumstances."[32]

Even with the end of the Cold War, the United States continues to operate with the legacy of a heavy anti-Communist bias. Even in President Clinton's proposals for fiscal year 1996, most of the refugees will come from Communist or formerly Communist countries: the former Soviet Union, Southeast Asia, and Cuba.[33] Thousands of Haitians seeking to escape a brutal regime were turned away from the United States, often by direct interdiction in the ocean as they tried to maneuver their boats to Florida. Many were not given an opportunity to present their case for asylum and were forcibly returned to Haiti. Others were detained under grim conditions at the Guantánamo naval base in Cuba while their appeals were slowly being considered. Refugee advocates were bitterly disappointed that the Clinton administration in 1993 continued the same policies toward Haitian asylees as President Bush in direct contradiction to Clinton's campaign pledge.

Current U.S. Refugee Policy

It is difficult to disentangle refugee policy from immigration policy and to give clear, straightforward accounts of what the policies are. This is complicated business, reflecting the complexity of the issues addressed in these policies. Nonetheless, let us make the attempt.

For fiscal year 1996, the Clinton administration has proposed the ceiling for refugee admissions at 90,000, a reduction of 20,000 from 1995. Which refugees will be admitted? Each year Congress and the executive branch of the federal government determine a geographical pattern of distribution. For example, 45,000 is proposed for the former Soviet Union and Eastern Europe, and 25,000 from East Asia.[34] The old pattern continues. Even now, if this proposal is adopted, most refugees admitted to the United States will come from the former Soviet Union and Southeast Asia.

U.S. refugee policy also establishes a set of priorities for determining which persons have the strongest claim for admission. The Clinton administration changed these priorities for 1995. The top priority was quite broad. First, it identified those who are in greatest need, in immediate danger of death, or especially vulnerable. Within priority one, the United States would draw more on referrals from the United Nations High Commission for Refugees (UNHCR) than in the past.

Second, however, was the expandable and possibly controlling category of "groups of special concern to the U.S. to be established as needed by nationality."[35] Additional priorities specified family reunification for immediate relatives, and for more distant relatives. Yet, in a welcome change, Clinton's proposals for fiscal year 1996 drop "groups of special concern" to the second priority.[36]

The location of the category of nationality groups of special concern to the United States is an important moral issue. When given high priority, this leaves the barn door open to admit refugees primarily on the grounds of foreign policy considerations, as anti-Communism functioned in the past. We have seen that 70,000 out of 90,000 refugees in fiscal year 1996 will likely come from the former Soviet Union/Eastern Europe and from Southeast Asia. Numbers from other parts of the world remain proportionately small, all the more so since the regions of Near East/South Asia and Africa have almost 80 percent of the world's refugees.[37] While the new set of priorities seems to give greater weight than before to the most vulnerable persons, it is morally imperative that this criterion shape the overall geographical allotments as well as the decisions about which persons are admitted from specific regions.

How are determinations made about who qualifies as a refugee and receives priority attention? U.S. refugee policy favors an orderly procedure which requires refugees to apply for admission to the United States from within their home country. Their applications are considered outside the United States. If they are approved, then the refugees are resettled in the United States. The U.S. government provides funding to states, localities, and nongovernment organizations to assist in the resettlement. Religious organizations play a major role in this challenging task. This means it is often religiously motivated persons who are involved in assisting refugees as they seek to establish a new home. Refugees are legally permitted to remain permanently in the United States and are eligible to become U.S. citizens.

This policy seeks to normalize a movement of persons which by definition bursts out of orderly procedures. Persons who fear for their lives are not likely to be able to take the time to file an application, wait for it to be considered, and do all this within a country from which they are desperately seeking to escape. Moreover, this approach deals better with individuals who are subject to persecution than with large numbers of persons whose group identity puts them at severe risk. Refugee advocates also point out that a relatively small percentage of admissions are granted to persons in refugee camps. Although the refugees may be safe from direct threat in these camps (they are not always safe from attacks from the outside, or from violence and intimidation from within), their suffering may be acute and camps make for a miserable long-term home.

An alternative to in-country processing in U.S. refugee policy is *asylum.* A person may escape to the United States and then file an appeal to be granted asylum. The person must prove that she or he has a well-founded fear of persecution back home and therefore merits asylum. If the claim is approved, the person may remain in the United States and work for income. The number of asylees who can seek citizenship is limited to 10,000 per year. Additional stipulations have been written into the law, which grants protection for only a specified length of time for designated asylees such as Salvadorans. If asylum is not granted, the persons are subject to deportation.

Asylum has become the target of a great deal of recent criticism in the United States and Western Europe because increasing numbers of persons are just showing up, whether immigrants or genuine refugees, and claiming asylum if apprehended. The very practice of asylum is in jeopardy as countries try to stop asylees before they arrive in the country, as the United States has done with Haitians. For refugee advocates the right to asylum is essential if these desperate persons are not to be sacrificed to the cynical interests of nation-states.

The number of refugees admitted to the United States is not great when compared to the number of legal and nonlegal immigrants. But it is the case that refugee resettlement requires more specific funding and programs and that refugees are more likely than immigrants to require social welfare services. This is hardly surprising when one considers the traumas which bear so heavily on refugees' lives. One deeply moving story is the young Cambodian refugee who became hysterical in class when the teacher played "hangman" to help teach spelling. The teacher learned later that the girl had seen her father hanged in Cambodia.[38]

An effective refugee resettlement policy depends not only on government support, but also on the readiness of persons and communities to receive refugees with hospitality. Lest we think that the American people are more likely than the officials of U.S. government

41

to welcome refugees, we have seen that on occasion the government has acted to receive refugees even when popular support was lacking. The moral challenges posed by refugee policy are not solely at the level of federal government policy but in local communities among the persons who make their homes there.

Issues in U.S. Refugee Policy

WHO IS A REFUGEE?

In the historical review of U.S. refugee policy, we referred to the United Nations definition of *refugee* and emphasized that this definition was written into U.S. law in the 1980 Refugee Act. To some, definitions seem important only to lawyers and scholars. Who could care about defining *refugee* when there are so many persons forcibly uprooted and forced to flee their homes? The task, to them, is not to define refugee but to assist refugees. Indeed that is the paramount moral imperative. But in an international system, tragically disordered as it is, which persons can call on the international community to provide protection? Which persons are we in American society obligated to protect? How do we choose? Does each person have an equal claim for protection? Does it matter what the circumstances of their flight might be?

The question of how *refugee* is defined is not pedantry or triviality. It is the effort to identify who those persons are in the human community who are in greatest need of safe haven and who present an especially compelling moral and legal challenge to others who are more securely settled. There are people who are included in some definitions and excluded in others. This can make the difference in who can appeal for international assistance or who can appeal for asylum, and who are excluded from such recourse. Still as we consider definitions it is crucial to remember that we are dealing with human beings and not mere cold abstractions.

In international law a refugee is one who seeks safe haven outside the boundaries of the home country due to "a well-founded fear of being persecuted for reasons of race, nationality, religion, membership of a particular social group or political opinion."[39] Persons who are refugees according to this definition have certain rights in international law that other migrants cannot claim. Clearly there are weaknesses in the capacity of the United Nations to enforce the stipulations of international law. But there are also debates about the definition itself.

Critics of the existing definition maintain that it no longer covers adequately the character of current forced migration. The U.N. definition, according to this view, reflects a "European bias," whereas today the greatest number of forced migrants come from third-world countries where a variety of factors are exerting potentially lethal pressures. What about the meaning and adequacy of persecution for defining refugees? It is clear that someone is persecuted when she is tortured or threatened with death because of her political beliefs. But what about a community of persons whose lives are threatened by the violence of civil war? Or by environmental degradation so devastating that persons can no longer survive where they are? And also what about persons who are victimized for factors other than religion, race, nationality, political opinion, or membership in a particular social group? For example, women are raped as part of a campaign of intimidation and terror, or girls are subjected to genital mutilation; and gay and lesbian persons may be targeted because of sexual orientation.

This has led the authors of one influential book to distinguish between three types of refugees. First is the classic type of refugee, the activist, whom the state wants to kill or expel because of some type of activity. Second is the target who may be a member of a group, for example, religious or racial, that is designated for abusive treatment by those wielding state power. Third, however, is a person who is not included in the current definition. He is the victim, one who is uprooted by violence that endangers his life but is not directed at him individually.[40] Is his need for safe haven any less than one who is specifically targeted for persecution?

Zolberg, Suhrke, and Aguayo propose that refugees be defined "as persons whose presence abroad is attributable to a well-founded fear of violence" and "who can be assisted only abroad, unless conditions change in their country of origin."[41] This definition shifts away from a focus on persecution to that of violence. In the authors' view, famine or the inability to survive materially could constitute life-endangering violence in addition to political or military threats.[42] The point is that if a nation does not protect its peoples from such violence, or indeed may be an agent of it, then these persons are "stateless" and therefore deserve international protection (i.e., refugee status).

Another influential alternative for defining refugees was adopted in 1969 by the Organization of African Unity (OAU). This definition

43

gives special attention to the role of outside countries and the dynamics of war in forcing people to move:

> The term "refugee" shall also apply to every person who, owing to external aggression, occupation, foreign domination or events seriously disturbing public order in either part or the whole of his country of origin or nationality, is compelled to leave his place of habitual residence in order to seek refuge in another place outside his country of nationality.[43]

In this proposal also, the determination of persecution is no longer the exclusive criterion for refugee status. Compelled movement is more important.

PERSONS WHO ARE INTERNALLY DISPLACED

Another factor in forced migrations that has had disastrous consequences for many people is displacement within the borders of a given nation. That is, should refugees only be those who leave the boundaries of their homeland, as the current definition requires? Or should persons who are forced to leave their homes and flee to another part of their own native country but without requisite resources for survival also be regarded as refugees? These persons are frequently referred to as the "internally displaced." In Sudan, for example, it is estimated that 500,000 civilians have died since 1986 because of famine and the violence of war.[44] Approximately four million Sudanese are displaced within their own country.[45] Among other displaced persons are two million Angolans, and one million or more in each country of Afghans, Rwandans, Bosnians, Liberians, and Iraqis.[46] Should international protection extend to them also?

Shacknove, among many others, believes they should be regarded as refugees. He argues that people may be forced to move for three reasons: persecution, vital economic subsistence, and natural calamities.[47] Whether or not they cross borders is not the critical element. Rather, the chief question is this: Is the state protecting the basic rights of persons subjected to any of the three threats identified above? If it is not fulfilling its legal and moral responsibility, then these persons may seek international protection (i.e., refugee status).

In international law, refugees have the right to seek safe haven in other countries. They may also call on the "international refugee regime" for protection and subsistence assistance. The chief agent of this regime is the United Nations High Commission for Refugees (UNHCR). In fact, in recent years UNHCR has operated with a broadened definition of refugees rather than holding strictly to the criteria in international law. This change in response to critical needs of persons provides compelling evidence for the need to bring the definition into accord with what is happening concretely to persons. Indeed, Deng favors the adoption of a specific United Nations convention on the internally displaced to mandate international action for protection and assistance when other efforts have failed.[48]

REFUGEES AND INTERNATIONAL LAW

Even with a broadened definition, however, the international regime is still far too weak an instrument to deal adequately with the massive character of refugee movements. Although refugees have the right to *seek* safe haven in another country, there is no corresponding obligation on the part of other countries to *receive* refugees. Among international agreements only the Organization of American States declares that refugees also have the right to be granted asylum.[49] So refugees may *seek* but they may not *find* a place to go. The strongest international instrument in refugee law is the principle of *nonrefoulement*. This means that states have the obligation not to return refugees to the home countries from which they have fled. It is inhumane to return refugees to the places where they face the probability of persecution. States are not required to admit refugees, but legally and morally they cannot deport them. This principle, though often violated by states, represents a firm agreement among nation-states, an accomplishment that needs to be built on, not undermined.[50]

Although persons who are designated refugees have some rights in international law, further weaknesses are built into the international system of state sovereignty. Not only does state sovereignty create refugees, it resists effective response to the refugees' plight. We have seen that states are not obligated to receive refugees. But they also have the authority to determine who is or is not a genuine refugee. Thus, states such as the United States frequently give refugee status only to those they wish to admit for other reasons (such as an anti-Communist foreign policy), and they withhold refugee status from those who come from so-called friendly countries. For example, if the refugee definition had been impartially applied, it is certain that

45

more Haitians and fewer Cubans would have been granted refugee status in the United States in the 1970s, 1980s, and 1990s.

The United Nations can publicize what it regards as clear-cut violations of international refugee law, but it has little enforcement capacity. The primary pressure is political and moral. This should not be underestimated, because most states go to great lengths to try to show that their actions are indeed in compliance with international law and human rights standards, another instance of the tribute that vice, on occasion, pays to virtue. Still the sovereignty of states takes precedence over international agreements. Response to the plight of refugees depends heavily on the cooperation of nation-states, which is often severely lacking, and on the efforts of an underfunded and understaffed UNHCR and other international assistance organizations.

REFUGEE IDENTITY: MAINTAIN, EXPAND, OR TRANSFORM?

Who is a refugee? Should the definition of refugee be broadened so that larger numbers of forced migrants could seek international protection? On the face of it, the case for this change seems compelling. If persons are forced to move in order to escape life-threatening circumstances and their national governments are either unwilling or unable to protect them, then international protection seems morally imperative from almost any ethical perspective.

However, the chief argument against changing the definition is an important one. That is, it is unrealistic to expect nation-states to become more hospitable to refugees by changing the definition in international law. As it is, nation-states often fail to comply even with the more narrow definition. It is better, according to this argument, to maintain the existing definition and to seek more rigorous compliance while using additional international aid channels to assist the forced migrants who do not meet the strict criteria. It would be better to keep the existing definition with the expectation that nations can adhere to it rather than to broaden the scope beyond the point of likely implementation. Moreover, the effort to obtain agreement internationally on an expanded definition, however worthy, would be better expended on developing alternative forms of protection and assistance.

A more fundamental and radical question is whether or not being granted refugee status is truly beneficial to the refugee. Shacknove maintains that refugee status can make the difference between life and death.[51] Therefore who gets included in the definition is terribly

46

important. Without this formal recognition, exceedingly vulnerable persons have no claim at all on the international system for protection. Yet others have maintained that "refugee" is a label that some, for good reason, do not want to claim for themselves. It frequently implies a helpless and dependent type of existence which is not sufficiently self-affirming and empowering. Refugee is a signification that renders persons as objects of assistance rather than subjects of their own lives. Roger Zetter argues that the refugee designation serves better the requirements of the aid agencies than it does the well-being of refugees themselves.[52] To be regarded as refugees may keep persons isolated and contained. Refugee identity does not convey the sense that refugees can shape their own responses to their desperate life situation. The centrality of moral agency and empowerment needs to be reflected in whatever designation or categorization is used.

REFUGEE OR ECONOMIC MIGRANT?

The question about how best to define refugee centers most often on the distinction between "genuine" refugee and "economic migrant." Indeed, the most common way for the U.S. government to dismiss asylum claims or refugee applications is to maintain that they are economic migrants, not true refugees. Many Central Americans and Haitians were turned away on these grounds. Perhaps the most influential way to differentiate the two is volition. Refugees are forced to leave home because of threats against their life. Economic migrants, on the other hand, choose to leave their native countries in order to seek better life opportunities elsewhere. The refugee is *forced* to leave whereas the economic migrant *chooses* to leave.

Although this distinction is helpful, it is not as free from ambiguity as one might think. It is not always so clear who is forced and who chooses to leave. The notion that persons are forced to leave may also give the impression that they are passive victims in a tragedy in which they play no active role at all. To be forced from one's own home does not mean that one has no choice. One can choose to stay, choose even to die. Certainly there are persons who do this.

It may be that volition is less important in distinguishing refugee and economic migrant than is the desperateness of the life-threatening conditions from which individuals choose to escape. It is important to emphasize the moral agency of refugees, even as circumstances force them to make a crisis decision of grave importance. If they

47

decide they must move in order to survive and be safe, they are still active agents in their own decision to become refugees. They are not mindless hordes who are driven only by external forces. They are not without volition.

Yet there is a difference between the family who would like to remain where they are but whose lives are endangered because of an appallingly brutal civil war, and the underemployed young person who is adventurous enough to migrate to another country in search of a job and income. One may have empathy for this person while still recognizing the more pressing claim of the family. The differences between refugee and economic migrant are important even as they are not free from ambiguities.

It is also the case that economic deprivation and environmental catastrophe can be a direct threat to life and, when not alleviated, lead to death. People who are forced to move by such circumstances are surely just as much genuine refugees as are those who are escaping political persecution. The primary distinction, then, should be not between the refugee and the economic migrant but between the refugee more broadly defined and the migrant whose circumstance is not life-threatening. The former may be dealt with in refugee policy, and the latter in immigration policy.

Not everyone agrees that refugees and immigrants need to be distinguished on moral and political grounds. Joseph Carens, for example, presents a moral argument for open borders.[53] For Carens, each individual is of equal moral value. Settled peoples do not have the moral right to defend privileges for themselves by using force to keep other people out. Borders enforce an unequal ordering of human communities based on the happenstance of birthplace. Why does one have to remain in one's own country where life opportunities are severely restricted rather than move to another country where the possibilities are greater? In this essay, the distinctions between refugee and immigrant do not matter. Persons should be free to move across borders.[54]

Carens understands that such a perspective is a long-range vision rather than the beginning point for developing more morally defensible refugee and immigration policies today. While the above view provides a lure and a challenge, Carens agrees that in the existing world the right of refugees to be granted safe haven is more morally compelling than the admission of immigrants. This is not only because the need of refugees is greater, but also "because the moral legitimacy of the state system depends on the provision of some safe state membership to everyone."[55] A great deal is at stake in the readiness of the international community to act on its moral responsibility for persons that goes beyond the restrictiveness of national boundaries. The human tragedies of refugees disclose lethal flaws in the nation-state system of international organization and the moral imperative for border-transcending responses.

REFUGEES AND ASYLUM SEEKERS

Another important distinction in refugee policy is between refugee and asylum seeker. Simply put, a refugee seeks entrance into a country by submitting a claim from outside the country. The United States establishes a maximum number for refugee admissions each year along with regional ceilings. When the United States grants refugee status, the refugee receives government assistance to resettle in the United States. Refugees are eligible after a period of time to become naturalized citizens.

Asylum seekers enter another country to seek safe haven and then argue for their right to remain. There is no limit to the number of persons to whom the United States may grant asylum. However, no more than 10,000 asylees per year may be granted permanent residency. Other asylees are able to remain in the United States until it is safe for them to return home, or until they can be resettled in some other country.

In fact, the treatment of persons seeking asylum in the United States has often been appalling. After all, to apply for asylum is not a crime. It is a right enunciated in international law. Yet when asylum seekers were imprisoned ("detained") while their applications were being considered, denied a fair hearing for their claim, and deported when they did not fit within the ideological test of anti-Communist foreign policy, they were not even granted the rights available to persons charged with crimes.[56] Often asylees have been coerced into accepting "voluntary repatriation," that is, cooperating with deportation proceedings, without being given an opportunity to apply for asylum. These kinds of practices led religious activists in Arizona and Texas to provide sanctuary to asylum seekers from Central America in the 1980s.

In addition, asylum has been rarely granted to women who claim that they have been subjected to gender-based persecution. The reluctance of officials to view rape as political persecution is a terrible blot on the asylum record of the United States. One striking example is a Salvadoran woman who was denied asylum in 1987. Her family

49

had been involved in the political struggles in El Salvador. An armed group came into the family's house, murdered the men and forced the women to watch, and then raped the women, including the woman applying for asylum. All the while one of the murderers was "chanting political slogans."[57] Yet the court (Board of Immigration Appeals) denied the woman asylum on the grounds that it was not clear that the rape was politically motivated. Although there is some indication that the INS finally is seeking to improve its record on gender-based persecution, the United States should be doing far better.

Affluent Western countries have become exceedingly nervous about asylum seekers. They worry about floods of new immigrants entering their borders under the label of asylum. For example, the United States interdicted Haitians in the ocean before they could get to the United States to apply for asylum. Refugee advocates vehemently maintained that this practice is contrary to international law regarding the rights of persons seeking asylum; yet the U.S. Supreme Court upheld the legality of this action according to U.S. law. Great Britain seeks to stop asylees at airports in order to prevent them from arriving inside its territory. In 1993, Germany changed its policy of liberally granting asylum to persons seeking protection inside its borders. It too has taken a more restrictive turn. The U.S. government is worried also about a large backlog of asylum claims that enables asylees to remain in the United States for years, and perhaps to disappear into the general population, before the claims are heard.

These countries want to control the flow of newcomers in order to keep the numbers small and manageable. They use not only interdiction but also detention, appallingly sometimes referred to as "humane deterrence," in order to discourage other persons from seeking asylum. The policy is basically this: "We shall make it as difficult as possible for you to seek asylum here. If by chance you get here anyway, you will likely be detained for a long time, the burden of proof will be on you to prove that asylum is compelling in your case, and the likelihood of your being granted asylum is very small. Thus you would be advised not to try."

These practices respond to understandable anxieties in Western countries. Asylum claims can become a way for individuals to bypass refugee and immigration procedures and get a foot in the door of a country where there is greater opportunity. To seek asylum can be a way for people to leap over the long queue of those waiting their turn for admission from outside the United States. Certainly there are

50

those who seek asylum protection whose claims are spurious, and their presence undermines the credibility of asylum rights.

Yet the chief purpose of asylum policy is to provide an option of protection to persons whose lives are in danger. It is not to figure out ways to make it more difficult for such persons to find safe haven. Asylum is often absolutely necessary to endangered persons. If a person fears for his life, he may well not be able to wait safely in his country while an application for refugee status moves slowly through bureaucratic procedures and long lists of other applicants. He must move quickly and then hope that he can make his case successfully. Because of the urgency and character of his flight, he may not be able to secure documents that could give vital evidence for his need for a safe haven. He may arrive in the United States with only his own story about circumstances back home that make him seek to escape.

The asylum option is designed for persons like him. Yet the asylum procedures conspire against his being granted asylum. Not only is he victimized in his homeland, but his chances of being able to find asylum in another country seem minuscule and all too arbitrary. Among the powerless in a world of many injustices, the genuine asylum seeker is certainly among the most desperate and vulnerable.

It is a new situation for the United States to be a country of first asylum. When the 1980 Refugee Act was passed, the principle of asylum was enacted in U.S. law for the first time, yet it was not regarded as a central issue. Since that date, asylees have come chiefly from third-world countries, especially Central America and the Caribbean. The response of the U.S. government to asylum seekers has been exceedingly ungenerous, except to Cubans, in shocking contrast with the national mythology that the United States readily admits those who are subject to persecution. The days when the United States was not sought by asylum seekers are over. What to do about asylum is one of the hottest contemporary questions in U.S. refugee policy deliberations.

The clear preference of policy administrators is for the orderly, one-step-removed approach of "normal" refugee selection. This at least provides some appearances of order, illusory as it likely is, amid the disorder of refugee existence and refugee-producing contexts. The bizarre notion that Haitians could apply for refugee status in Port-au-Prince and await an orderly processing of applications under the nose of their tormentors illustrates the unreality of the policy. It was the imposition of a false order by those who were safe and secure on the dangerous disorder experienced by Haitian asylum seekers. The more unruly pattern of asylees does not fit well into such procedures. Asylees are treated more as a problem to the United States that must be minimized and contained rather than as a human challenge to be fairly and effectively confronted. The specific stories of pain and struggle, fear and courage, initiative and stamina, are pushed aside in order to fit people into institutional constraints.

Howard Adelman has suggested that the traditional distinction between the refugee as a long-term entree and the asylee as a temporary status is no longer very accurate. Asylees also do in fact tend to remain for a long time. Instead the difference is better understood as "state-selected" refugees and "self-selected" refugees.[58] In his view, both are legitimate refugees and national policy should develop procedures appropriate to both types. Tragically, the movement of refugees is a persisting characteristic of the international situation, even as the characteristics of such migrations change in different times and places. The United States needs to adopt policies and practices that ensure fair and hospitable treatment for both refugees and asylum seekers.

ADDITIONAL CATEGORIES FOR REFUGEES

The phenomena of refugees and the pressures they exert on the United States has led to the proliferation of categories. Refugees and asylum seekers have not been sufficient. For example, in 1980 President Carter granted admission to many Cubans and Haitians under a new classification called "special entrant" rather than under the terms of the newly adopted 1980 Refugee Act. This meant at the time that they were not eligible to become permanent residents.[59]

Another category is "extended voluntary departure" (EVD), which enables persons to remain in the United States until it is safe for them to return to their home country. This status does not permit persons to stay permanently or to apply for U.S. citizenship. The 1990 Immigration Act gave legislative sanction to this option, now called "temporary protected status" (TPS). TPS was related specifically to Salvadoran asylees who were able thereby to remain in the United States for eighteen months longer, subject to renewal, while conditions were still too dangerous for them to return home.

Provisions such as EVD and TPS are a matter of some debate among refugee advocates. Some maintain that short-term provisions for safe haven undercut the intentions of refugee and asylum law.

They worry that the United States and other states will adopt short-term commitments in place of the stronger provisions for refugees. For example, instead of hearing carefully the claims of persons for asylum, the U.S. government could simply grant TPS and then subject persons to deportation after a short time if they do not return voluntarily. Supporters of TPS, however, believe this provides the basis for a more flexible and humane U.S. response to crises in other countries that may be relatively short in duration. In fact, TPS has now been applied to persons from places other than El Salvador, such as Liberia and the Middle East.

One of the leading scholars in international refugee law has argued that something like TPS should become the international norm for protecting refugees. The hope that refugees could be resettled in "third countries" has become realistic for only a small number of the world's refugees. It would be better to expect states to accept refugees temporarily until the refugees could safely return home rather than to presume that states will grant refugees permanent residence and citizenship. In other words, Hathaway argues for the right of first asylum but not for the right of resettlement.[60]

In my judgment the argument against TPS is too perfectionistic and the moral case for TPS as one option in refugee policy is more persuasive. Still, the primary test is historical and contextual. How will TPS actually function? Will it provide a cloak for evading responsibilities for refugees, or will it provide an invaluable haven until conditions in home countries are genuinely more safe? Will it enable persons to remain in the United States without having to live in limbo for a long time until asylum claims can be heard?

CAUSES OF REFUGEE MOVEMENTS

Few would dispute the notion that the primary moral and political imperative is to prevent the generation of refugees in the first place. Prevention-oriented policies are needed above all. Yet in order to know how to prevent the creation of refugees we must know what causes the forced movement of persons. A preventive strategy must deal with causes, not manifestations.

The causes of refugees may be many and are the subject of debate. This discussion is similar to the question of how *refugee* should be defined. Some contend that refugees are caused primarily by totalitarian and politically repressive regimes. A root cause strategy, responding to this analysis, seeks to replace these governments with democratic ones that protect the civil liberties of their citizens.

U.S. refugee policy has been greatly influenced by this view. Yet, in practice, the United States has identified totalitarianism almost exclusively with Communist regimes and has virtually exempted "friendly" right-wing repressive governments from its human rights critiques. In a post–Cold War world, the opportunity is better than anytime since World War II to exert pressures on behalf of democratization as a consistent feature of U.S. policy. The resistance to this is not simply the strong inclination to criticize "enemies" and to be silent about the abuses of allies. It is also the failures of the U.S. government to uphold the human rights standards it selectively applies to others. For example, the United States criticized Asian countries for turning Vietnamese boat people away from their shores, but the United States itself interdicted Haitian and Cuban boat people to prevent them from entering the country.

Another version of the repression thesis is that refugees are caused by political and cultural factors related to the construction of national states. Ethnic conflicts are rife in many parts of the world, in the Balkans and former Soviet Union as well as in the third world. Those who are on the losing side in struggles for power are subject to severe discrimination and even overt wars of displacement, expulsion, or extermination. Most recently formed nation-states were constructed by victorious outsiders who drew boundaries in ways that took little account of historical and cultural factors of the people themselves. Moreover, colonizing powers frequently exacerbated ethnic tensions by exploiting differences in order to maintain their power. "Since World War II, struggles for political power within a state by a dominant group, and persecution or discrimination as a result of competition for limited resources have been at the root of refugee flows."[61]

Others have argued that the core factor in creating refugees is economic deprivation. The problem is "underdevelopment." The solution, therefore, is "development." Since most refugees come from third-world nations, it is not surprising that many see poverty as the primary generating factor. In this analysis, as poverty is reduced and economic opportunity increased, fewer refugees will be created.

Yet others have challenged this influential thesis. They maintain that it is not poverty as such, but violence that produces refugees. Certainly in the Cold War years, the United States and the USSR provided military support for contending factions in a given country, thereby intensifying and escalating the violence of civil war within those countries. Moreover, economic deprivation itself can be a form of violence which creates genuine refugees, not just economic migrants. Loescher concludes that "the majority of contemporary refugee movements in the Third World are caused by war, ethnic strife, and sharp socioeconomic inequalities."[62]

Another cause needs to be specified as well—environmental degradation. Jodi Jacobson identifies environmental refugees as "those forced to leave either their homes or their homelands due to environmental causes."[63] This is a particularly potent factor in sub-Saharan Africa. While natural disasters such as earthquake and severe drought can force people to move, the devastation of agricultural land, deforestation, and toxic waste contamination, which occur as a result of human policies, are increasingly generating flight. This too is frequently the result not just of factors internal to a country but of transnational political and economic influences that are putting at severe risk the natural ecologies on which persons depend for their livelihood. Causes of forced migration, then, have to do with a complex interplay of contextual factors that generate violence against peoples. Frequently these violent actions are aided and abetted by other countries.

Not surprisingly, debates about causes of refugees frequently reflect the different outlooks of affluent and powerful countries in the Northern hemisphere and the more marginalized countries in the Southern hemisphere. The northern nations maintain that causes are primarily internal to countries in the South. The implication is that the refugee-generating country in the South needs to put its own house in order. The South argues, however, that transnational factors are causing the problems that create refugees. Therefore, the international community, especially the influential countries to the North, have primary responsibility to change the policies that produce refugees (e.g., arms trade, gap between rich and poor, support of repressive regimes, environmentally destructive development). Surely, both views convey some part of the truth. Causes are rooted in complex mixtures of internal policies and external influences. Cuban refugees, for example, were caused by an interlocking set of factors, including policies both by Castro and by the United States, such as the embargo and explicit welcome to the United States to embarrass Castro's regime.

It is clear that long-term strategies to deal with the human tragedies of refugees need to be oriented toward removing the causes. Yet these responses, as important as they are, do not help the millions of current refugees. Thus refugee policies must also be directed at immediate needs and imperatives. The long-range policies will need to accompany present-oriented responses, not replace them. It is also likely that the creation of refugees is endemic to the international order of nation-states. Although the numbers can be reduced and responses to their condition can be far more effective and humane, refugees are likely to remain as a permanent feature of the international scene even over the long term.

RESPONSES TO REFUGEE MOVEMENTS

While it was the hope and expectation of post–World War II internationalists that refugees represented a temporary challenge, the persisting generation, and indeed escalation, of refugees gives a far more sobering picture. Most refugees are from the third world, especially Asia and Africa, although the human catastrophe in the former Yugoslavia tragically shows that other continents are not immune from a sudden creation of refugees. It is also important to emphasize that by far the greatest number of refugees are residing in third-world countries, not affluent nations of the North.

Current international responses to such large numbers of people are painfully inadequate. The United Nations High Commissioner for Refugees (UNHCR) is the international agency charged with the responsibility for assisting refugees. Its budget is considerably less than what the United States alone spends on its own refugee programs and procedures.[64] Fortunately, UNHCR does not spend a great deal of time trying to determine if forced migrants fit exactly the international definition; UNHCR seeks to get aid to them, often working with private relief organizations. The immediate response, then, is to deliver life-sustaining aid to refugees who are organized into camps both to provide a more orderly way to distribute assistance and to protect the host country from a sudden inundation of new residents.

Generally three strategies are identified for responding to the plight of refugees. First is voluntary repatriation. This means that the refugee chooses to return to her home country when the fear of persecution is no longer present. Of course, most refugees would have preferred to remain in their homeland in the first place and want to return as soon as possible. Coerced or forced repatriation, however, is vigorously repudiated in international law and by human rights advocates. And for good reason. Forced repatriation could be exceedingly dangerous, as many Vietnamese boat people who were sent back against their will feared. Moreover, after refugees have lived away from their countries for some years, they sometimes prefer to live where they are rather than return, even though it may now be safe.

With the end of the Cold War, many more refugees were able to return home. For example, about 2.5 million refugees were repatriated in 1992.[65] But merely to return home does not end the refugees' struggles. The home environment may not be entirely safe after all. Even more difficult, the internal conditions in the home country may be so devastated that its capacities to incorporate large numbers of returning refugees are severely limited. Repatriation may be desirable, but if it is to be humanely practical, it will require ongoing international commitments.

A second response is incorporation into the country of first asylum. Refugees kept in camps for long periods of time may find work opportunities and social networks within the country outside the camp. They may prefer to move out of the camp and live as residents of that country if they are able to figure out a way to do it. This too is a limited option, because nations of first asylum contend they cannot absorb large numbers of refugees. Again, this seems to be available to only a small number of refugees, not the great majority.

A third response is resettlement. Refugees are moved from the country that first gave them protection to a "third country" where they may establish legal residence. The presumption here is that resettled refugees will remain in the third country, although it is possible for them to return to their home country when it is no longer dangerous. Unfortunately, the resettlement response is available to only a small percentage of the total number of refugees. Still this represents a critically important element in U.S. refugee policy.

The inadequacy of these responses to the tragedies of refugee existence is overwhelming. Most refugees remain in camps or find ways to fend for themselves in a temporarily protected place (sometimes called "self-settled"). It is important again to emphasize that by far the most refugees are protected in third-world locations, not in the affluent North. The striking current exception is the large number of refugees from the Balkan region seeking to move into European countries. In actuality the enclosed refugee camp has become the primary international response. Yet this is a highly problematic situation. The camp is not intended to be a permanent home but a

57

station for direct assistance and temporary haven on the way to a genuine home. Sometimes it is more like a prison to keep refugees from flooding the host country. Indeed the camp may help to provide immediate relief, but it is terribly inadequate as a long-term solution.[66]

We must remember that, in most cases, the refugees' escape from their home country is exceedingly traumatic. Not only do they have to pull up roots and establish a life in a strange place, they often have experienced violence or were vividly fearful of it. Physical and emotional wounds are gaping. Moreover, in refugee camps they probably are not able to carry on the occupations they had before. Opportunities for children are severely limited. Strains on families are intense. Women are all too frequently left out of leadership positions and denied opportunities to participate in plans about such essential matters as food distribution. They do not have money, as men may, and they are often the last to get food. Moreover, they continue to be subjected to male violence, even within this purportedly protected environment. Camps may even be managed as a part of a deterrence strategy. For example, in the 1980s, authorities in Hong Kong intentionally fostered miserable conditions in refugee camps to discourage (unsuccessfully) Vietnamese boat people from seeking asylum.[67]

Furthermore, in camps refugees tend to be placed in a dependency role where they are recipients of aid rather than being able to provide for themselves.[68] Indeed, some refugee scholars maintain that the camps better serve the interests of the international humanitarian assistance regime than they do the needs of refugees.[69] Thus, refugees and refugee advocates increasingly are calling for empowerment patterns of assistance which maximize the opportunities for refugees to make decisions about their communal organization and governance. Arguing that "the whole administrative machinery of camp aid distribution and practices is founded on the undermining of the refugees' autonomy and self-determination," these scholars advocate more self-settlement models of refugee organization or at least programs of aid distribution that are directed by the refugees themselves.[70]

Ethical Reflections

We have surveyed a broad number of issues that help us understand the plight of refugees today and the kinds of responses that the international community and the United States are making to this massive challenge. The major question, however, is one without a satisfactory response. How can peoples ensure places of safety, livelihood, and belonging for refugees in the short term and prevent the creation of refugees in the long term? While we plead and pray for answers, there is no clear solution. It is a political, ethical challenge of tremendous complexity with fateful human consequences for millions of people in the world. In chapter 5 we shall examine possible policy responses, but let us recognize that there is no substitute for the moral character of peoples that is rich enough to sustain persistent efforts to fashion evermore satisfactory responses.

One set of theological and ethical issues concerns perceptions. How are refugees perceived? Frequently they are viewed as burdens. As such, the overriding policy response is often directed toward avoiding such burdens, pushing the burden on someone else, or distributing the burden more equitably. Frequently, refugees are perceived as "different," "strange," "other than us." As such, the response to refugees is often shaped by feelings of threat, fear, discomfort, and insecurity. A Christian perspective will need to address especially the question of how refugees are to be perceived and valued.

Another set of theological and ethical issues concerns the relation of national boundaries and the human rights of refugees. Few would disagree with the conviction that refugees should have a right to safety and to other basic needs. But who has the responsibility to ensure that these rights are secured? How weighty are these rights when they are in conflict with the principle of national sovereignty? Do nations have a right to secure their borders against persons outside who seek refuge from life-threatening violence? Even though one might answer these questions by giving greater weight to the rights of refugees, assertions about the prerogatives of national sovereignty are, in fact, much more influential in the behaviors of states.[71] This too requires Christian ethical reflection.

There are other ethical issues as well. *Should we continue to distinguish between refugees and immigrants?* If so, what is the distinction and what are the implications of this distinction for refugee policy? We have anticipated this discussion by pointing to debates about how refugees should be defined. Those who argue for such a distinction believe the contextual factors behind refugee movements provide a greater moral claim than that of immigrants. We shall also consider this issue in the discussion of immigration.

59

What, specifically, is the United States' responsibility with regard to refugees? What kind of commitment should the United States make to the resettlement of refugees within its borders, and which refugees should be given priority? For example, one might suggest that we have a greater responsibility for refugees within our geographical region than for those from far away (Cubans and Haitians rather than Sudanese). Or perhaps the United States has a greater responsibility for refugees it has helped to generate as a result of U.S. foreign policy than for those the United States has not directly caused (Indo-Chinese rather than persons from Myanmar [Burma]). Not only do we need to consider which criteria of selection should govern U.S. resettlement of refugees, but we also must consider what the U.S. international role and responsibility are in response to the majority of refugees who will not be resettled here.

Still other issues need attention. In light of the fact that the United States cannot admit all the world's refugees, *how many should we admit?* We have emphasized that most of the world's refugees are protected in third-world countries. *What, then, is fair and equitable burden sharing among the various countries in the world, including the United States, especially given huge disparities in power, resources, and capacities to respond?* Finally, we need to consider what refugee reception means to persons and communities in the United States. Some contend that our first responsibility is to the poor and powerless who already live in the United States and that the focus on refugees diverts attention from and further expands the existing underclass. Moreover, *what are the limits to the capacities and responsibilities of U.S. peoples to incorporate refugees in their communities?*

I believe a Christian perspective provides a way to interpret these questions and to develop responses to them without providing any specific policy answers. *Christian ethics affects the way Christians view refugees and their rights, the claims of nation-states, and the responsibilities of national communities for the protection of refugees.* Christian ethics especially affects the church and its discernment of what faithfulness to God requires in response to the desperate plight of refugees. Finally, I believe that Christian ethics can make a vital contribution to wider public deliberations about refugee policy. That is, Christian ethics shapes the character of Christian communities and also the character of its public witness and advocacy. These ideas will be developed in greater detail in chapters 3 and 4.

2

U.S. IMMIGRATION POLICY: LAND OF OPPORTUNITY OR FORTRESS AMERICA?

Acentral element in the U.S. national self-understanding is its immigrant character. It is inconceivable that a rehearsal of the national narrative would not include immigration as an integral element. Without doubt the narrative still has power. Americans believe the United States is a heterogeneous unity forged out of the immigration of many diverse nationalities and cultures. Most seem proud of it. They believe Americans are a generous people who want to keep this country at least somewhat open to newcomers. Americans value the contributions immigrants have made in the past to scientific and technological inventiveness, economic development, and cultural richness. Moreover, the democratic principles and polity of the United States seem to fit better with an inclusionist orientation toward immigrants than with exclusionist barriers.

Even in the face of mounting anti-immigration feeling, political representatives have a difficult time enacting rigidly exclusionist legislation. It would seem somehow "un-American." Still, the standard American immigration story, which highlights the national openness to immigrants, often does not accommodate the other side of the story. How many know about exclusionist laws that specifically kept out Chinese and Japanese? How many know about the establishment of explicitly racialist quotas to keep the United States "white" and systematically exclude peoples of color? How many know about a long period in recent U.S. history in which few immigrants were admitted?

If the truth be told, the anti-immigration sentiment is just as "American" as the shined-up positive image. Both anti-immigration and pro-immigration traditions are powerful forces in U.S. history. Both have had an impact and continue to be expressed by passionate advocates. While sometimes the ideological line that divides one side from the other is clear, often it is blurred at best. In current debates, for example, it cannot be assumed that liberals are pro-immigration and that conservatives are anti-immigration. In each era, some arguments strike familiar themes; others accent new notes. Although the debate intensifies or cools in different periods, immigration has periodically evoked intense partisanship and controversy. Clearly, we are in the middle of another such time now. Immigration is changing and recreating America, and there is sharp disagreement about whether or not this is a good thing.

Until the latter part of the nineteenth century, the United States had a basically open and unrestricted relation to immigrants. This is not to say, however, that immigration was free from controversy and some efforts at control. The Alien and Sedition Acts of 1798 reflected tensions with France and fears that persons influenced by the French Revolution would be dangerous subversives. These laws also were attempts by the Federalists to attack the growing political power of pro-Republican immigrants. Both of these reasons for seeking to control immigration—that is, to keep out subversives and immigrant groups that would strengthen the opposition political party—crop up again at other times in U.S. history.

More portentous, however, was the earlier Naturalization Act of 1790. This Act explicitly specified that non-"white" immigrants were not eligible to become naturalized citizens of the United States. Only free "whites" could become naturalized citizens.[1] Incredibly, this prohibition was not changed until 1952. As Ronald Takaki points out, Chinese workers who were recruited to help build America were excluded from its polity. Not only were they denied citizenship, certain states denied them the right to vote or own property.[2]

> Study of the history of citizenship and suffrage disclosed a racial and exclusionist pattern. For 162 years, the Naturalization Law, while allowing various European or "white" ethnic groups to enter the United States and acquire citizenship, specifically denied citizenship to other groups on a racial basis. While suffrage was extended to white men, it was withheld from men of color.[3]

U.S. experience with immigration is inextricably connected with the dominance of racist categories for signifying "others."

The first large-scale immigration to the United States began early in the nineteenth century. Maldwyn Jones points out that "the five million immigrants of the period 1815 to 1860 were greater in number than the entire population of the United States at the time of its first census in 1790."[4] During these years, there were times when antiforeign feeling reached high levels of intensity. Especially strong was the hysteria of some Protestants toward Catholic immigrants. They regarded the growth of the Catholic church as a fundamental threat to American democratic institutions and Protestant hegemony. Some of the worries about immigration that became more influential in subsequent years began to be expressed during this time as well. Immigrants were tied to poverty and criminal behavior; their political influence was decried; and their tendency to stick together and persist in exhibiting strange customs was criticized.

In 1886 the Statue of Liberty was dedicated, inscribed with the now famous poem by Emma Lazarus welcoming the "huddled masses yearning to breathe free." However, almost at the same time the United States was for the first time enacting laws to control immigration. The most restrictive law was directed at the Chinese in California, outlawing Chinese immigration. A generation later the Japanese were the target of racist reaction on the West Coast and were subjected to the same kind of exclusion. The winds of immigration restriction were beginning to blow across the United States, although the full legislative impact did not occur until the early 1920s.

The antiforeign feeling directed especially at people of color or darker complexioned "whites" with different customs is often referred to as nativism. John Higham, one of the leading scholars on the history of nativism, defines it as "intense opposition to an internal minority on the ground of its foreign (i.e., "un-American") connections."[5] In Higham's interpretation, there are three primary traditions of nativism in U.S. history: anti-Catholic, antiradical, and Anglo-Saxon. Sometimes one tradition predominates; at other times all three may be powerful forces. Nativism often erupts when citizens experience economic hardship and social turmoil.

Around the turn of the century, a "new" immigration began to replace the old pattern. Instead of coming primarily from the British Isles, Germany, and Scandinavia, immigrants were now arriving from southern and eastern Europe. They looked different and acted different. Although anti-Catholic feeling and fear of anarchists and

63

socialists continued to exert an influence, nativism became increasingly controlled by racist doctrine and reaction. Feelings of white superiority joined with purportedly scientific conclusions about the qualitative differences among races to generate widespread concern about maintaining the racial purity of America. Should America "be peopled by British, German and Scandinavian stock, historically free, energetic, progressive, or by Slav, Latin and Asiatic races, historically down-trodden, atavistic, and stagnant?"[6]

In 1924, the United States adopted a rigidly restrictive and racially constructed immigration policy. Nationalities were to be assigned quotas based on the percentage of their numbers to the existing population of the United States as a whole (called the "national origins" system). Overall immigration was limited for the first time. Asians were excluded. Countries in the Western Hemisphere were not included in the quota assignments because their numbers were not yet regarded as significant. Clearly the policy was intended to maintain white dominance through controlling the racial composition of American society. In fact it accomplished this goal, and immigration as a whole was greatly reduced.

The national origins system remained in place for more than forty years. It was not changed until the Act of 1965, which instituted a very different system. This policy set numerical limits for each hemisphere and also for each country within the Eastern Hemisphere. Certain criteria for selecting which migrants to admit from within the quotas, now familiar, were established at this time: family unification, needed skills, or refugee status. While the Act was intended to keep the number of immigrants at about the same level as before, in fact the numbers increased sharply. Noteworthy also was the increase in immigrants from third-world countries. Especially large numbers of Asians and Mexicans entered the United States after 1965.

In the post–1965 period, the primary debate in the U.S. immigration policy was not the overall number of immigrants or the criteria by which they were selected. Instead, the debate focused on illegal immigration, especially from Mexico. Large numbers of undocumented workers (often called "illegal aliens") were entering the United States each year, although exactly how many is very hard to determine. The Immigration and Reform Control Act of 1986 (IRCA) attempted to deal with this by granting amnesty and an opportunity for citizenship to many undocumented persons already living in the

United States, and by penalizing employers who knowingly hired undocumented workers (called the employer sanctions provision of IRCA). Attempts have also been made, with debatable results, to tighten the enforcement of immigration law along the border between Mexico and the United States.

While certain voices expressed grave concerns about the number of illegal immigrants, the wider public did not yet seem greatly alarmed. In fact, in 1990, the U.S. Congress passed another immigration law that, among other things, raised the annual ceiling on immigration. This law also increased considerably the number of immigrants who could be admitted on the basis of skills. Still, however, most immigrants would be admitted for purposes of family unification. The 1990 Act also eliminated previously existing exclusions of homosexuals, persons with AIDS, and Communists.

Since the passage of the 1990 Act, however, the public pendulum seems to be swinging back toward anti-immigration sentiments. Support for severely restricting legal admission is growing. Still, illegal immigration continues to inflame the most vocal reactions, and California is the location of some of the loudest outcries. Pete Wilson, reelected governor of the state, has helped mobilize those who favor harsh measures to stop illegal immigration. The fact that Proposition 187 won the approval of the California voters by a sizable margin reflects the strength of anti-immigration views. This action, currently being tested in courts for its constitutionality, would deny education, health, and other social services to undocumented immigrants. Advocates for immigrants responded sharply to these views by claiming that "the proliferation of anti-immigrant initiatives and legislative proposals are linked by the desire to scapegoat immigrants, especially the undocumented, for the current economic hard-times hitting the U.S. economy."[7]

In the past, the United States did not revisit and change its immigration laws very often. Benchmark legislation can be counted on one hand. But the pressures to reexamine immigration policy have been occurring frequently in recent history; indeed, it is becoming an extended process in which it seems less and less likely that any one Act will settle the matter for long. The U.S. Congress established a special committee in 1978 to study immigration and make recommendations for changes. Yet another commission was mandated in 1990, chaired by Barbara Jordan, which sent its interim report to Congress in the fall of 1994. If immigration admission policy is a way that the United States "defines what an American is,"[8] then to arrive at a definition seems now to require continual struggle and negotiation. Controversies press and reveal core convictions and values. We will not soon be done with policy debates about immigration!

Current U.S. Immigration Policy

Before we explore the contemporary debates about U.S. immigration policy, we need to clarify what the policy is and what some of the characteristics of immigrants are. *How many immigrants enter the United States legally each year?* For 1995, the ceiling was set at 675,000, with some additional categories of persons exempted from the quota. With so many persons around the world wanting to emigrate to the United States, *how is the selection made?*

First, there is the same ceiling for every country: 25,000 persons. This fascinating system was put in place in 1965, although at the time it applied only to Eastern Hemisphere countries. Ironically, this was intended by some of its supporters to maintain the racial identities and national origins of past immigrants. Instead, the law established a criterion of multicultural and multinational diversity, radically different from the racist policy enacted in the 1920s. Rather unintentionally a very important normative principle was introduced, namely, universal equal treatment.[9]

Second, a preference system was put in place to determine which persons should be given priority. Up to now, primary preference has been given to family members, often called family reunification. The strong emphasis given to family-based immigration has been supported by church organizations involved in immigration and refugee ministries. Second to family unification in priority is immigrants who have occupational and entrepreneurial skills valued by the United States. The 1990 Act provided for proportionally more openings for needed workers than before, reflecting the influence of those who favor a more economics-based than family-based immigration policy. In summary, the United States developed "a system of quotas and preferences that favored family-based admissions, allowed for those with needed skills, authorized the same admissions level for all countries, and established an annual worldwide quota."[10]

A particularly controversial feature of the 1990 allotment of economic visas was a special category for major investors. One congressman, John Bryant from Texas, labeled this feature "the sale of American citizenship to anyone with one million dollars." Another congressperson commented, "However beneficial the investment may be . . . America would, for the first time in its history, be granting a statutory preference for citizenship based on wealth."[11] Such opposition notwithstanding, the provision was adopted.

Since 1965 the great majority of immigrants have come from Asia and the Americas. Anxiety over the racially and culturally transformative effect of this pattern also found legalized expression in the 1990 Act. Some members in Congress were worried that European countries especially have been underrepresented in recent immigration flows. So a certain number of visas are set aside annually to enhance greater "diversity," which really means peoples who are more like the majority U.S. population than the recent immigration population.[12]

It is estimated that in recent years slightly more than one million persons migrated to the United States each year, including legal immigrants, refugees, and illegal immigrants. The United States receives almost as many legal migrants each year as the combined total of all other countries.[13] Three-fourths of the immigrants come from ten countries: Mexico, Philippines, the former Soviet Union, Vietnam, Haiti, El Salvador, India, the Dominican Republic, China, and Korea.[14] What about the total number? Is the United States really being flooded? As usual, it depends on one's perspective. During the 1980s, the United States admitted a total of about 100,000 more immigrants than the highest previous decade, 1901 to 1910. But the percentage of newcomers to the existing population is 8 percent today, in contrast to 14 percent in 1900.[15] Restrictionists tend to cite the first set of statistics, and immigration advocates the second.

Questions People Often Ask

WHO ARE THEY?

It is difficult to summarize briefly the characteristics of immigrants. They are a very diverse population with differences between and within specific nationality groups. For example, although Koreans,

Chinese, and Indians are grouped together as Asian, there are important cultural differences between these nationalities. Some immigrants are highly educated before they arrive; others are not. Some work in jobs requiring manual labor; some work in professional positions as scientists, nurses, or engineers, while others are self-employed or entrepreneurs. While many immigrants are poor, they are rarely the most poor of their countries. They are persons who learn about opportunities beyond their own locality and who can imagine that a different life is possible. Immigrants are a self-selected group. By and large they are risk takers, hard working, and ambitious.

WHY DO IMMIGRANTS COME TO THE UNITED STATES?

Probably the most influential view is the "push-pull" theory. Push factors have to do with the circumstances in the home country that make persons want to leave. Perhaps they are unemployed or marginally employed, or perhaps they are highly educated but cannot pursue their occupation of choice. Pull factors are the magnets of the United States that lure the migrants. Jobs are available, wages are higher, and the opportunities are greater. For migrants from Mexico, the border is long and permeable enough to cross, and there may well be relatives and friends who can provide assistance.

Others suggest that push-pull forces are only part of the migration picture, especially when we consider the migration of low-wage workers. They point to the dynamics of the global economic system in which labor migration across borders is required. Conditions in both sending and receiving countries foster migration even though immigration policies may seek to discourage it. Sending countries need a release from the domestic pressures of an alienated unemployed or underemployed citizenry, and receiving countries need persons to take unpleasant work at a low wage.[16]

Moreover, migration patterns between countries often reflect a long history in which social networks have been established across borders. Some scholars have pointed out that the United States for decades has looked to Mexico and Puerto Rico to obtain unskilled and cheap labor. Employers have come to depend on flows of these workers, who often come from the same villages and regions. It is not solely or primarily the existence of poverty that produces migrants. Undocumented migrants tend to come from the same places in Mexico rather than being spread out in a roughly equal way throughout the country. The flows "are rooted in the history of prior economic and political relationships between sending and receiving nations."[17]

In fact, according to Gerald Lopez, this history is one of vigorous encouragement and promotion of migration from within the United States, even when it has been illegal. Established traditions are now strong enough that overt recruitment is no longer necessary.[18] The recent boatloads of undocumented immigrants from China show the same pattern. A disproportionately large number came from the Fuzhou area of the Fujian province of China, where the United States had sought seamen for its vessels in World War II.[19] It is misleading, therefore, to claim that the magnet of U.S. affluence and opportunity "naturally" pulls poor persons out of other countries with no active U.S. role when, historically, the United States has been drumming up workers from outside its borders.

WILL IMMIGRANTS MIX WITH THE REST OF AMERICAN SOCIETY?

Behind this question is often the image of the United States as a melting pot. There are many reasons why this is unsatisfactory. For one thing, it suggests settled Americans *want* immigrants to melt, when often they have vigorously tried to enforce patterns of segregation. For another thing, it implies that American society is a static, homogenized entity into which immigrants melt with no remaining trace. Instead, immigrants change America, and America changes immigrants. Immigrants often retain characteristics of their original nationality and culture as a feature of American society, not as something separate from Americanness. America may perhaps best be expressed in such metaphors as tossed salad or mosaic, or even as a rich and hearty brew in which diverse groups contribute unique ingredients to its ongoing fermentation and changing flavor.

But the question also points to anxieties about the concentration of immigration peoples in certain locales, especially in large cities. Does this indeed portend the fragmentation of American society along ethnic and linguistic lines? In fact, the spatial concentration of immigrant communities aids adaptation in the long run. It often provides jobs, information, and savvy about managing in a new country, and invaluable social and emotional support in a stressful transition. Ethnic solidarity also frequently becomes the chief avenue to political participation by immigrants. As Portes and Rumbaut put it, "the reaffirmation of distinct cultural identities—whether actual or

69

invented in the United States—has been the rule among foreign groups and has represented the first effective step in their social and political incorporation."[20]

SHOULDN'T IMMIGRANTS HAVE TO SPEAK ENGLISH?

This is one of the most volatile issues in the immigration debate. The reasons are not trivial. Part of the concern is the public expense and effort that are expended in multilingual communication. But perhaps a deeper concern is symbolic, the feeling that American unity is being undermined by apparently underwriting the perpetuation of separate linguistic enclaves. According to a recent study of the relation of newcomers and residents in six American communities, language is the greatest source of conflict. Language is a matter of tension not only between those who speak English and those who speak a different language. It is often also a source of conflict between and within immigrant groups.[21]

Language not only provides a means of communication to carry on the practical business of living. It also provides a sense of identity and a way of grasping and interpreting experience. Language carries a tradition and a worldview that is communal but not universal. To be required to give up one's language is to be required to give up a part of oneself and one's group identity. To have one's language discounted is to be discounted oneself. Some of us can remember our own experience in public schools when Mexican children were not permitted to speak Spanish. But changing languages is not like changing clothes. It is really like entering another world. It is not surprising, then, that the retention of language is important to groups that share a common language. And it is not surprising that language is a point of conflict and tension between different linguistic groups.

But behind the criticisms of immigrants is the assumption they do not want to learn English and will only do so if they have to. But immigrants do learn English, especially the children of first-generation newcomers. Success stories still abound. The 1988 U.S. National Spelling Bee champion was Rageshree Ramachandran, who was born in India, and the second-place winner was a Chinese-American boy. In 1985, the winner was also a youth born in India, whose family spoke Tamil at home.[22] In Denver, a Spanish-speaking Serbian-Croatian-American received the 1994 award for National Bilingual Teacher of the Year.[23]

At a time when many English-speaking parents want their children to learn other languages in school and indeed are proud of them when they spend a year abroad becoming fluent in a second language, it is ironic that there is such a negative feeling toward immigrants' retention of non-English languages. Moreover, there is solid evidence to show that students who are bilingual perform better academically than those who are monolingual.[24] First-generation immigrants may well have difficulty learning English. Those of us who have attempted to speak a non-English language when traveling outside the United States should have some appreciation for how difficult this is. But learning English is not a prerequisite for the first-generation immigrants' economic progress.[25] And monolingualism in a language other than English is rare in the second generation.

English is not in any danger of being replaced as the common language. The question is whether or not immigrants will be both helped to learn English and encouraged to retain their original language. The two work together. If the goal is to help immigrants learn English, then this can be better done by making language education available, not by isolating and stigmatizing them for not being able to speak English. Retaining the original language is important not only for fostering linguistic richness in a multicultural America, but also for a healthy group and self-image.

DO IMMIGRANTS BURDEN THE WELFARE SYSTEM?

One of the new ingredients in the immigration debates since 1965 is the existence of the welfare system in the United States for the poorest members of society. Are immigrants coming to the United States now to take advantage of the welfare system rather than to work? Professional economists cite statistics to support sharply different conclusions about the economic impacts of immigration. Statistical analyses do not settle the argument but further fuel it.

Donald Huddle argues that several studies in 1992 showed that immigrants used considerably more public money than they paid in taxes.[26] In analyzing the 1990 Census, he maintains that "the poverty rate of immigrants is 42.8 percent higher than that of the native born." Moreover, "on average, immigrant households receive 44.2 percent more public assistance dollars than do native households."[27] Similarly, George Borjas believes evidence supports the contention that poverty rates and utilization of welfare are high among unskilled immigrants.

71

In the changing work situation in the United States, they will have an increasingly difficult time establishing themselves economically.[28]

The Urban Institute, in a study based on 1990 Census data, asserted instead that immigrants generated far more revenue than they used. The analysis also held that 2.3 percent of legal immigrants (not including refugees) drew on public benefits during the 1980s, whereas 3.3 percent of persons born in the United States used these benefits.[29] The heaviest use of welfare is by refugees and elderly immigrants. We have seen why refugees are more likely to need this assistance. Elderly immigrants are not eligible for Social Security, so some form of public support is their only recourse for retirement income. For understandable reasons, undocumented immigrants do not draw heavily on public benefits. For legal immigrants, welfare use actually decreased in the 1980s. Even for refugees, the use of welfare decreases steadily over time.[30]

Another study compared the use of public assistance in Los Angeles County by Latinos (16.9 percent) and non-Latino whites (41.7 percent).[31] It is estimated that the amount of money spent on educating the children of illegal immigrants is 2 percent of the total expenditure on education.[32] The Census Bureau recently reported that while many immigrants start out poor, many also move quickly out of poverty.[33] Julian Simon argues that immigrants do not use more social welfare services than natives, and that immigrants contribute more in taxes than they use in social services.[34] In further support of this contention, a business-oriented publication reported that immigrants pay more than $90 billion in taxes in contrast to their use of about $5 billion in welfare.[35]

It needs to be emphasized that the primary debate about economic consequences is focused on unskilled immigrants rather than those who enter the United States at skilled and professional levels of employment. But what are we to do with these discrepancies? Analysts of data bring assumptions to their work. Different sets of data can lead to different conclusions. And often in analyses about immigration, the data are incomplete. Costs may indeed be greater at city and county levels since the state and federal governments receive most of the taxes, but this is also true for nonimmigrants.[36] The most serious issue may well be welfare dependency and economic justice for the poor. That also is not primarily a problem of immigrants but of a large underclass of U.S. poor, which also includes some immigrants.

72

At the least we can say that the economic consequences of labor immigration are disputed. This should lead to skepticism about alarmist claims that immigrants are a heavy burden on U.S. society. They may in fact continue to be an economic benefit. Howard Adelman maintains on economic grounds alone that the admission of refugees and immigrants is a good investment, yielding a return higher than most comparable capital investments.[37] Similarly, *Business Week* concludes that "by any economic calculus, their [immigrants'] hard work adds far more to the nation's wealth than the resources they drain."[38]

DO IMMIGRANTS DISPLACE U.S. WORKERS?

When we look at unemployment figures, it seems logical to assume that more Americans could be employed if there were not so many immigrants taking the jobs. Characteristically the U.S. labor movement has favored restriction on immigration precisely because of the assumption that immigrants compete for jobs and are usually willing to work for low pay, presumably driving down the wages that American workers would receive.

Vernon Briggs is one of the most influential proponents of this view. He maintains that even though a number of studies do not provide hard evidence for significant displacement, they are not entirely adequate for measuring recent labor impacts. He quotes former U.S. Secretary of Labor, Ray Marshall, who asserts "there can be little doubt that immigration displaces workers" and "elementary economics suggests that at a time of high unemployment, increased labor supplies depress wages and reduce employment opportunities for legal residents unless you completely segregate labor markets."[39] Briggs emphasizes especially the impact of immigrants on employment opportunities for citizens and resident aliens in heavily impacted urban areas.

Yet, surprisingly, there is not a great deal of evidence that immigration has this negative effect. Borjas contends on the basis of empirical research that "immigrants have little impact on the earnings and employment opportunities of natives."[40] Similarly, Julian Simon maintains that, generally, immigrants have little negative effect on jobs, but there are some instances in which particular groups of U.S. workers may be hurt by particular immigrants.[41] It may be that com-

73

petition is greatest with residents who have dropped out of high school and have minimal skills.[42]

Immigrants, however, also create new jobs and start new businesses. They take jobs that natives do not want. They contribute to overall economic productivity with their work and their spending. Immigrants have revitalized decaying sections of large cities.[43] Immigrant labor, undocumented as well as legal, has been vital in the survival of certain industries such as textiles, garments, and footwear in Los Angeles and New York.[44] With declining population growth rates in the United States, Americans may need the immigration of young workers to fuel the economic system and to finance the Social Security system, especially when large numbers of baby boomers hit retirement age.

These considerations of economic interest, even when they are read in a positive light, are not without morally troubling features. If sectors of the U.S. economy depend on economically marginal people to fill undesirable jobs at rock-bottom wages, then this is exploitive even though they are eager to do the work. It may be because of immigrant labor that certain businesses can survive and prices for certain services and products can be kept low, but this can hardly provide the basis for moral celebration. Immigration raises questions about fair wages, fair prices, and humane working conditions that pertain not only to immigrants but to all those who work in semiskilled and unskilled jobs. All the more troubling is the prospect of large numbers of unskilled immigrants and other working poor helping to finance retirement benefits for an aging and affluent population.

Again, most questions related to the economic impact of immigration point to manual laborers. Rarely are questions raised about U.S. reliance on immigrants who are highly educated professionals. Yet this too is morally troubling. Countries abroad invest resources in the education of their young, and the United States reaps the benefit. Sometimes this is referred to as the "brain drain." But it is not just that the United States may lure the best and brightest from other countries. Instead of relying on its own education system to equip its citizenry to fill occupational needs, the United States is using without compensation the educational institutions of others. It would seem the United States should be investing more heavily in its own peoples, especially in historically marginalized communities, to provide educational and occupational incentives and hope and to fill national occupational needs.

WHAT ABOUT ILLEGAL IMMIGRATION?

The most difficult question in U.S. immigration policy is what to do about illegal immigration. Persons who are in the United States illegally are without visas or the green card (signifying resident-alien status) or have stayed beyond the time period permitted. Some simply live without legal documents. Others obtain false identification papers. If these persons are discovered, they may be deported. They live an underground existence, trying not to do anything that would call attention to the fact that they are undocumented. Fear and anxiety are daily companions. Under these circumstances, it is not surprising that they do not often seek out public assistance. They are not legally eligible, and they may be discovered. Of course, when they have children born in the United States, these children *are* U.S. citizens; and they are eligible for public assistance.

Although not all illegal immigrants come from Mexico,[45] it is this movement that generates the most controversy. In legal terminology, these persons are referred to as "illegal aliens." This designation is objectionable on two counts. First, "alien" has come to mean something different than a person with a different nationality. It conveys the notion of a being who is not really human, someone radically "other" and possibly dangerous. Migrants are human beings, and our language should convey this recognition. Similarly, migrants are not illegal. They may be inside the United States illegally, but they are not themselves illegal. Therefore I shall use the term *undocumented workers* or *undocumented migrants*. This communicates more accurately that these immigrants are in the United States without legal documents, and most have entered the United States because they want to work.

Concern over the number of undocumented workers from Mexico became publicly significant in the 1970s, generating a flurry of studies and policy proposals. Eventually (1986) the Immigration and Reform Control Act (IRCA) was passed primarily to deal with this particular phenomenon. Two features were prominent. First, undocumented persons who had lived in the United States prior to 1982 (or 1986 for agricultural workers) were granted legal standing and the opportunity to seek U.S. citizenship. The fact that they entered the United States illegally would not be held against them. The offer of amnesty

75

was a recognition that large numbers of undocumented persons would be better dealt with by an acceptance of this reality than by attempts to identify and deport them, or to leave them hidden. Amnesty also represented a moral acknowledgment of the contributions of undocumented workers and their functional membership in local communities and the national society. Legalization of their status would help to protect them against abuses by employers who sought to take advantage of their vulnerability.

The second major feature of IRCA is the so-called employers sanction provision. This makes it illegal for employers knowingly to hire undocumented workers. At best this provision prevents employers from exploiting undocumented workers; it requires employers to hire persons who are legal residents or citizens; and it provides a mechanism to discourage illegal immigration that would work in tandem with immigration controls at the border. Yet critics argue that it is simply ineffective as a way to prevent illegal immigration. They also contend that it is inappropriate to expect employers to be enforcement agents of national immigration policy. Especially important from an ethical perspective, employers sanction has contributed to discrimination against Hispanics in the United States who are legal residents or citizens. And finally, employers in many instances have not been held accountable to the law and continue knowingly to use and abuse undocumented workers.

Whatever conclusions one arrives at regarding IRCA, it did not resolve concerns about continuing migration of undocumented workers from Mexico. For some, the ongoing influx means that "the United States has lost control of its borders." That is, the United States seemingly cannot screen effectively those who enter the country legally from those who enter illegally. Border towns in California and Texas are most heavily affected, even though the immigrants can be found eventually in many different sections of the country.

The fear is that without effective control, the United States is subjected to a "tidal wave" of poor Mexicans looking for a better life, inundating U.S. communities with large numbers of persons who do not speak English, and who draw heavily on publicly financed education, health, and welfare services. Not only are many persons worried about the social impact on local communities and the economic impact on public funding, some immigration advocates worry that large numbers of undocumented persons undermine public hospitality for legal immigrants and refugees. Restrictionists believe that many Mexican women cross the border to have babies in the United States so that their children can be U.S. citizens, and that others are drawn by the prospects of obtaining government benefits.

Advocates for undocumented workers counter by maintaining that these persons are unfairly blamed for economic and social distresses that are not caused by the migrants. They become convenient scapegoats for a whole host of problems. Scapegoating becomes all the more virulent when it is combined with racist sentiments about Mexicans and other Hispanics. The outcry against undocumented workers is often seen as an expression of xenophobia—the fear and hatred of "others" who are not "like us."

Advocates contend that Mexican migrants contribute more to American society than they cost. Most are young adults who are adventurous enough to take the uncertain and often risky journey north. They come because they want to work and are willing to work at the most unpleasant and lowest paying jobs. Often they send a portion of their income to families back home in Mexico. Often, also, they come from locales in Mexico where networks of labor migration have been in operation for a long time, frequently with the encouragement of employers in the United States.

Although the migration of Mexicans into the United States is clearly at the forefront of public attention, several recent events have expanded public discussion. It is estimated that large numbers of undocumented Chinese immigrants enter the United States each year and settle primarily in New York. The dramatic and heartrending story of the three hundred Chinese immigrants on the freighter *Golden Venture* captured public attention in the United States. These persons had paid smugglers to bring them to the United States, and even after arrival they continued in a kind of indentured servitude to the smugglers to pay for their voyage. On this occasion, they had been on the freighter for four months, traveling in miserable conditions, and were eventually dumped in the bitterly cold waters off one of New York's beaches. Several persons died in this appalling act of cruelty.[46]

According to various accounts, the trafficking of human beings has become big business. Similar appalling stories abound about the treatment of Mexican migrants by "coyotes," the term for persons who are paid to get undocumented persons across the border to the United States. Clearly immigration policy must now seek to prevent

77

the smuggling of persons and to prosecute vigorously those who do. The public outcry to the *Golden Venture* tragedy is a response to the misery of the immigrants and the cruel ways they are exploited. But this incident has also been another cause for alarm for a public who has been led to think the United States is besieged by illegal immigrants coming by land, by air, and by sea. In fact, although immigrant smuggling must be dealt with effectively, the alarm is frequently far out of proportion to the numbers involved.[47]

The Contemporary Immigration Debate

Immigration is one of the most inflammatory issues in America in the nineties. Exclusionist pressures are becoming more influential again after thirty years of selectively admitting significant numbers of immigrants. But immigrant advocates are also vocal, some in fact contending that the issue of immigrants' rights is the civil rights movement of the nineties. It may be that immigration policy is similar to debates about abortion. How one views the matter may have little to do with rational arguments or empirical studies. One may be disposed either to favor or to oppose immigration on the basis of perspectives and values that may be more unconscious than conscious.

Certainly persons' experiences with immigrants, positive or negative, or a more complex combination of both, will have an important influence on their view of the matter. Marilyn Hoskin maintains that Americans who have interacted with immigrant workers are more likely to be positive than those who have not had this experience. Although income level does not correlate with attitudes of Americans toward immigrants, less education and "lower" occupational status does tend to correlate with anti immigration views. Higher education, especially in the liberal arts, tends to foster more positive attitudes. It may be, as Hoskin points out, that the difference is not only a matter of exposure to ideas that promote cultural diversity but also the level of vulnerability people feel toward the presence of immigrants.[48]

Whatever the reasons are for the intense disagreements about immigration policy, deeper levels of conviction and value are often disclosed even when they are not articulated. These debates have to do with meanings and definitions of America, notions about the good society, alternative visions of the future, the character of Americans, and rankings of conflicting values—all of which contain implicit if not explicit ethical content. As with most public policy debates, ethical considerations do not lead simply to one side or the other. Ethics is intertwined with personal experience, notions of personal and group interest, and analysis of information in virtually indistinguishable patterns.

We shall now outline briefly the debate between, to state the matter rather too baldly, the inclusionists and the restrictionists. We have already discussed some of these differences in the previous section, but now we shall seek to set forth the chief terms of the debate in a more unified way.

INCLUSIONISTS

America was founded on democratic principles that affirm the equal dignity of each individual person. Freedom is perhaps America's highest value: freedom from despotism and persecution, and freedom to pursue personal aspirations and happiness, under law to which each is equally accountable. America is a nation that has been formed by a cosmopolitan mixture of the world's diverse peoples, not by people of a single race, culture, or religious creed. America is an immigrant nation. The contributions of immigrants have made America what it is. America continues to welcome newcomers who share the dream of freedom, especially those who are persecuted, oppressed, and in grave personal danger.

Since generous immigration policies are relatively exceptional among nation-states, this characteristic is justifiably a matter of national pride for Americans. To shut out immigrants is to violate the very character of America itself. Restrictive views are not congruent with the nation's best moral tradition. Throughout U.S. history, restrictionists have appealed to the worst features of the American people: white racism, national xenophobia, cultural ethnocentrism, and economic selfishness.

It is the very diversity of immigrants that makes America a strong and dynamic society. The challenges that immigrants pose to settled communities create tensions, but they are the ones that generate creativity and vitality. Immigrants bring a belief in the "American dream" that revitalizes over and over again a hope in the future of American society. The American dream may be tarnished for many

79

long settled in the United States, but for many immigrants it is still compelling. The dream is believed, and there are enough examples of dreams being realized to make these beliefs credible for others.

Immigrants bring a diversity of customs and perspectives that enrich American society. The popularity of cultural fairs gives evidence of this, with a fascinating and invigorating array of different foods, clothes, arts and crafts, languages and accents, and physical characteristics. Crowds gather to hear a Peruvian musical group while munching on a falafel sandwich or Chinese eggroll. After all, what is American culture, anyway? It is certainly not a Euro-American creation alone (itself a multicultural mix). For example, many regard the hot dog as characteristic American cuisine. Yet this is a contribution of German immigrants and was not an entirely welcomed dish during the years of anti-German feeling in World War I.

American culture already reflects the characteristics and contributions of diverse peoples. Continuing openness to cultural change through the interaction of the world's peoples *within* a single society is central to the promise of the American experiment. America is not yet completed. Moreover, an inclusionist orientation to the multicultural character of immigration can provide a far better window to the challenges of diversity in the rest of the world than the constrictive view of restrictionists.

Immigrants also bring tangible economic benefits. It is curiously inconsistent for Americans to value hard work and economic ambition and then criticize immigrants for using their ingenuity to get to the United States to try to create a better life for themselves and their families. Immigration requires strong motivation, persistence, and courage. The fainthearted do not make the attempt. The rest of the United States benefits from both the highly skilled and the unskilled work of immigrants, especially over the long term. Immigrants work in existing jobs, create new jobs, buy goods, and pay taxes. They should be valued and welcomed rather than subjected to discrimination and hostility. While a selective admission policy needs to be humanely enforced, the United States must continue to have a generous immigration policy.

RESTRICTIONISTS

It is true that the United States is an immigrant nation. Americans may indeed take pride in this. But the situation today is very different than it was in the nineteenth and early twentieth centuries. The United States no longer needs an expanding labor force to work in burgeoning industries. The United States no longer needs additional people to populate the countryside. There are limits to how many people can be humanely incorporated into American society. Immigration puts increasingly severe strains on large cities. Overpopulation and damage to the natural and physical environments go hand in hand. Overcrowding along with the clash of diverse cultures creates major social tensions and human distresses in cities like Miami and Los Angeles.

Immigration also threatens the unity of American society and the cultural supports that are necessary for democracy to flourish. Immigration is creating a balkanized society in which ethnic communities are more concerned with their separate identity than with the common good of the whole. A proliferation of different languages makes communication among peoples exceedingly difficult. Those who come may not have any experience with or commitment to the responsibilities of living in a democratic polity. Immigration is eroding the cohesion of American society, which is rather fragile in any case. There are serious conflicts not so much between whites and people of color as between peoples of color themselves.

Resentment among citizens and legal residents is increasing. It is wrong to read this as ethnocentrism or racism. Rather it is an excessive number of newcomers that strains the capacities of communities to absorb and integrate them. The inclusionist viewpoint is often the stance of an educated elite who are themselves removed from the direct consequences of too many immigrants. It is elitist not to take into account the views of ordinary Americans.

It is the responsibility of nations to control their borders. This is a legitimate and necessary function of national sovereignty. Nations must ensure an orderly pattern of migration into their midst. Otherwise the well-being of those already living and working there may be undermined. "Our first duty is to our own citizens."[49] Without effective control of borders, the United States is in danger of being flooded by people from poor and overpopulated third-world countries. The potential flow is inexhaustible. There is no way that the United States can admit all the people in the world who would like to migrate here.

Immigrants often take jobs away from Americans. They may drive the wages down for American workers and make the organization of workers for better conditions and wages more difficult. They tend to increase the already severe problem of unemployment. They often end up on welfare services, thereby deriving benefits from the tax-paying citizens. They are frequently a social and economic drain on communities' resources. It is not national selfishness to protect Americans from excessive immigration. Other countries need to take responsibility for their own people's well-being. It is clear that immigration must be restricted and that restrictions must be effectively enforced.

ANALYSIS OF THE DEBATE

A great deal of the public debate is utilitarian in character. Does immigration bring, on balance, beneficial or harmful results for American society? We have discussed aspects of this question earlier. Of course, inclusionists maintain that immigration is largely beneficial, and restrictionists argue that it is more harmful. Sometimes each side points to economic benefits or liabilities. Other times the argument is about cultural pluses or minuses, namely the values of multicultural diversity or the negatives of cultural fragmentation. As we have seen, it is difficult to agree on the data by which utilitarian comparisons can be made. It is also problematic to make comparative judgments about nonquantifiable cultural benefits or liabilities. Consequences must certainly be taken into account and debated, but there are other ethical issues lodged in the debate that are just as important.

Race

In light of U.S. history, it would be naive to think that race is not a factor in the debate, even if it is not explicitly articulated. Even though Tocqueville in the nineteenth century could describe America as "a society which comprises all the nations of the world,"[50] this statement is much more true today.

America is indeed a multiracial country, and the changed character of immigration since 1965 has made it even more so. Since by far the largest number of immigrants in the past thirty years have been persons of color (primarily Asian, Latin American, Caribbean), it is difficult to disentangle a restrictionist view from issues of race and racism.

In his influential study of nativism and U.S. immigration policy, John Higham identified Anglo-Saxon racism as one of its chief sources and manifestations.[51] But explicitly racist arguments about immigration are not *publicly* acceptable today in the way they were in the early twentieth century. Where racist sentiment drives anti-immigration views, it generally must find a different and more publicly acceptable face in public policy discourse. Racism has largely gone underground, at least in public debate. While its moral illegitimacy in the public arena is to be celebrated, its continuing virulence in more disguised forms makes it more difficult to identify and confront.

There is some indication, however, that this is changing. Some are beginning to draw explicitly on racialist reasoning to support a restrictive position on immigration. Brimelow, for example, argues that multiracial societies just do not work. He does not assert innate white racial superiority over peoples of color. Rather he maintains that a unified America requires a strong white ethnic majority. Immigration, by rapidly changing the ethnic composition of American society, is a threat to cultural and national solidarity. The cultural differences embodied in the racial identities of recent immigrants are too great to be incorporated in this nation.[52]

Is it possible to be a restrictionist without also being a racist? Is it possible to favor strong measures to prevent illegal immigration from Mexico without being driven by xenophobia? I believe it is. There is a morally credible case to be made for more restrictive policies. This position should not be branded as inherently racist. The restrictionists raise legitimate concerns that must be carefully addressed, not simply dismissed out of hand. Many Hispanic Americans favor greater restrictions along the U.S./Mexico border. Some restrictionists maintain that the first responsibility of the United States is more effectively to open opportunities to its own people of color in the underclass rather than to expand further their numbers.[53]

Restrictionists might also argue that immigration can foster competition between communities of color within the existing social system rather than enhance the prospects for a cooperative mobilization for racial and economic justice. Cities have experienced conflicts between Koreans and African Americans, between African Americans and Latinos/Latinas, and between Latinos/Latinas and Southeast Asians. To be sure, these conflicts occur in the context of white racism in American society as a whole. Still, immigration may foster and intensify racial ethnic conflicts. Immigration may contribute to the separateness of diverse racial ethnic communities rather than lead to a more inclusive multiracial and multiethnic national community.

Whatever may be the merits of the above views, restrictionists must still deal directly with the force of white supremacy in American history. Restrictionists have the moral responsibility to oppose explicitly racist impulses in the restrictionist movement. They must also demonstrate that their own views can be disentangled from racism. When restrictionists express alarm at the growing population of "ethnic minorities" and the declining birthrates of Caucasians, the racist assumptions are all too clear. When fears are expressed about increasing violence within and between communities of color without addressing the continuing realities of racial injustice in American life, white racist assumptions are evident. When growth in the Hispanic population in certain states is viewed as a threat to American cultural unity, this reflects the racist notion that Caucasian homogeneity is the cultural norm. When certain immigrants are singled out for especially punitive treatment, as in California's Proposition 187, it is difficult to deny the force of racism in its appeal and effects.

Why is there such resistance to a Hispanicization of certain areas along the southern border of the United States or even to a Hispanic majority in the state of California? Apparently some Americans perceive a growing Hispanic minority as a threat to the dominance of white culture. Yet many American citizens are Hispanic, and many Hispanics are (North) Americans and have been for generations. Whatever American culture means, it must already be inclusive of Hispanic influences. Whatever American culture means, it must be inclusive of African Americans, Native Americans, Asian Americans, and Arab Americans. The notion that there is a white cultural hegemony in the United States to be maintained in the face of immigrants of color is a morally repugnant expression of Anglo-Saxon racism.

Racism has been called the Achilles' heel of American democracy, the deepest and most egregious contradiction between American ideals and American reality. It is not simple to know how in public policy both to affirm the distinctive identities of racial ethnic communities and to shape a unified and just multiracialist democracy. But it is one of the most profound ethical challenges of our current historical situation. Immigration policy is a place where this challenge must be engaged.

Cultural Unity and Diversity

Nativism has often been an influential component in American restrictionism. In addition to Anglo-Saxon racism, nativism in the past has also been driven by anti-Catholic and antiradical sentiments.[54] Today these elements are not very important. Anti-Catholic views are simply not a factor in contemporary restrictionist rhetoric. It may be that anti-Jewish feeling is still operative in reaction to the admission of Jewish refugees from the former Soviet Union, although this has little bearing on policy deliberations. It is more likely that anti-Muslim views affect some attitudes toward immigrants from Muslim countries, especially since the Muslim population in the United States is growing. Again, however, anti-Muslim feeling is not often articulated in current immigration debates.

Antiradical views continue to rise in influence from time to time, although overall such views do not seem to be a major factor at this time. The chief expression of antiradicalism is the worry about terrorists. For example, Arab immigrants have sometimes experienced suspicion and hostility when Arab organizations have been tied to terrorist acts. In the 1980s the concern that some Central American refugees were Communist fed into the national debate. But this sentiment was not nearly as potent as the charge that there were too many economic migrants flooding the country. The religious faith and political ideology of immigrants have just not been major elements in recent restrictionist efforts.

The deeper cultural issue in the 1990s is the relation of unity and diversity. Is immigration contributing to the fragmentation of American society into culturally distinct ethnic units with little sense of identification with the wider national society? Restrictionists frequently use the word *balkanization* to depict what is happening. Although the rhetoric is inflated, it is used precisely to draw parallels between immigration patterns in the United States and the ferocious violence taking place between ethnic peoples in the former Yugoslavia. The fear is that ethnic communities care more about maintaining their cultural distinctiveness than adapting to the traditions and mores of their new home. The fragmentation feeds competition and conflict between groups rather than cooperation.

Restrictionists also contend that immigration should be curtailed or stopped until the United States has had time to incorporate newcomers successfully into its communities. A representative of this

85

view is Roy Beck, who wrote recently about the experience of Wausau, Wisconsin, in receiving sizable numbers of refugees and immigrants. He quotes one local woman as saying, "This was a very nice thriving community; now immigration problems have divided the town and changed it drastically. . . . Neighborhood is pitted against neighborhood."[55] The question here has to do with the capacity of American communities to absorb cultural differences. Beck argues that the 1924 restriction on immigration provided time for recent German immigrants to be integrated with older New England Yankee residents. They were able to fashion a cultural unity that could sustain the admission of some additional newcomers but not the large numbers of recent years.[56]

For restrictionists, the societal requirements for cultural unity are being strained to the breaking point. The United States keeps admitting new people whose cultural and linguistic differences from much of American society understandably generates tensions and conflicts. It is not possible for a society to continue to cope successfully with the escalating problems this necessarily introduces. Cultural alienation of immigrant communities and cultural backlash of established communities are the regrettable, but not surprising, consequences of unrelieved pressures from large numbers of newcomers. The absorptive capacity of American culture to receive and incorporate newcomers has about reached its limit.

Inclusionists, on the other hand, believe restrictionists greatly exaggerate the tensions generated by immigration. For inclusionists the cultural diversity represented in immigrant communities is a national treasure. Diversity does not need to be feared or resisted. Instead it deserves to be valued and supported. The most powerful tendencies in American culture are toward the homogenization of differences, not the survival of ethnic distinctiveness. The latter is in fact the more urgent challenge. The diversity of immigrants does not undermine or threaten the unity of American society. Groups that settle here do in fact overwhelmingly want to live within the laws, send their children to school, and work in the economy. They value the freedom and opportunity that the United States affords. Societal unity does not need to be built on cultural uniformity.

From an inclusionist perspective, a way to characterize the relation of immigrants to American society is incorporation. The United States should not seek to assimilate or absorb newcomers. Instead it should seek to incorporate (in-body) immigrants in the wider American community. They become part of a corporate body that is continually re-creating itself. They contribute to it and are influenced by it. They can maintain their distinctiveness while also becoming valuable members of the society as a whole. They have a place. They are welcome. They belong. They should be encouraged and even assisted in the transition. But their diversity should be respected and valued. The price of admission to the United States is not to hand over their cultural distinctiveness. They are invited to participate in an ever-changing American culture and society, not to fit into an already finished cultural product.

A strong cultural identity and ethnic self-affirmation in fact are important for the mental health, educational achievement, and eventual incorporation of immigrants in American society. Ethnic solidarity is partly a response to immigrants' experience of marginalization and rejection in the dominant culture. But it also helps immigrants negotiate the stressful passage from one home to another. The flip side of this picture is that the immigrants who seek most fully to assimilate into dominant American culture experience higher degrees of mental and social disorders.[57] For inclusionists, the cultural diversity that immigrants bring is healthy for both immigrants and the wider society. It does not undermine societal unity but in fact contributes to a dynamic unity that is stronger than one built on cultural uniformity.

The cultural conflict today between restrictionists and inclusionists is deep and frequently bitter, but it is not entirely new. Social historians of the twentieth century point out that it is an ongoing debate in American life. When immigration policy becomes contested, these clashing perspectives surface again and again. Monists, or assimilationists, believe the establishment of a normative cultural identity for the United States is essential for a healthy society. People who choose to come to the United States should be prepared to adopt this identity for themselves rather than to perpetuate cultural characteristics of the former home country.

Ethnic pluralists, on the other hand, believe that the U.S. cultural identity is best understood as cosmopolitan, a free interaction of diverse peoples in a dynamic societal project. After examining these polarized options, Higham proposes a mediating position called "pluralistic integration." By this he means there should be respect for cultural particularities while also keeping ethnic boundaries permeable and valuing the importance of a common culture.[58]

What actually is happening in the relation between newcomers and residents? The Ford Foundation study of six communities in the United States focused on this question and provides some illuminating responses.[59] For one thing, the researchers found that overt conflict is rare. Instead newcomers and residents tend to maintain distance from each other. The need is to foster greater interaction in the pursuit of common goals, not to assume that diversity leads automatically either to conflict or to harmony. Effective incorporation of newcomers requires intentional strategies. "Participation works."[60]

Rapid economic and political changes are occurring in American communities, and immigrants are part of the change but not the cause of it all. It is too simple to attribute tensions between newcomer and resident to the relation of subordinate ethnic culture to the dominant American culture. Instead, these relationships involve a complex interaction of diverse ethnicities, races, and cultures along with the dynamics of class, gender, and power. In Miami, for example, the notion of white dominance is anachronistic. Established African Americans increasingly find themselves in subordinate positions to Latinos, especially Cubans, who are more recent arrivals. In Monterey Park, California, some Chinese immigrants came with money, which gives them positions of influence over many of the longtime residents.

American society is really multicultural. According to the researchers, in order to deal more effectively with increasing diversity "a new political discourse may be needed that focuses on efforts to organize diversity, to build activities that involve many groups working together."[61] The answer does not lie in stopping immigration or in seeking to enforce some kind of cultural uniformity. In fact, many good things are happening that need as much media attention as the dramatic conflicts. Key values in the incorporation of newcomers are democratic participation, cooperative interaction, and overcoming persisting inequalities.

National Moral Traditions

It is difficult to assess how important the moral heritage of the United States is in shaping the perspectives of its members. Still, however frequently it has been violated or ignored, the image of the

United States as a place of safety and opportunity for the world's downtrodden seems to have a potent influence. Even when anti-immigration sentiment increases, it is like rowing upstream for restrictionists to argue that immigrants should now be kept out. It is much harder to build the exclusionist theme into a moral narrative to which specific appeal can be made, because generally the reasons for exclusion have not been ones that can withstand public moral testing. This is not to say that a moral case cannot be made. But it is hard to find a strong moral argument today based on normative American self-understandings to justify a severely restrictive stance on immigration. The inclusionist perspective can much more readily draw on America's moral tradition.

The meanings of America that immigrants themselves bring generally thicken the moral basis for inclusion. A recent study of the impact of newcomers on residents cites the experience of an immigrant woman trying to enroll her son in school. After spending eight hours in moving through the "bureaucratic maze," she said to the person helping her: "Thank you so much. What a wonderful country you have to let my child in school. This is why we are here and what makes this country great. Everyone has the opportunity to go to school."[62]

When inclusionists draw on America's self-understanding to support admission of refugees and immigrants, the moral basis moves beyond a utilitarian calculation of costs and benefits. Inclusion becomes a moral good to which the United States aspires, even when the admission of newcomers creates problems. Short-term costs are less important than moving in ways that are congruent with the substantive vision of the good society. Costs represent challenges to be addressed but are not sufficiently weighty to alter the vision itself.

Inclusionists may also talk about welcoming refugees and immigrants as a moral obligation, not only as a vision of the good society to which Americans aspire. The motif of obligation pertains especially to refugees seeking a safe haven. But it can also apply to immigrants. That is, the United States is obligated by its immigrant heritage and its privileged position among other nations to be especially generous in admitting immigrants. To be sure, the United States cannot receive all those who seek freedom and economic opportunity, but it is obligated to receive some of them as one among many responses to global injustices. A restrictive policy, even if it makes prudential sense, is unjustifiably selfish.

For inclusionists, there is little that contradicts America's moral self-understanding more egregiously than some plans to control the border between the United States and Mexico. The symbolism as well as the concrete reality of building walls to keep people out is appalling, all the more so because of the evolving interdependencies in international relations. The notion of a "fortress" America is morally repugnant. Either the United States can continue to welcome immigrants, or it can give up on its self-image as a land of freedom and opportunity. Restrictionism is, in a real sense, a challenge to the normative meaning of America.

Restrictionists are at a disadvantage when appeal is made to America's moral heritage. They are more likely to focus on utilitarian arguments such as economic costs and negative societal consequences. But underneath these claims are moral views that are not identical with utilitarianism. Restrictionists are asserting the right of the American national community to protect itself, its institutions, and its way of life. For them it is not national selfishness to restrict immigration but a recognition that there are finite limits to America's capacity to incorporate newcomers. There is nothing inherently unjust about protecting borders because this is necessary to preserve the health of the American national society.

Restrictionists *do* make consequentialist judgments that recent immigration is having such a negative impact that America's right to self-protection must be invoked. America must protect its settled communities in heavily impacted places from the disruptive changes brought about by large numbers of immigrants. America has a right, indeed an obligation, to incorporate its existing underclass more fully in the American polity. But it is not fair to expect American people to pay taxes to provide basic needs and social services for immigrants, especially undocumented immigrants, when taxpayers are burdened, the welfare system is fostering dependency, and so many residents remain mired in poverty.

The United States does have a certain obligation to seek the eradication of poverty, unemployment, and human rights violations in other countries. But immigration cannot be the answer to the desperate plight of so many of the world's peoples. And the first responsibility of the United States is to its own people and to the perpetuation of its own distinctive national experiment among the diverse nations of the world. When immigration conflicts with this primary national responsibility, it must be curtailed or stopped so that American society may flourish and, at best, continue to be an experiment that inspires other peoples.

Clearly the differences between inclusionists and restrictionists involve judgments about the costs and benefits of immigration. It is a mistake, however, to label inclusionists as idealists and restrictionists as realists. Both support their views by pointing to the consequences of immigration for American society. But both also appeal, at least implicitly, to notions of obligation, principles of justice, and normative understandings of American nationality. There are ethical issues and perspectives that are lodged in the public struggle over immigration policy.

Christians, of course, can be found in both camps and at all points in between. In the past too many white Christians promoted Anglo-Saxon racism, and too many Protestant Christians propounded anti-Catholic hysteria. Christian complicity in American nativism is a historical record that requires honest engagement and heartfelt repentance. But Christians have also sought to welcome newcomers and assist them in getting settled in the United States. They have established social service and advocacy ministries for immigrants in large cities. Churches continue to play a major role in the resettlement of refugees and in supporting organizations that work with immigrants.

In more recent years, churches in their public policy witness are generally aligned with an inclusionist perspective. Churches are advocates for refugee and immigrant rights and for a generous admissions policy. But what is the ethical perspective that Christians may bring to immigration issues? How does a Christian perspective engage the national debate about immigration? The policy questions are numerous and complex, and Christian ethics does not provide simple answers. But Christians should bring their convictions to expression in the public arena and make their contribution to public moral discourse about appropriate national policies.

As we examine proposals for immigration policy in greater detail in chapter 6 we shall need to consider the question of how many immigrants the United States should admit and what the basis for selection should be. We shall also need to evaluate various proposals for dealing with the immigration of undocumented workers. One of

91

the most controversial proposals is the use of a national worker authorization card or at least a verifiable social security number that every citizen and legal resident would have to possess to prove eligibility for employment. Before we examine specific options for immigration policy, however, we turn to a discussion of the ethical issues and the perspectives of Christian ethics on these issues.

3

THE ETHICS
OF HOSPITALITY
IN A WORLD
OF NATION-STATES

Christmas eve, 1982, the Quaker mystic and activist Jim Corbett agonized about the dangers that were facing Central American refugees:

> But Herod's slaughter of the innocents casts the shadow of the cross on the Christmas story. I couldn't help remembering, from two weeks earlier on the Mexican-Guatemalan border, the grief in Mother Elvira's eyes as she told of just such a baby boy, nine months old, whom Guatemalan soldiers had mutilated and slowly murdered, forcing his mother to watch. Only at the risk of wounding the mind can one learn about the methodical torture of dispossessed persons that the United States is sponsoring in Latin America.
>
> The victim might have been the baby in my arms. And it might yet be. As a Salvadoran refugee, he is considered an illegal fugitive and is hunted by those in league with the military terror that drove his family from its home.[1]

Experiences such as hearing Mother Elvira's unbearably horrible story and holding this sleeping baby while anxiously waiting for the young mother who might get caught trying to cross the border prompted the initiation of the sanctuary movement in the United States. Refugees desperately tried to enter the United States, but the U.S. government was sending most of them back to dangerous situations in their home countries. What should Christians do?

The sanctuary witness is a lived manifestation of a Christian perspective on migration policy. I suggest we begin here in exploring the primary elements of Christian ethics.[2] Feminist thought especially has rightly urged that the starting point for ethical reflection is concrete engagement with the realities of human suffering.[3] Sanctuary activists opened themselves to encounter with refugees. They responded in a way that was motivated and informed by their faith. And they engaged clearly and courageously the laws and policies of the U.S. government. Christian ethics is not identical with the "moral majority" in American life; it is not subservient to government authority. Christians should bear witness to their faith in public life. In this chapter and the next, we shall look at what this entails for refugee and immigration policy.

Encounter with Refugees and Immigrants

The standard way to view refugees and immigrants is through a national lens. The needs and interests of the nation are dominant. The circumstances and claims of migrants are very much subordinate. Even refugees, those persons whose claim is purportedly most influential, are generally selected because they fit government foreign policy objectives rather than because they are in the greatest danger. But, for Christians, encounter with the personal presence of migrants is primary. The cry of the migrant for protection, assistance, or admission is the central moral question. What will we do when someone presents herself with this appeal? It was exactly this personal encounter with the refugees' distress that challenged sanctuary workers to go deep to discern what Christian responsibility required.

Encounter with migrants means something else as well. It means that migration policies are rooted in relationship, relationship between the migrant and the resident. Is the relationship to be defined by national identifications or by the moral power of the migrant's story? For Christians, the primary question cannot be, What should the government do? The primary question concerns personal and interpersonal responsibility. What is the appropriate response to the concrete challenge of migrants as persons with whom we are related in the family of God? Of course the answer carries implications for government policy, and the character of government policy is exceedingly important. But the relational nexus is the starting point.

The legal scholar Peter Schuck contends that the relational perspective of sanctuary workers is not an isolated one. He believes that immigration law is being transformed from the bottom up by "palpable" encounters between residents and newcomers. Informal linkages, functional ties, and human rights commitments are increasingly more important than legalistic government restrictions. Schuck puts it eloquently:

> By regarding all who arrive here not as strangers but as members, along with Americans, of a universal moral community in which abstract principles of exclusion yield to the more palpable claims of actual and potential human linkage, communitarian values deprive administrative deportation efforts of the moral legitimacy that the classical order managed to sustain for so long.[4]

A Christian perspective is not a nationalistic one. The migrant presents himself as an enfleshed story with sacred significance. Chung Hyun Kyung writes powerfully about the sacred textuality of Asian women's lives in a way that illumines the encounter with migrants as well: "The text of God's revelation was, is, and will be written in our bodies and our peoples' everyday struggle for survival and liberation."[5] In our encounters with migrants God is disclosing the claims they are making on our lives and the opportunities they are opening up before us. The conviction that the liberating God was active in the struggles of Central American refugees influenced many of the sanctuary workers. Indeed, Christians are often challenged to view migrants in unconventional ways. How migrants are imaged makes a great deal of difference. In fact, this may be the place where a Christian contribution is most powerful.

INFLUENTIAL INTERPRETATIONS OF MIGRANTS

Two interpretations of migrants are very common in public discourse. First, migrants are frequently pictured as a burden, a major headache. Whatever else they might be, they are burdensome to the receiving society. They are perceived as culturally burdensome because their cultural identity is different from the societal norm. This tends to disrupt the ethos of settled communities and weaken the connective tissue that binds members of a society together in a common life. Migrants are perceived as economically burdensome because they may require public assistance of some kind. They are politically burdensome because they are seen as part of a growing problem of mass migration from the third world to the first world, threatening the security of national borders.

95

Another manifestation of this image is that migrants tend to be viewed as a nameless and faceless part of a horde of people seeking to cross the border. The lament that "we have lost control of our borders" is a reflection of this perception. Migrants are an imminent tidal wave, a ticking time bomb. One migrant is no great problem. If we were considering the individual migrant seeking refuge or greater economic opportunity, we would not be setting off any alarms. An influx of one hundred thousand or two million migrants, however, is quite another matter. The moral differences between face-to-face relationships between individuals and policies that order the actions of large groups of people are not insignificant.

The second image is something of a counterstrain, generally less audible. According to this alternative perception, migrants are beneficial to the receiving society. They contribute their labor and pay taxes. They buy goods. They launch new economic enterprises and rear children with a zest for accomplishment. Migrants bring valued personality characteristics such as inventiveness and ambition, courage in the face of severe threats and massive obstacles, willingness to work, and boundless energy. In contrast with many jaded or disillusioned residents, migrants often believe in the "American dream," which renews hope in the American future. Finally, migrants often bring an ethnic identity that contributes to a richly variegated fabric of multiculturalism, which is more something to celebrate than to berate.

Whichever images are dominant, the tendency in American life is to view the migrant through the lenses of utilitarian calculus. In what way will he or she bring benefits to us, or constitute burdens? Which is greater—cost or benefit? With this perspective, we view migrants as objects to be assessed in terms of their value to us. But, of course, the calculus is never very precise. Neither moral nor economic arithmetic gives an unambiguous answer. It is telling to compare the widely varied estimates and assessments of demographers and economists. If sanctuary workers had sought to make a decision by such means, what would they have done?

The truth of the matter is that migrants are probably both burdens and benefits. But just because something is burdensome does not mean that we should not do it. Nor do presumed benefits automatically settle the question of what we should do. Moreover, the attempt to compare burdens and benefits can be very dicey. How do we compare the public costs of resettling refugees with the public benefits of incorporating persons in our communities who understand the meaning of freedom at depths beyond most of us? I am not arguing that a consideration of consequences is unimportant. That would be foolish. But I am contending that the prevailing utilitarian and nationalistic moral discourse is deficient as an ethical perspective on refugee and immigration policy. A Christian perspective approaches the questions from a different angle.

NARRATIVE ETHICS AND THE CHALLENGE OF THE STRANGER

Viewed from a Christian perspective, migrants are not perceived simply as burdens or benefits. They are persons created in the image of God, loved by God, and related to us in the inclusive community of God's reconciling grace. Narrative ethicists have helped to remind us that Christian ethics is communicated in the story(ies) of the Christian tradition, principally the biblical tradition. While we understandably pull out principles and doctrines from these accounts, it is above all in the narrative itself that Christians gain an understanding of God and Christian moral responsibility. And it is this narrative ethic that Christians today should continue to live out in their witness to society.

In Christian thinking about migrants the biblical stories and images about sojourners and strangers are often lifted up. Indeed it is difficult to deny the force of exhortations about welcoming and loving the stranger. But *what is the force of these stories today?* Are they commandments? Analogies? Ideals? I suggest below that they provide dynamic ways to perceive migrants along with appropriate moral responses. In summary, the place to begin our ethical reflections on migration policy is with the concrete encounter of migrants and residents. How we perceive migrants and our relationship with them will largely shape our response to this encounter.

The narratives of the Hebrew Bible and the New Testament convey varied tales of migration, relationships with "others," and moral responsibility. Abram's trek from Haran to Canaan was an act of response to God's promise (Gen. 12:1-9). Yet, some years later, Abram and Sarai were forced to travel to Egypt because of a severe famine in Canaan (Gen. 12:10-12). In the first passage migration is an opportunity; in the second it is a necessity. Both convey continuing realities of migration. Although Abram's behavior toward Sarai in Egypt is morally repugnant, it reflects the pressures migrants face to accommodate to the power of rulers in order to survive, and the fact that women often suffer most grievously from such vulnerability.

Migration stories also include pictures of hospitality. As we read in Genesis 18:1-16, Abraham is now the host rather than the refugee. The text provides a full account of the hospitality toward strangers that God expects. It involves both gestures (such as bowing) and the best provision Abraham can offer. He remains with the visitors while they eat, and he even accompanies them for a while "to set them on their way." Although Abraham initially did not know these travelers were messengers from God, the fact always remains a possibility when strangers appear. On this occasion, they bring the startling news that Sarah will have a son. This motif about the surprising identity and wonderful news of strangers is echoed in the book of Hebrews: "Do not neglect to show hospitality to strangers, for by doing that some have entertained angels without knowing it" (13:2). In fact, Christ himself may appear in the person of the stranger (Matt. 25:31-46; and the appearance of the risen Christ as a stranger to grieving disciples on the road to Emmaus in Luke 24).

Migration stories further depict the sins of inhospitality. In Genesis 19, Abraham's nephew, Lot, also extends hospitality to visitors. But here the residents of Sodom, instead of offering a welcome, want to do violence to the strangers. This cruel violation of hospitality brought about Yahweh's destruction of Sodom and Gomorrah, an action so vivid and harsh that it continued throughout the Old Testament to convey the seriousness of God's judgment.

Yet even more central to the story of Israel is the oppression of Hebrews as foreigners in the country of Egypt. Once again, this time the family of Jacob, Hebrews migrated to Egypt to escape the desperate conditions brought about by famine. Providentially, Joseph was in a politically influential position to render assistance. But eventually the Hebrew foreigners were enslaved. According to Patrick Miller, the account takes on the character of an "*anti-sojourn* story, a depiction of inhospitality to strangers."[6] To note analogies with current debates about migration policies is irresistible. The Pharaoh was in a double bind. He was worried about the political threat of an increasing immigrant population. But he also did not want to lose the cheap labor of the Hebrew slaves. In a utilitarian calculus, which was greater—burden or benefit?

The central event in the history of Israel takes place in this context. Yahweh delivered the oppressed immigrants in the mighty event of the Exodus. Teachings about hospitality to strangers were rooted above all in this experience of oppression and liberation. Sanctuary workers were indeed reappropriating a central theme of their faith narrative when they viewed Central American refugees in light of God's liberating activity in history. "You shall not wrong or oppress a resident alien, for you were aliens in the land of Egypt"(Exod. 22:21).

In the Old Testament several different terms refer to strangers or foreigners. The Hebrew words *zar* and *nokri*, translated as "stranger" and "foreign," refer to persons who are not a part of Israel. Specifically, *nokri* refers to "a foreigner who has not entered into any lasting relationship to the land or the people."[7] *Ger*, on the other hand, is translated as "sojourner," "stranger," or "alien," and points to someone who comes from outside the community but who now settles within the community.[8] The *ger* may reside for a short time or long time. This person is the subject of important covenantal obligations in Israel. The *ger*, unlike *zar/nokri*, is one who has established a relational bond with residents. The terms of the relationship are a matter of moral significance.

The *ger* is very much like what we today call "resident alien." He or she may be a refugee or an immigrant, settling into the community but still as an outsider who brings a different communal identity. Within the covenant community, however, this difference does not justify a double standard of justice. First, resident aliens are viewed as persons alongside widows, orphans, and the poor, who are particularly vulnerable. They do not have the structures of security that many others have, and so special provision for their needs must be assured. Thus the *ger* should be allowed to glean in the fields or receive tithes of food to make sure he or she has enough to eat.

Second, the resident alien should receive justice in Israel, whether in the courts (Deut. 24:17) or as a refuge from vengeance (Num. 35:11-16). Sanctuary workers clearly drew on this image in which protection of the endangered person is a mirroring of Yahweh's own activity as a deliverer and provider of refuge. Miller contends that the slave law in Deuteronomy 23:15-16 provides even stronger warrant for a sanctuary witness. The slave seeks protection, and the community is obligated to provide it.

In the present formulation of the law, it is envisioned that such fleeing slaves are refugees from outside the country who come into Israel seeking sanctuary. Protection and the opportunity to settle wherever the refugee slave desires are the specific safeguards of this statute.[9]

Third, the resident alien is included in the celebration feasts central to the worship life of Israel. When the community brings its gifts to Yahweh and gives thanks for Yahweh's blessings, the poor and the rich, the stranger and the resident, are invited to the meal. In some ways this is the most powerful image of all, a foretaste of the messianic banquet in which all come to the table to enjoy food and friendship.[10] There is one law in Israel, not a different one for strangers and residents. Again, the force of the narrative is to make Christians morally suspicious of contemporary efforts to institute a different standard of treatment for migrants in our midst.

We have seen only a glimpse of the variety and richness of Old Testament stories about migration. Migration may be a response to the beckons of God; or it may be a forced exile, which makes people vulnerable to abuse. Our traditions depict God's judgment against and deliverance from inhospitality. Stories also give pictures of the hospitality that God requires of those who have experienced God's mercy. This narrative account of migrants, migration, and hospitality indeed displays something of what love of these neighbors entails. As Miller puts it, love for the stranger "provides one of the earliest examples of its extension beyond the neighbor, or one might say that here the definition of the neighbor receives its extension."[11] The stranger or sojourner is neighbor rather than outsider, with all the moral expectations that come with this relationship.

> When an alien resides with you in your land, you shall not oppress the alien. The alien who resides with you shall be to you as the citizen among you; you shall love the alien as yourself, for you were aliens in the land of Egypt: I am the LORD your God. (Lev. 19:33-34)

Miller directs us to one additional characteristic of Hebrew literature that has imaginative implications for viewing and treating migrants. This is the role of the Levite as a sojourner in Israel. Levites were dependent on the community for the provision of basic needs. Accordingly, they provided the ongoing occasions for members of the community to practice hospitality. Even more, however, their dependent

100

role conveyed concretely the dependence of the community on the blessings of God.

> The sojourning of the Levite in the midst of a people demonstrates the possibility of a communal life in which those whose circumstances keep them outside the usual structures of economic and social accessibility experience a well-being out of dependence, a dependence that is built into the system not as a necessary evil but rather as a reflection of the dependence of all the community.[12]

This way of viewing the migrant is certainly out of sync with current public discourse. Here the migrant is a personal symbol of the dependence that is characteristic of human existence. Provision for migrants should not be begrudged but gratefully embraced as a requirement of community. Life and its prerequisites are gifts from God. Migrants also are gifts of God, reminders to Israel "that it lives in dependence on the Lord, without a final claim on the material good of this world."[13] Instead of railing against dependency, these Hebrew narratives convey a moral realism about the insecurities and vulnerabilities of human life. And they show how a community sought to structure its life in a way that reflects God's own hospitality.

In narrative ethics, these accounts of hospitality are normative above all for contemporary heirs of God's covenant with Israel. They do more than spell out rules for conduct, although rules for treating sojourners and strangers are emphatically stated. Christians today are challenged to situate themselves in the context of this narrative in which love for the sojourner figures so prominently. Whatever nation-states do or don't do, Christians are to exemplify a readiness to welcome the sojourner as a neighbor, remembering imaginatively our own past history as sojourners, and remembering gratefully our present dependence on the generosity of God. The force of the narrative is to shape the way Christians see and respond to the refugee and immigrant.

In the Old Testament, hospitality to the stranger is one of the clearest expressions of the commandment to love God and neighbor. Already the stranger is transformed into neighbor in the light of covenant faith.[14] This tradition is continued and intensified in the New Testament. In one of his most influential parables, Jesus describes the faithful as those who welcome the stranger (Matt. 25:35). Conversely, inhospitality is an act of unfaithfulness that brings God's judgment (Matt. 25:43). More strikingly, Jesus identifies himself with the stranger, saying, in effect, "As you welcome the stranger, you welcome me." Jesus is present in the person of the stranger. Now Christians are entreated to respond to the stranger as they would respond to Christ himself.

In this imaginative construction, Christ is the neighbor, the neighbor is Christ. For the stranger to be regarded as neighbor carries rich ethical import indeed. The migrant may be different or foreign, but he or she is also one of us. The migrant is not to be treated solely as a helpless, dependent object of paternalistic assistance but as a person, a moral agent whose life story can challenge and transform the lives of hosts. This giving and receiving in the relationship between resident and migrant takes a variety of complex forms. While the host may have the provisions to grant hospitality, the migrant is not just a recipient; he brings himself as a gift, welcomed or not, for the hosts to receive.

Whose giving is greater? Whose receiving is greater? In the mutuality of neighbor relation such a calculation is misplaced. Giving and receiving are shared in an indistinguishable flow. What complicates the pattern of mutuality, however, is the unequal power relation between the migrant and the host. The disparity is often immense. The migrant *is* vulnerable and dependent, a sign of the condition that all humans share at a fundamental level. The host is in a position to offer or refuse hospitality. Genuine neighbor love resists and transforms unequal power relationships so that the mutuality of giving and receiving may flourish. Love seeks justice.

In Matthew 25, Jesus identifies with the stranger and challenges Christian communities to welcome the stranger as they would welcome himself. Although this teaching challenges the imagination, another parable is even more shocking. The good Samaritan story is so familiar that it often loses its startling character (Luke 10:29-37). But let us look at it again. The lawyer asks Jesus what he has to do to inherit eternal life. With some prodding by Jesus, the lawyer rightly identifies the love of God and neighbor as the answer to his question. But the lawyer pushes for more specificity about who the neighbor is whom he is required to love.

Jesus proceeds to tell the familiar story of the despised Samaritan who compassionately assists the wounded traveler. But Jesus does not conclude by asking or answering the lawyer's question: "Who is my neighbor?" Instead, Jesus shifts the ground from object to subject. "Which one proved to be neighbor to the injured man?" Jesus does not define the neighbor who then can be loved as legalistically specified by the commandment. Rather the reader is given a picture of neighborliness, of neighbor love, which opens outward to an unspecifiable range of implications and applications. The parable provides an imaginative perspective about neighbor love rather than legalistic prescriptions.

Furthermore, in this parable it is not Jesus the stranger to whom assistance is given. It is the stranger, the Samaritan, who models Christlike love to the faith community whose own leaders failed to fulfill the law. Remarkably, it is the stranger who may disclose to the "faithful" what love of neighbor entails. Therefore, it is not just that Christians are called to be "Christs" to strangers, or to give aid to the Christ who is present among the most vulnerable. It is also that the stranger may be Christ to us, disclosing to Christians the embodied reality and summons of God. It may be that the stranger is the teacher, the one whose gift to hosts is more valuable than proffered food and shelter.

In Christ, the stranger may prove to be neighbor beyond what we might be able to imagine. This image communicates the sense of wonder and expectation which appropriately characterizes the encounter between resident and migrant, recalling again the motif that the stranger may be a divine messenger. Activists in the sanctuary movement often witnessed to this powerful insight when they talked about how much more they had received than they had given in their encounter with Central American refugees. In a narrative ethics Christians will relate to migrants with a readiness to learn, even to be surprised.

Narrative ethics in a Christian mode addresses Christians and churches above all. The stories of Israel, Jesus, and the church are authoritative for the Christian life. They communicate the ways of God and the ways of human faithfulness. The ethicist Stanley Hauerwas has made a great contribution in holding Christian communities accountable to their own narrative faith, emphasizing that their ethics is often in sharp conflict with conventional societal norms.[15] The thrust of narrative ethics is to shape the moral character of churches and of Christians so that they may live in faithfulness to God. What is less clear is the import of narrative ethics for social structures and public policy, a question we will return to later.

For now, however, let us stay with the challenge of narrative ethics. Christians should place their own interpretations and responses within the narrative traditions of their faith community. No specific blueprint is provided for how Christians should deal with the agonies and dilemmas of contemporary migration. That is not the point. But Christians should only respond in a way that fits the story of God's love for the stranger and the faith community's responsibility to love the neighbor through extending hospitality.

It makes a profound difference if the moral character of Christians is such that they are disposed to love the migrant as themselves, to respond compassionately and generously to the most vulnerable persons that they encounter. The Christian mind and conscience are to be formed by empathetic identification with the oppressed Hebrews in Egypt, the deliverance by God in the Exodus, the flight of Jesus, Mary, and Joseph to Egypt as refugees from King Herod's murderous policy, and Jesus' identification with the stranger and sojourner. A Christian perspective is shaped by these stories of suffering and liberation, threat and promise, with the conviction that it is more important to serve God than the national interest.

Yet it is not quibbling to point to hermeneutical complications. A narrative ethic is dynamic and historical, not literalistic and legalistic. Again the sanctuary witness is illuminating. Sanctuary activists drew on Old Testament traditions about protection and justice as manifestations of covenant faithfulness. They imaginatively appropriated these texts as they sought to respond to the cries of Central American refugees. This imaginative hermeneutic is narrative ethics at its best. It is not a wooden application but a matter of permitting narrative traditions to speak in fresh ways to current challenges. What hospitality means and requires must be worked out in response to contexts.

The contexts of contemporary migration are different, and these differences must be taken into account. In the biblical traditions, the hospitality ethic is rooted in a nomadic agricultural ethos. Today, one might be a resident and in a position to extend hospitality, but tomorrow one might be forced to leave and need to rely on others' hospitality. Expectations regarding the treatment of sojourners emerged in a context of mutual vulnerability and dependence. In today's world, the refugee especially is, if anything, even more vulner-

104

able than yesterday's sojourner. In an increasingly urbanized world carved up in often arbitrary ways into nation-states, there is little in the way of a shared ethos of reciprocated hospitality. And there are massive numbers of people who are on the move, who need a place to go, but precious few places where they can go.

Biblical texts on migration do indeed provide dynamic analogies with contemporary challenges and remain remarkably pertinent. Certainly the radical vulnerability of migrants, especially refugees, is as true today as yesterday. People are still driven off their land and from their homes as a result of injustice, violence, and natural disasters. The narrative continues to shape in powerful ways a Christian perspective on migrants and migration. But we shall still have to press forward the question of what Christian responsibility requires in our own context.

THE MIGRANT AS STRANGER

We have seen that the migrant, or the resident alien, is often referred to both as sojourner and as stranger in the Old Testament. These words tend to be used interchangeably in translations of *ger*. Yet it is fruitful to give some further attention to the significance of the image of stranger for the way Christians view migrants. Recent philosophy and theology have emphasized the importance of "otherness" for moral selfhood and community. "Stranger" is a metaphor for many "others" who open new realms of experience to persons who assume their ways of life are normal and normative. Yet, more specifically, "strangers" is a very influential metaphor for migrants in current discourse, such as "a nation of strangers," "strangers or friends," "strangers within your gates," and "strangers to these shores."[16]

Migrants enter established communities as people who are different in nationality and often in physical appearance, language, and customs. This difference, sometimes called cultural distance, is a very powerful element in Americans' attitudes, frequently evoking negative reactions of fear, resentment, and hostility. When this negative reaction is particularly harsh and intense, it is characterized as xenophobia. While xenophobia is by no means an exclusively American trait, it has frequently erupted in the history of Americans' response to migrants. Xenophobia is usually tied to racism as well, with racial "differences" representing the facet of otherness most likely to generate hostile reactions by resident Americans.

Yet the notion of stranger is not without its problems in viewing contemporary migrants. Are Mexican, Guatemalan, Cuban, Vietnamese, Korean, and Nigerian migrants best seen as strangers? After all, we do know and relate publicly to Mexicans, Guatemalans, Cubans, Vietnamese, Koreans, and Nigerians who are already living in our communities. Many families who bore these national identities in the past have lived in the United States for some time and are now U.S. citizens. It is not as though current migrants are total strangers culturally or even personally. "They" are "us."

There can be an element of racial arrogance in referring to migrants as strangers. It may suggest that whiteness is the norm for comfort and familiarity in the United States, and migrants, because they are in recent years primarily people of color, are "different," "strange." Who is strange to whom? Ronald Takaki points out that, to American Indians, the European looked strange: "The native peoples were struck by the 'ugliness' and 'deformity' of the strangers."[17] Perhaps, then, it is better to jettison the metaphor of stranger. A migrant who is a stranger to me may be received as a friend or relative by others within Denver.

Still, while recognizing the ambiguities and the necessary qualifications, the metaphor of stranger is morally significant from a Christian perspective. This is not just because Jesus identified with the stranger and indeed was himself stranger in a hostile environment. It is also because we need to take seriously the phenomenon of otherness in human relationship. The neighbor often presents herself to me, not as someone who is just like me, but as someone who is different. How am I to view this difference? And this question becomes magnified in the case of migrants who are seeking admission to this national community where acceptance means a great deal. This question may indeed be the most potent one in current debates in which recent migrants *in their difference* are viewed as rending the cultural unity of America.

One moral response to the stranger is to love her *in her differentness.* H. Richard Niebuhr states this eloquently in his powerful essay on the meaning of Christian love: Love "rejoices in the otherness of the other. . . . As reverence love is and seeks knowledge of the other, not by way of curiosity nor for the sake of gaining power but in rejoicing and in wonder."[18] In Niebuhr's view the otherness of the neighbor is not only to be respected but reverenced, prized, treasured. In love one seeks relationship with the other with a valuation that is far richer than a calculation of the neighbor's utility.

A second response is the need that persons have for the gifts of otherness in order to be more whole. In this notion, persons are incomplete until they are able to integrate the otherness of neighbors in their selfhood. Instead of shutting otherness out because it is perceived as threatening we should incorporate it into our very being. This does not need to be viewed in only an individualistic way. As a person who has been shaped by a national society of economic affluence and military might, I might well need (or our national society might well need) the perspective of others who mediate the experience of suffering and defeat. This I believe is the thesis of the wonderful Mexican poet, Octavio Paz. He believes that alienation between Mexicans and North Americans will not be overcome until each encounters the "otherness" of the other and discovers that the other is oneself. I quote at some length from his classic, *The Labyrinth of Solitude:*

> The North Americans are credulous and we are believers; they love fairy tales and detective stories and we love myths and legends. The Mexican tells lies because he delights in fantasy, or because he is desperate, or because he wants to rise above the sordid facts of his life; the North American does not tell lies, but he substitutes social truth for the real truth which is always disagreeable. We get drunk in order to confess; they get drunk in order to forget. They are optimists and we are nihilists. . . . We are suspicious and they are trusting. We are sorrowful and sarcastic and they are happy and full of jokes. North Americans want to understand and we want to contemplate. They are activists and we are quietists; we enjoy our wounds and they enjoy their inventions. They believe in hygiene, health, work and contentment, but perhaps they have never experienced true joy, which is an intoxication, a whirlwind. In the hubbub of a fiesta night our voices explode into brilliant lights, and life and death mingle together, while their vitality becomes a fixed smile that denies old age and death but that changes life to motionless stone.[19]

A third way to view the stranger calls into question the self-referential character of Paz's perspective. Perhaps the other is *not me*. The other is genuinely other. And the encounter with the stranger is necessary to overcome the self's illusions that she or he is the center of reality. The other is morally significant precisely *because* I cannot integrate him into my selfhood. He does not exist for me, simply to be absorbed into my life projects. In the stranger is an other who presents us with moral claims and opportunities that we are incapable of generating out of ourselves alone. Encounter with the otherness of the stranger is a beckon to leave security behind and embark on a moral adventure. Perhaps the deepest reason why we resist strangers is not because of their potential threat but because we might be changed by the encounter.

In this interpretation, the challenge, indeed the tension, that one experiences in encounters with strangers is precisely what one needs to be opened to God's summons. One's narrow world is expanded, one's self-protective and spiritually deadening security systems are broken open, and one's ways of life are tested and possibly transformed. Ethnocentrism is shattered. Narcissism collapses. The stranger brings news that Christians must hear if they are to be God's faithful witnesses in the world. How can we know the "truth" of strangers without personal encounter, without extending hospitality?

It is always possible that the encounter with the stranger will change our lives. Openness and receptivity to the sacred textuality of strangers' lives are indispensable virtues of Christian existence.[20] For Christians the stranger is the enfleshed news that God brings into our midst, often as a disturbing challenge, as a disruption of our orderly and routinized lives, as an invitation to adventurous faithfulness.

I am suggesting that a Christian perspective on migration begins with the encounter between migrant and resident. Christian interpretations of this encounter are imaginatively shaped by stories and images that make up its narrative traditions. For Christians, hospitality to the sojourner and stranger is a rich moral metaphor for the Christian life and has particular normative pertinence for responses to migrants.

Of course, it is important not to use these interpretations in a way that romanticizes the stranger. Strangers can be unpleasant, even dangerous. Migrants are flawed human beings, as each of us is. Nothing will doom a church's ministry with migrants faster than the expectation that the encounter will be smooth and free of difficulties and frustrations. That is life. So what else is new? The point is that Christians can construct safe environments for hospitable responses without remaining behind self-protective walls. And learnings and changes can occur in the midst of conflicts and struggles. Hospitality to strangers does not promise trouble-free existence but the kinds of troubles that Christians are called to engage.

In a Christian perspective, it is a distortion to view migrants in terms of their usefulness. Migrants are created and loved by God. In their vulnerability, they are to be treated compassionately and justly. In their differentness they are to be reverenced. They are neighbors with whom to enter relationship, open to the future in which we may all be changed. Christians should resist depictions of migrants as scapegoats for complex community ills or as faceless statistics. It is, after all, the personhood of migrants and the relational challenges posed by their presence that make migration policy a moral question and not merely a statistical one. The narrative ethic of extending hospitality to the stranger does indeed collide with many powerful forces in contemporary American life.

THE MESSIANIC BANQUET AND MULTIRACIAL COMMUNITY

In the narrative traditions of Christian ethics, hospitality to the stranger carries the force of a moral obligation. The command is lodged in the covenantal history of Old and New Testaments and originates in the actions of God in this history. The deontological dimension of ethics always has its place in a narrative context. But narrative ethics also contains teleological motifs. That is, Christians are directed to a future in which God will establish *shalom.* There are good ends to be sought because they fit the character of the new order that God has initiated in Jesus Christ and will yet bring to fulfillment.

Narrative ethics, though rooted in the past, is future-oriented. It is this facet of Christian ethics that speaks especially to questions of multiracial and multicultural diversity in current debates. Which moral vision will be normative? The alternatives can be starkly put: Rudyard Kipling's "East is East, and West is West, and never the twain shall meet,"[21] or the words of invitation to the Lord's Supper, "People will come from east and west, and from north and south, and sit at table in the kingdom of God." In a Christian perspective, the reconciling promise of God in Christ opens up new possibilities for human community. Rich and poor, black and white, east and west, women and men, are welcome at the table of God to share food and conviviality.

The Lord's Supper anticipates the gathering of diverse people at the banquet of God. Breaking bread is an image and ritual of justice,

109

in which the gifts of God are shared with all for their mutual empow-erment.[22] This is an earthy and simple image of God's future. Distinc-tions are not obliterated, but they no longer divide. Now people can sit down together and share the food that is provided by a gracious and merciful God. These folk from every area of the world may not yet be intimate friends, but they can no longer be enemies. At the Lord's Table, persons receive and celebrate the saving grace of Christ, and they experience a taste of the fully realized reconciliation yet to come. Christians are challenged to affirm gratefully and to seek resolutely manifestations of this wonderfully diverse and inclusive community in their own histories. The vision of reconciliation in the Christian narrative is not parochial but is inclusive of all (Col. 1:15-20).

In American life, and perhaps elsewhere as well, attacks against multiracialism and multiculturalism seem to be increasing in volume and number. Derided as "politically correct," inclusiveness is the target of invectives from those who want to maintain white domi-nance. Peter Brimelow has thrown down the racialist gauntlet in arguing that American culture is "white" and should be protected from further migrations of peoples of color. He says it is

> a plain historical fact: that the American nation has always had a specific ethnic core. And that core has been white. . . . It is simply common sense that Americans have a legitimate interest in their country's racial balance. It is common sense that they have a right to insist that their government stop shifting it. Indeed, it seems to me that they have a right to insist that it be shifted back.[23]

I believe from a Christian perspective such arguments about diver-sity are better dealt with by an ethics of vision than by an ethics of obligation, by the teleological rather than the deontological cast of narrative existence. Because of its eschatology of reconciliation, Christians are biased in favor of multiracial and multicultural com-munity. In theory, a relatively homogeneous society could treat all its members justly and relate justly to other societies that are different culturally and racially. But, in a Christian perspective, homogeneity as a goal is morally suspect. Suspicion turns to vigorous moral criticism when we attend to the United States, which is, in fact, already a multicultural and multiracial national society and which must decide whether to claim it or negate it.

110

A narrative ethic seems at first glance a curious location for addressing the furious debates over diversity in America. Thomas Ogletree, however, has convincingly shown that Paul's theology led to a breakthrough on how to regard cultural diversity.[24] For Paul, unity is no longer found in adherence to the Law but now in creative response to God's reconciling grace in Christ. There are a number of facets to Ogletree's interpretation which need to be emphasized and elaborated.

First, Ogletree maintains, rightly I believe, that the social or communal focus of New Testament ethics is the church, not the broader society or political order. There are social dimensions of the gospel. The church is to embody in its life the new era, the new historical possibility, which Christ represents and initiates.

New Testament traditions struggle with how this new reality is to be manifested in the church. Narrative ethics is indeed directed at the church. The church is to be the bearer of the historical reality it has experienced in Christ. This does not mean that the narrative today *only* addresses the church, as Hauerwas argues; yet in the context of the New Testament itself we look to ecclesiology to grapple with the social impact of Christ.

Second, Ogletree gives special attention to Paul's response to the knotty conflicts between Jews and Gentiles in the young churches. At stake were the terms of the "new" community established in the name of Christ. Would adherence to the Law still serve as the unifying bond? Paul replaced the Law with promise as the basis for a new community possibility. Whereas the Law tied people to the past, promise stretches toward the future. A new social form can emerge in response to the unifying reality of Christ. Being bound to Christ frees believers to invent different ways of living together that may not even have been imagined before.

Third, this theology makes possible an affirmation of the values of cultural diversity. Indeed, cultural diversity does not have to give way to foster community. The two are not incompatible. Unity in Christ relativizes without disvaluing the cultural differences among persons in the community. My cultural traditions are not normative for you, but I am not required to give them up unless they subvert the unity we share in Christ. Paul's "grasp of the possibilities of community among culturally diverse peoples" is, for Ogletree, an original contribution to social ethics.[25] Now, circumcision is not required of Gentiles, though Jewish Christians may continue the practice (Gal. 2:1-10; 1 Cor. 7:18-20). Now, eating meat identified with pagan sacrifice is not prohibited, but Christians should be sensitive to others in the community whose faith might be undermined by the practice (1 Cor. 8:1-13).

Because the church's unity is in Christ, Gentiles do not have to conform to culturally relative characteristics of Jewish Christianity, and Jewish Christians are permitted to retain distinctive practices so long as these expressions of cultural freedom do not divide and weaken the community. The gospel of Jesus Christ does indeed break down walls of division and hostility, making it possible for persons once estranged now to be friends. A genuinely new kind of community is made possible. "The gospel summons us to celebrate pluralism, to welcome it into the internal life of the community of faith."[26] Indeed Paul is working out the practical implications of what is present also in Mark's ethics. For Mark, followers of Christ fashion a new community in loyalty to Christ rather than on the basis of customary ties of kinship and nation. Christian communities should be "open to peoples of all races and nations."[27]

Fourth, although Paul does not hesitate to offer advice (!), the terms of the new community are to be worked out through negotiation. Christian freedom permits new forms of relationship that are yet to be created. Paul does not seek to impose a new set of rules or laws. The practice of negotiation is a response to the theology of promise, and it values the presence of diversity without privileging one over another. In Ogletree's interpretation, Paul's ethics "suggest the negotiation and continual renegotiation of patterns of relationship among diverse peoples until arrangements can be devised which allow all to flourish, and flourish in their diversity."[28]

Fifth, Paul's theological ethics of promise and reconciliation may be extended beyond the church to the world. Admittedly, this requires an expansion of Paul's own moral focus. Paul was prepared to see the radical implication of Christ for the relationships of men and women, slave and free, Jew and Gentile, within Christian communities (Gal. 3:28). But he did not extend his vision to institutions and communities outside the church. Regrettably, churches soon adapted to hierarchical patterns of surrounding societies rather than maintaining the ecclesiological radicalism of Paul.

Does this mean *we* should not make this extension as current participants in the ongoing narrative of Christian existence? This issue is hotly debated in contemporary Christian ethics. Hauerwas maintains that the narrative ethics of hospitality to the stranger and of peaceable community are normative only for the church. The church has the responsibility to witness to the truth of this narrative in a world that will forever regard it as foolish and foreign.

Instead of this interpretation, however, I agree with the position of Ogletree. God is active in the world in all its various spheres, not solely in the church. The new order that Christ represents and initiates is already dynamically operative in the world. Loving the stranger, making friends with enemies, freeing the oppressed, negotiating community with people who are different—these are signs of God's transforming work.

The radical challenge to the church is to live out the promises of the new age in the present, and *also* to discern and respond to signs of the new age in other spheres of God's world. Especially germane to the study of migration, Ogletree sees "movements, organizations, and institutions which are open to the plurality of human cultures and lifestyles, which are ready to negotiate patterns of community of significant diversity" as analogous to the new order of human relationship opened up in Christ.[29]

CONCLUSIONS

A Christian perspective on migration issues is shaped by the narratives that churches regard as holy scripture. Narrative ethicists are right to emphasize the particularity of Christian ethics. Christians are part of a historical community that holds certain stories to be authoritative about the ways of God and of human moral responsibility. To be sure, there are many motifs in narrative traditions, defying reductionism or neat harmonization. Narrative ethics will not supply specific answers to complex dilemmas about migration policy. But such images as hospitality to strangers and culturally diverse communities provide indispensable insights for a Christian perspective.

Narrative ethics contains both deontological and teleological features. To love the neighbor, to seek justice for the marginalized, to extend hospitality to the stranger, carry the force of moral obligation rooted in God's own gracious generosity. At the same time, God's future calls Christians to seek those patterns of community that

113

respond to the reconciling reality of Christ. Yet narrative ethicists rightly emphasize that even more basic than an ethics of obligation or of goals is an ethics of character. The moral force of narrative is to form Christian communities and personhood for faithful existence.

More than anything else, the future of American migration policy will turn on the moral character of its peoples. Will we be disposed to welcome people who seek safety here from life-threatening violence? Will we seek to shut down and turn back an openness to cultural and racial diversity? How will American peoples perceive their encounters with refugees and immigrants? The witness of Christians and churches is a very important part of this societal debate. Clearly a narrative ethic speaks to the ways churches are to embody hospitality and inclusiveness in their own lives. But I believe a Christian narrative ethic also can be articulated in public discourse and advocacy as a perspective that can have a wider societal impact.

National Community and Inclusive Community

Borders have guards and the guards have guns. . . . To Haitians in small, leaky boats confronted by armed Coast Guard cutters, to Salvadorans dying from heat and lack of air after being smuggled into the Arizona desert, to Guatemalans crawling through rat-infested sewer pipes from Mexico to California—to these people the borders, guards and guns are all too apparent. . . . On what moral grounds can these sorts of people be kept out? What gives anyone the right to point guns at them?[30]

"What gives anyone the right to point guns at them?" The angry and anguished tone of this question is exactly right. Something is terribly askew here. How in the world can one move from an ethical perspective of hospitality and inclusive community to a justification of pointing guns at needy strangers to prevent them from entering *our* country? From a nationalistic perspective, it is not very difficult to support the enforcement of restrictions. From a Christian perspective, it would seem to be impossible to close the borders to persons who are fleeing for their lives. It would seem very difficult to justify keeping poor people out of the United States in order to maintain or improve the standard of living of North Americans.

114

One influential approach, of course, is to argue for a large gap between the norms of love and justice, between the Christian ideal and the politically possible. The argument goes like this. The ideal calls for open borders in a world where persons are free to migrate when they cannot meet basic needs and secure basic rights in their homelands. Love for neighbor requires the reception of needy migrants with compassionate hospitality. However, in reality, national societies would never permit open borders. Settled Americans look resentfully at newcomers when there are too many of them. Like it or not, there are practical constraints on the number of migrants Americans are willing to admit and incorporate in their communities.

Thus, in the real world, some restrictions must be enforced. Because of people's sinful tendencies to seek their own interests above the interests of others, the concerns of settled Americans will always predominate over the needs of those who want to enter. So the pragmatic task is to maneuver between total exclusion and total inclusion in order to admit a selected number of migrants, especially those who can clearly bring benefits to the United States. Restrictions on migrants, in this way of thinking, are a moral concession to the preferences that persons naturally have for their own national compatriots, and for their own stake in the welfare of the national society.

Although this viewpoint contains some unavoidable features of a Christian perspective on migration, it does not provide a satisfactory response to the plight of Haitians, Salvadorans, or Guatemalans. It does, at least, recognize that in the contemporary world migration must be viewed in the context of national communities and nation-states. A truism in conventional discourse about migration is: a nation-state has the right to control its own borders. Let us examine this claim and then evaluate it from a Christian perspective.

NATION-STATES AND RESTRICTIONS ON MIGRATION

Historians trace the beginning of the nation-state system of international relations to the Peace of Westphalia in 1648, or to the Napoleonic revolution at the beginning of the nineteenth century. The sense of "nation" is exceedingly elusive. It may be based on polity, like the Constitution in the United States, or on ethnicity, religion, language, or history. Nation reflects a civic and cultural identity of a people that is expressed in their way of organizing themselves politically. *State* is the governing apparatus of the nation. *Nation* and *state*

115

are not identical. The state at best seeks to represent the national community's values, promote its welfare, and protect its security. But it is also possible that the state will serve to enhance itself and its own power at the expense of the national community.

In a nation-state system, the nation-state has sovereign authority over the territory of the national community. In theory (as seen in the membership of the General Assembly of the United Nations), each nation-state is equal. Each is free to determine its own internal policies without interference by others. Of course, the powerful nation-states have always interfered and intervened when it suited them and when they could get away with it. Still, it is not hard to understand how this development could be energized by a revolutionary ideology: freedom from imperial or colonial or external control by outsiders, so that at last we can be in charge of governing ourselves according to our own values and aspirations. The notion of *sovereignty* is paramount. No authority beyond the nation-state itself determines what happens within its borders.

The nation-state has sovereign authority over who is permitted to enter its territory. Migrants may be pushed out of their own country, but the doctrine of sovereignty says that the nation-state doing the pushing cannot be interfered with. At the same time, the sovereignty of the nation-state over the territory to which the migrant might seek entrance permits it to block the door. In this system of nation-states, the migrant is rendered insignificant, subject above all to considerations of national interest.

This system is particularly tragic when migrants are refugees. Although they are citizens of a state, their state does not protect them and may even persecute them. But they may not be able to gain entrance into another country because they have a different nationality. Again, in the words of Joseph Carens:

> Refugees are the orphans of the state system, or more accurately, they are the victims of serious abuse by those in charge of the social units to which they have been assigned by birth. Their plight reflects a failure, not only of the particular state from which they are fleeing, but also of the system of dividing the world into independent sovereign states and assigning people at birth to one of them. (Indeed, this sort of failure may be an inevitable by-product of the modern state system.)[31]

Contemporary political scientists vigorously debate whether or not the system of nation-state sovereignty is eroding in the face of recent historical developments. Clearly, nation-states have established certain internationalist structures to deal with problems that require cooperative efforts. Standards of universal human rights have been promoted and even enacted into international law that qualifies absolutist notions of national sovereignty. Yet even with attempts to develop international agreements about refugees, the authority over refugee admission continues to reside with officials of the nation-state. Refugees and asylees are at the mercy of those whose dominant interests are to keep them out. Nation-state sovereignty protects the interests of those who have secure membership in their own countries. It does not protect those whose lives are endangered or those whose well-being lies in seeking opportunities elsewhere.

Joseph Carens is a political philosopher committed to the principles of democratic liberalism. From a normative perspective he is very critical of the dominance of nationalistic attitudes toward migrants. Carens begins with the conviction that individuals have equal moral worth. In a bold and provocative essay, he presents an ethical case for open borders.[32] If each person is equally valued, then there is no compelling moral basis for preferring national citizens over outsiders, especially when the outsiders are much poorer than residents.

Carens compares citizenship today to feudal privilege in an earlier era. Borders keep persons locked within a territory and its polity. We have nothing to do with our birthplace, yet birthplace has a profound impact on persons' life chances. To argue that a Haitian must spend the rest of his life in Haiti, and that I as a U.S. citizen am justified in keeping him out of the United States is very much like the arguments for feudalism. He is confined to a station in life. Whatever opportunities are permitted him must be found within this station. Life is constricted for him because of a condition that has nothing to do with his choices, abilities, and aspirations.

Border restrictions, in this system, function to the severe disadvantage of those who do not want to be confined involuntarily in the place where they were born. Borders protect unjust privilege. Carens points out that if we adopt John Rawls's theory of justice, we need to view the question of free movement from the perspective of persons who would be most disadvantaged by restrictions. Carens concludes: "In the original position, then, one would insist that the right to migrate

117

be included in the system of basic liberties for the same reasons that one would insist that the right to religious freedom be included: it might prove essential to one's plan of life."[33]

A different ethical perspective on these issues is provided by Michael Walzer. Walzer does not begin with the premise of the equal moral worth of each individual. Rather, he stresses the moral significance of the national community and its right to choose members in accord with its character. Restrictions on the admission of immigrants is a crucial expression of the community's right of self-determination.

> Admission and exclusion are at the core of communal independence. They suggest the deepest meaning of self-determination. Without them, there could not be communities of character, historically stable, ongoing associations of men and women with some special commitment to one another and some special sense of their common life.[34]

Walzer clearly values the communal character of human existence and the genuine diversity of communities. In his thinking, the United States as a democratic country is morally required to treat people equally who are within its territorial borders. But it is not morally required to treat people outside its borders according to the same standard of equality. However, national communities do have a limited moral responsibility to render "mutual aid" to needy outsiders.

The mutual aid principle would commit U.S. citizens to help those whose need is especially severe and who can be helped with a minimum of cost and effort. Those who seek asylum in the United States have a particularly strong case for assistance. But beyond this limited responsibility, the number of migrants could be so large that the national community would be swamped. Thus the community's right to restrict immigration is primary, and the principle of mutual aid qualifies it in only a limited way.[35]

From Walzer's ethical perspective, current U.S. immigration and refugee policy would seem to be justified. The United States does seek to restrict admission. The United States admits some refugees, and is legally committed to protect asylees. In its policies, it gives priority to the reunification of families, recognizing that the admission of individuals also involves a moral commitment to their primary relationships.

For Walzer, the restrictions of U.S. policy are quite within the moral prerogatives of the country. Who we do or do not admit cannot be

118

critiqued by criteria beyond the nation's own determination. This means that normatively, as well as functionally, U.S. citizens may make admission decisions on the basis of the kind of national community they want to fashion. A nation's particular identity, character, and self-understanding are normative for migration policy, not universalistic principles. But citizens, including Christians, can morally contest the definitions of nation that are morally determinative for the nation's life.

CHRISTIAN ETHICS AND NATIONAL CONTROL OF BORDERS

A humanitarian version of nationalism in the nineteenth century expected that each national society would contribute something distinctive to a united world community. But this optimistic vision has been dashed on the rocks of the twentieth century. In this recent era of nation-state world organization, we have experienced devastating wars, the Holocaust, the refinement and extension of state repression, millions of refugees, and the development of weapons of destruction. Kenneth Boulding, expressing moral outrage against the destructive manifestations of nationalism, puts the challenge to Christians with unmistakable clarity: "We have wars because people love their country: that's why. And suppose the Church came and said: 'Your country is not worth loving.' Who wants to be a German after Hitler? Who wants to be a Frenchman after Napoleon? Who wants to be an American after Hiroshima and Vietnam?"[36]

Maybe Boulding's denunciation is too harsh, but many Christians have all too readily adapted their faith to ideologies of nationalism and national sovereignty. In the United States, loyalty to God and to country have often been viewed as the same thing. It can be difficult to determine if there is in fact any difference between Americanism and Christianity in many of our churches. In England it is common to see memorials to notables in military garb in magnificent cathedrals which laud them for serving God, king, and country. With the privilege of historical hindsight, we today may ask whether or not they were serving God when they killed or were killed on behalf of the king (and maybe a few of his lucky subjects).

One part of a Christian assessment of nationhood, therefore, is religious and moral criticism. The modern tendency has been to deify the nation, the national cause, and the power of the state apparatus. As H. Richard Niebuhr pointed out, the nation (or nation-state) often

119

serves as the center of value for persons in an era of nationalism.[37] But it is a false god, a dangerous idol, because it has so much power over peoples' lives and because it excludes so many and so much. The nation may be deeply valued in Niebuhr's view, but only as it is valued in relation to a wider range of relationships that extends far beyond its borders.

For Christians, then, the nation is not the center of reality. The authority of the nation-state is not absolute. It is not the ultimate arbiter of morality. National claims are relativized. The nation is entirely too limited as a community to be granted moral supremacy. The nation and presuppositions about national interest must be viewed in relation to a wider community, which includes other nations, peoples, and species, both past and future. While the notion of sovereignty in political discourse is self-limiting to the degree that it applies only to a specified territory and people, it nonetheless confers a quasi-religious legitimation to the nation-state, which too readily becomes idolatrous. For Christians, the claims and interests of nations should always be evaluated by reference to the God whose love and justice is the center of astonishingly inclusive relatedness.

The second part of a Christian perspective is that human particularities are valued. Christian ethics does not, in my judgment, lead to a preference for abstract universalism in which differences do not matter. Humans are social-historical beings, situated in time and place. We are culture-creating and culture-bearing peoples. We develop a sense of who we are by being related to particular communities, whose identity we come to share. Even though I might presume to claim an internationalist rather than a national identity, I would wear it in a way that looks very North American to people from other countries.

In biblical traditions there is a recognition of both the unity of the human family in God and the diversity of the peoples of the earth. Both are contained in Paul's sermon in Athens, a text that historically has often been cited in support of immigration: "From one ancestor he made all nations to inhabit the whole earth, and he allotted the times of their existence and the boundaries of the places where they would live" (Acts 17:26). God is the creator of all human beings through their common ancestor Adam. Indeed, all of us are relatives. Yet nations with their boundaries also reflect God's ordering activity.

120

The narrative traditions that shape a Christian perspective do not present a single model for organizing and governing human communities. We should distrust them if they did, given the historical character of human existence. In fact, these traditions give us an ambiguous evaluation of the establishment of Israel as a nation and its emergence as a regional power. Some traditions legitimate this development and others denounce it. Some traditions regard Roman government as ordained by God while others view it as anti-Christ.

Biblical traditions do, however, bequeath perspectives that still annoy and illumine. The authority of government is often highly valued and carries the mark of divine approval, but it may also be oppressive and evoke God's judgment. Borders between peoples seem to be accepted, but the faithful are often rebuked for being too exclusivist in their orientation to others. The particularity of human communities seems to be embraced in God's ordering and saving work in history, but this is in tension with the universality of God's loving relatedness.

For Christians these are tensions to live with and within as we struggle with immigration and refugee policy. An important legacy of biblical traditions is to affirm the values of particularity in the economy of God's ongoing creativity. Indeed God is pictured as working through particular, covenanted communities. The organization of human beings in national communities is not inherently evil. Nations may be valued in their particularity. But the values of nation may not be absolutized nor may they demand exclusive loyalty from their members.

The nation-state system is a human invention, a historical creation, a way to organize and govern dispersed and diverse human communities. This particular organization is not mandated by God. It can be changed and surely will change. The nation-state stage of world history has been characterized by humane creativity and monstrous cruelty and destructiveness. Any future political invention is likely to exhibit similarly ambiguous manifestations. Currently there are pressures on the nation-state system that move in two entirely different directions: the federalist organization of European states in the Maastricht agreement, or the breakup of nation-states into smaller entities. Whether the system is one of national communities or some alternative, Christians can affirm the legitimacy of community particularity while always qualifying its authority from a more inclusivist ethical vision.

Many of these comments apply also to a moral assessment of national borders. Particular human communities are necessarily bounded in some sense. For Walzer, the determination of membership is a basic boundary. In the case of political communities, so is territory. It is important to emphasize that national borders, also, are human constructions. They are not eternally fixed by either nature or deity. Borders are notoriously arbitrary, often reflecting which country had greater power at a particular time in history. For example, the border between Mexico and the United States was established by the victor over the vanquished and constitutes by almost any standard unjust acquisition of territory by the United States.

Because borders are inventions that bear a weight of emotional intensity and historical grievances, their demarcation should be determined by negotiations and mutual agreements, not by conquest or intimidation. But borders are not inherently evil. A Christian vision of the world is not necessarily one without borders. Borders mark off discrete human communities. They may serve valid purposes. A world in which genuinely diverse human communities can flourish requires also some legitimate sense of boundedness.

But borders need to be kept under moral suspicion by Christians. For Christians, the territory within national borders is not finally ours to possess and own. The treasures and resources of the land are gifts of God that are held in trust for all persons now and into the future. Borders also should not become like fortresses that breed hostility and enmity among neighboring peoples. In the context of the Cold War, John Bennett often made the important point that American people should not be prevented from human contact with persons from Communist countries. Even if governments are adversaries, the people should be able to interact with each other, pointing to a relatedness that transcends the immediacy of political conflict.[38] Borders are provisional and negotiable constructions for the sake of just and humane order and can only be justified by an ethical vision that is wider than nationalism can provide.

In the world system of nation-states, refugees and immigrants are among those who are most disadvantaged and powerless. A secure national membership counts for a great deal. Without it, a person is exceedingly vulnerable with precious few options. The nation-state system conspires against them. I suggest in this chapter that Christians are disposed to see and respond to migrants through the lenses of their narrative faith. Images of hospitality and inclusive community are to shape the moral practice of churches and Christians. In our current nationalistic ethos, Christians are called to relativize the authority of the state and qualify the claims of the national community. Yet Christians may also participate in shaping the character of the national community. We may affirm the values of government and the existence of genuinely diverse national communities.

Christians are shaped by an ethic of hospitality that is not delimited by national borders; rather, it extends to a world of national communities. We are seemingly back to the virtually unbridgeable gap between Christian ideals and political realities. But this is not our only recourse. In the next chapter we shall look more specifically at some of the implications of Christian ethics for U.S. migration policies.

4

NEGOTIATING COMMUNITY:
THE QUEST FOR A JUST AND
HUMANE MIGRATION
POLICY

Christians are disposed to extend hospitality to strangers because of their relation to a compassionate and just God. Moreover, Christians are inclined to seek communities in which diversities can be incorporated through negotiation. These images and themes from Christian tradition shape the encounter of residents and migrants. Migrants are viewed not primarily in terms of utility value but as persons with lives of sacred worth. The appeal and claim of migrants require a response, both at interpersonal and at policy levels. In Christian ethics, we reflect on these appeals and our responses from a Christian perspective.

This faith relation necessarily de-centers the claims of national communities and nation-states. Nationalistic ethics may be dominant in the world of nation-states, but it cannot be dominant for Christians. Christians need to draw more tautly the tensions between membership in the national society and faithfulness to God. It is not acceptable to view migrants primarily through national lenses. National claims are relativized; and they are replaced by the cries of the poor and powerless. We are members of a universal family in which each person is equally valued by God and individuals are related to one another through God's love. Still, we are also members of particular communities and polities that are integral to our lives as social and historical selves. National communities also make valid claims on their members.

As we consider U.S. migration policy, we cannot avoid the tensions described above. The tensions are there in the differences between Carens and Walzer, who approach ethics from certain philosophical commitments. For Carens, the equal moral worth of each individual is more weighty than the rights of national communities. For Walzer, the rights of national communities are greater. Similarly, for Christians, the equality of persons in the family of God and the specific claims of the poor are often in tension with the interests and priorities of particular national communities. In this chapter we will consider some ways that Christian ethicists and political philosophers deal with this tension. Then I shall present what I believe to be the implications of a Christian perspective for U.S. migration policies.

Perhaps the most influential way to deal with this tension is provided by human rights discourse. Human rights perspectives challenge the dominance of nationalistic ethics. It is a way to articulate universally binding norms while also respecting differences among nations so long as they do not violate those norms. There is no question that human rights ethics qualifies and relativizes the sovereign authority of nation-states. From a human rights perspective, nation-states should be held accountable to a transnational ethic, which is both more person-centered and more universally inclusive. It is not surprising that Christian ethicists are often among those who are contributing to this development.

In international relations, the most influential human rights documents are often referred to as the International Bill of Human Rights.[1] According to these standards, persons have the right to move from their homeland to someplace else, and they have the right to return to their homeland. Persons have the right to seek refuge from persecution, and they have the right not to be returned to the country from which they have fled (called *nonrefoulement*). Yet, as we have seen, nation-states can make their own decisions about whom to admit and whom to keep out, or whether or not to admit anyone at all. Only nonrefoulement is binding in international law, although nation-states have the *moral* obligation to assist refugees, whether by admission or aiding those countries that are providing the assistance.

In the international system of nation-state sovereignty, each nation-state has the responsibility to protect the human rights of its members. As Jack Donnelly makes clear, "implementing international human rights is largely a matter of national, not international, action."[2] But at least the *norms* to which nation-states are held accountable are not simply those that are chosen by national entities. Many human rights advocates, for understandable reasons, would like to see a stronger role for international institutions in implementing these norms.

What is clear is that migrants are rendered virtually powerless in this international scenario. Refugees have the right to seek safe haven, but nation-states are not obligated to receive them. Moreover, nation-states control decisions about who really is a refugee, thereby often avoiding the claims of desperate people by defining them as economic migrants. Internally displaced persons' are even more vulnerable because they cannot as readily call on the international community for assistance and protection. Although a human rights perspective lifts up the desperate plight of refugees and provides a normative basis for the "international refugee regime," the restrictiveness of nation-states rules the system.

So-called economic migrants, or immigrants, have even less international protection. They have the right to move, and the right to be treated fairly in countries where they find work.[3] But decisions are entirely at the discretion of nation-states. Migrants have to market themselves as a needed commodity or meet very restrictive admission criteria. Or they must seek to enter a country illegally, perhaps obtaining false documents, or living a kind of underground existence to stay away from the law. Should the right to move carry any moral weight on the policies of receiving countries? Are tight restrictions on entrance justified? Or should people not only have a right to move to seek protection, but also to work, to improve their standard of living, or to use their talents more fully?

Christian Ethics, Human Rights, and Migration Policy

In the previous chapter, we reviewed aspects of Christian narrative traditions that dispose Christians to relate to migrants with compassion and hospitality. One very influential way that Christians apply their faith to public policy is through the nation-transcending perspective of human rights. Christians believe that each person is created in the image of God and loved equally by God, therefore each person deserves to be treated justly. And human rights discourse is a way to specify what this entails in specific historical contexts.[4] Christian responsibility for migrants goes beyond the entitlements of rights, but it certainly includes these norms.

The interrelation of narrative ethics and human rights norms was embodied in the sanctuary movement. Christian activists drew specifically on the stories of God's liberating activity on behalf of marginalized people and of covenant responsibility to protect the lives of sojourners and strangers. This narrative of hospitality shaped their responses to the personal appeals of Central Americans for sanctuary in the United States. At the same time, Christian activists sought to hold the U.S. government accountable to the 1980 Refugee Act, which enacted international standards regarding the human rights of refugees. Moreover, Jim Corbett, Quaker activist in southern Arizona, explicitly appealed to human rights standards in critiquing the abuses of nation-states and in challenging communities to accept personal responsibility for protecting refugees.[5]

Narrative ethics is characterized by particularity, the particular faith traditions of Jewish or Christian communities. Human rights ethics attempts to formulate universalistic norms that can be affirmed by varied traditions in varied cultural contexts. For Christians, human rights becomes a way to articulate the universalizing implications of narrative ethics. Both are important aspects of a Christian perspective. As sanctuary activists discerned, narrative traditions and contemporary formulations of human rights cohere in the Christian public witness.

The clearest and most thoroughly developed Christian perspective on the ethics of migration is provided in Roman Catholic social teachings. There is nothing comparable in Protestant Christian ethics, although a number of denominations have prepared studies that develop a theological and ethical basis for policy recommendations. In this section I shall develop the thinking of two Protestant ethicists who give a prominent place to human rights norms, and then reflect on the implications of their theories for migration policy. Following this discussion, we shall consider the perspectives of Roman Catholic social teaching, which also relies heavily on conceptions of human rights.

COVENANT ETHICS AND HUMAN RIGHTS:
MAX STACKHOUSE AND JOSEPH ALLEN

Max Stackhouse regards human rights as inherent in Christian convictions about God. For Stackhouse, God is the holy other whose righteousness is the standard for ordering human communities. In the biblical tradition, there is a universal moral order, rooted in the righteousness of God, which is other than ordinary experience yet directly pertinent to ordinary experience; and human responsibility involves action toward the future that can reconcile the contradictions without dissolving the difference between the otherness of God and human reality.[6]

Human beings are created in the image of this righteous and loving God. Dignity is given to us as a gift of God's grace. Persons have rights because they are loved by God and are embraced in the universal fellowship of God's community. To believe in *this* God means that *nothing else* can be absolutized. Human beings are free from deterministic ideologies and schemes, and they are empowered by the hope that the current order can be changed.

For Stackhouse, we have the moral responsibility to relate to each other in ways that fit the character of God's love as we see it in Jesus Christ. This is normative not only for church life but for public policy and the ordering of social structures as well. We are morally required to value each person and protect each person's rights. Our understandings of community are transformed as well. Family, ethnic, or political bonds are not ultimate. Rather, persons are citizens of a universal community that creates new ties and responds to a different set of loyalties. We are called to care for each other as members of the community of God—a re-created community that overcomes the conventional barriers that exclude and divide.

Stackhouse believes the Universal Declaration of Human Rights is a very significant accomplishment in the effort to articulate a universal ethic. In ways rather similar to earlier church councils, the Universal Declaration emerged from an assembly of representatives from many different places in the world. In this document, persons are not viewed as isolated individuals or as national citizens. They are "members of the human family" above all.[7] The relatedness of persons is affirmed, a relatedness that is universal in breadth. "Specific 'gene pools' are not the basis for human solidarity, identity, and 'membership'; voluntary bonding is."[8] The right of persons to move should be seen in this light. A person's membership should not be regarded as fixed by birthplace but should be subject to the principle of choice.[9]

Stackhouse does not directly address questions of migration policy. But his vigorous advocacy on behalf of universal human rights, specifically the right to move, has challenging implications. Presumably, similar to the view of Joseph Carens, even membership in national

129

societies should be based on choice, not on where one is born. But the ethical basis for this freedom is not solely the right of personal self-determination[10] but the realization of human relatedness in intentional covenanting. Persons should be free from absolutizing and deterministic systems to actualize their deepest convictions and values in community with others. Normatively this seems to apply not only to churches and other voluntary associations, but to national communities as well.

Stackhouse's cosmopolitan view of human rights and human community seems to lead to a relatively open-borders approach to human migration. Perhaps minimal restrictions could be justified to protect the health of the democratic polity, which Stackhouse regards as the kind of polity that is most responsive to norms of human rights. Still his interpretation of Christian ethics calls for an expansive notion of membership. Universal ties are morally stronger than national or ethnic ties. There does not seem to be a morally compelling reason to give preference to the interests of U.S. citizens over the appeals of persons from, for example, Haiti or Guatemala. "They" are just as much members of our family, the family of God, as national compatriots. Persons should be free to move to a new place, to form those associational bonds necessary for human flourishing with a different community than their birth community.

What is not as clear in Stackhouse's theory is the force of the right of a *community* to be self-determining. By what right or according to what limits may national communities say no to people who want to move here? If the right to move does not also include a moral obligation to receive people who want to move here, then the right does not amount to very much. Yet, on the other hand, the very act of covenanting seems to imply a mutual decision that involves the receiving society as well as the migrant. The positive valuation that Joseph Allen gives to special covenants is helpful in responding to this question.

Joseph Allen develops a theory of Christian ethics that directly addresses the tensions between the claims of the national community and broader moral responsibility.[11] He does so through the notion of covenant. God's inclusive covenant comprises all humankind. The national community, however, is one of a number of special covenants. Generally, the claims of special covenants are greater, because these are the settings in which finite human beings can most concretely live out their moral responsibilities. Yet when there is a conflict, the claims of the inclusive covenant have greater weight.

Allen believes the church has the special calling to proclaim the inclusiveness of God's covenantal relation with all humankind. But even officials of national governments have obligations to persons other than their own citizens. They should seek a balance between the interests of their citizens and those persons who reside outside their borders.[12] The national community has genuine value and is worthy of Christians' conditional loyalty and moral commitment. But the nation is not the center, nor is it the ultimate arbiter for political ethics. The claims and the requirements of special covenants must be rigorously evaluated from an inclusive ethical perspective.

Now, in Allen's theory, human rights are based on what is appropriate to each person's membership in God's inclusive community. A person's right to respect is absolute. Other rights may be in conflict and have to be weighted. Which rights or claims have priority? For Allen, human need is the primary measure of justice when various rights cannot be harmonized or balanced. God's love and righteousness is the ultimate standard. It is the inclusiveness of God's covenant that enables and requires Christians to move beyond self-interest and particular community loyalties.

What are the implications of this theory for migration policy? Potentially, it has radical implications indeed. Many arguments based on U.S. national interest would give way to the claims of needy migrants who have nowhere else to go for safety, work, and sustenance. Certainly, efforts to secure human rights for persons in their own homelands, including distributive justice, is a moral imperative. But it would also seem difficult to justify closing the border to needy neighbors who are not threatening the basic rights of Americans (which does not, after all, include the right to monopolize wealth and resources).

Yet it would also be possible to develop the implications of Allen's theory differently. Since particular covenants do have an important claim on their members, there is a special obligation to seek justice for the poor in one's own national community. It may also be necessary to place some restrictions on immigration in order to protect the cohesion and order of the national community.[13] A great deal rides on what kind of interpretation one gives to the notion of "order."

One could, of course, view order in either a "high threshold" or a "low threshold" way. A high-threshold view would be like that of restrictionists, who regard the American civil order as so severely threatened already that few migrants should be permitted to enter. A low-threshold view, which I believe to be more consistent with Allen's theory, is that the U.S. society is not yet threatened by current numbers of newcomers; thus a generous admission policy is warranted. Yet, if at some time U.S. cohesion and order are sufficiently threatened, then tighter restrictions on newcomers would be morally justified.

Allen's view of Christian ethics would seem to require a generous policy toward refugees and especially needy immigrants. The challenges of incorporating newcomers into U.S. society are not nearly as severe as the needs of others in God's inclusive covenant for protection and basic sustenance. In Allen's theory, it would also be difficult to justify the cosmopolitan principle of allotting immigration slots on the basis of national membership. His ethic seems to call for a policy in which individual need would be the primary criterion for admission to the United States, to be applied in a nondiscriminatory way.

Yet Allen also provides a positive interpretation of the moral significance of special covenants. National societies are not at core a necessary evil but a moral good and an ongoing moral challenge. Based on Allen's normative perspective, it is possible to argue that national communities have a right to protect themselves, their members, and their vital institutions. National communities have finite capacities for incorporating newcomers. Members are justified in giving priority to the well-being of those within the national community. Allen's interpretation both affirms the particularities of national communities and locates them in the context of a more inclusive vision in which the basic human rights of others also makes a powerful moral claim.

Nationalistic perspectives are so much a part of the air we breathe that it is difficult to entertain, much less act on, the inclusive vision of Stackhouse and Allen. A human rights perspective challenges governments to adopt hospitable policies toward those who seek membership in their societies, qualified only perhaps by a low-threshold principle of public order. The authority of the nation-state and the boundaries of national community are qualified and continually transformed by transcendent norms of universal relatedness.

Churches especially are accountable to God for their stewardship of this powerful ethical vision.

ROMAN CATHOLIC SOCIAL TEACHING

In Roman Catholic thought, the centrality of human rights is indisputable. Fortunately, a body of teachings has evolved over the years which relates a human rights perspective to issues of migration. If anything, the critique of the dominance of the nation-state system and advocacy on behalf of migrants is even stronger here than in any of the views we have considered thus far. For Catholics, human rights are rooted in the dignity of each human being. Each person is created in God's image; each is related to all others in the unity of God's family. The resources of the earth are created by God for the good of all people. People's membership, above all, is in the universal family.

Solidarity is a concept that expresses the interrelatedness of the peoples of the earth. Our lives are linked in our created sociality and in our common destiny. A recent statement on refugees by several pontifical councils challenges people to look beyond their own cultural and national particularity to wider ranges of relationship and responsibility. Solidarity "is a firm and persevering determination to commit oneself to the common good; that is to say to the good of all and of each individual, because we are really responsible for all."[14]

In Drew Christiansen's interpretation, Roman Catholic teaching has become increasingly critical of the nation-state system for its repeated violations of human rights.[15] Human beings should have the right to migrate (both to leave and to be received); instead, migrants are reduced "to disposable objects of state policy."[16] The right to move is based on the right of persons to a homeland where they belong and can provide for their families. For Christiansen, nation-states are justified in excluding migrants *only* in exceptional circumstances. As a rule, nation-states are permitted to *regulate* but not *exclude* the entrance of migrants.[17]

Belief in human rights requires pressing for increasingly open borders. Christiansen believes the implication of Catholic teaching is "that the United States and other nations ought to permit virtually open borders for all those who have serious reason to abandon their ancestral homeland and seek a new life elsewhere."[18] Yet a relatively open-borders policy does not extend morally to wealthy and educated citizens of third-world countries. They have the moral obligation to contribute to the humane development of their homelands.

In Michael Evans's view, the right to move is qualified somewhat more than it is for Christiansen.[19] Evans believes this right is limited by the norm of the common good, not only the universal common good but also the common good of sending and receiving countries. Presumably, a nation could be justified in limiting the number of immigrants if unrestricted immigration is threatening its capacity to secure the common good of its current members. For Evans, then, a just migration policy is one that balances the right of individual persons to move with the impacts of migration on the domestic common good of receiving communities. But when the need of migrants is grave, the moral presumption clearly swings to the right of persons to be received in a new homeland.

In Catholic social thought, the right to move encompasses economic reasons as well as the fear of persecution. For example, the right to work and to earn a living wage is well established. Reaching back to Leo XIII's encyclical *Rerum Novarum* (1891), Catholics may appeal to this right as a way to support the claim of immigrants as well as refugees. In the context of debates about undocumented migrants from Mexico, the National Conference of Catholic Bishops maintained that the U.S. government cannot morally ignore the right of persons to migrate in order to find work.[20] It certainly is not a criminal deed for them to cross borders to seek work, even though the United States might seek to restrict their entry. The very efforts of Mexican migrants are a courageous assertion of their dignity, too little respected among settled people to the north.

Even though it is harder and harder to distinguish between immigrants and refugees, Evans nonetheless believes the moral claims of refugees are weightier than those of other migrants. Persons and national communities have the moral obligation to assist refugees because all of us share a common dignity and humanity. When states engage in "egregious" violations of members' rights, then those persons have a right to seek international protection. Evans believes this protection should not be limited to persons who cross borders, but should apply to internally displaced persons as well. All those who are forced to leave their homes are refugees, whether the reasons are economic, environmental, or political violence.[21]

Although there are some shades of difference in interpretation, Catholic social teaching provides a clear and consistent ethical perspective on migration policy. First is the presumption that the migrant has a right to enter another country, unless that country has weighty moral reasons to prevent the entry. Simply to assert the rights of national sovereignty or the requirements of national interest is not enough. The national community must be able to justify morally its restrictions. A "foreigner" is in the deepest moral sense a member of the wider human community and so can validly move to a different national society from the one in which he or she was born. Catholic bishops in England and Wales have made the intriguing proposal that a nation-state's restrictions should be subject to challenge before an appropriate court.[22]

Second, the claims of refugees have the greatest moral weight. Moreover, the definition of refugee should be expanded to include the internally displaced as well as those who cross borders. It should be further broadened beyond the fear of persecution to include economically and environmentally uprooted people. As Christiansen puts it, "degrading poverty is as much a denial of human dignity as subjection to political tyranny."[23] In fact, in light of this principle, it would seem that the United States should admit a greater number of refugees overall and a greater number of refugees in proportion to the number of immigrants.

Third, implicit in the above principle is that the criterion of need is determinative in sorting out which migrants have the strongest claim for admission. Christiansen says that "the poor ought to have priority over other economic migrants in admission to the United States and in eligibility for U.S. citizenship."[24] Here, the poor are not only the economic refugees whose deprivation is life-threatening, but also the ones who scrape and struggle every day just to provide the bare necessities of life. In Catholic thought, the claim of these persons is weightier than more highly educated or professionally qualified migrants, or those relatively affluent persons who want to attain a yet higher standard of living. These more privileged persons, we may presume, have more options in their homelands and greater responsibility for contributing to their development than do the poor.

Fourth, Catholic thought supports the full incorporation of migrants into the receiving community. There is no justification for a double standard of justice. Migrants have the same rights as citizens—

135

for example, housing, education, social welfare, just working conditions.[25] Current U.S. proposals for denying public assistance to undocumented persons and for denying social welfare to new "resident aliens" are violations of human rights. Residents should treat migrants as members of the same human family. Discrimination is unjust, whether it is based on race, ethnicity, or nationality. Human rights are *human* rights, not merely American or Mexican rights. By implication, the U.S. government has the responsibility to protect the rights of persons in the territory over which it has jurisdiction, whether or not these persons are documented.[26]

At the same time, recent Catholic social ethics explicitly affirms cultural pluralism. That is, the kind of universalism that is advocated does not assume a "sameness" to peoples that denies the value of differences. Peoples in their relatedness are creators and bearers of culture. To respect persons also means to respect the specific culture in which they express their humanness. Catholic teaching affirms "the right of man [*sic*] to preserve and develop his own ethnic, cultural and linguistic patrimony."[27] In Christiansen's view, the Catholic church has a distinctive opportunity to affirm the cultural characteristics of immigrant groups while also helping them to become integrated into the wider society. In a unity that embraces diversity, the church models as well as advocates "possibilities of greater community than we ordinarily imagine are feasible, both within and across borders."[28]

In conclusion, Catholic social teaching provides a clear ethical perspective on migration issues. Furthermore, Catholic thinkers have related this perspective in quite specific ways to public policy questions. In many respects, this perspective is in sharp conflict with U.S. policies and in even sharper conflict with restrictionist trends in American public life. Less clear in Catholic social ethics, however, is which kinds of regulative measures would be morally justified. That is, the clear presumption is with the right of the needy migrant to be admitted into an affluent country like the United States.

But what may the United States justly and humanely do to regulate migration? The National Conference of Catholic Bishops opposes the employer sanctions provision of the 1986 Immigration Act.[29] Catholic Charities opposes the use of a national identity card.[30] While the moral direction of Catholic teaching toward open borders is unmistakable, it is important to be more clear about what can morally be done, if

136

anything, to limit migration into the United States. Among advocates of immigrants' rights, this question seems infrequently addressed. Yet, unless one does in fact favor unrestricted or even unregulated migration, the question of appropriate mechanisms of enforcement is unavoidable.

A Christian Perspective on Migration Policy

Christian ethics provides no simple solutions to dilemmas and ambiguities in a nation's migration policy. But it does provide a normative perspective on these questions that is not identical with the interests of nation-states. Churches, I believe, are those communities in history whose calling is to bear witness to the promise of the gospel. Their primary loyalty is not to the nation-state. Christian ethics is disciplined reflection on the vision of relatedness to God that churches seek to embody in their own lives and to realize in the world. Christian ethical reflection is indeed addressed centrally to Christians but also more broadly to the public arena, where diverse people should be encouraged to bring their deepest convictions in respectful dialogue and conscientious action.

The narrative traditions of Christians convey images of hospitality to strangers as concrete manifestations of covenant love. These traditions challenge us with the moral and religious significance of strangers. We are invited to participate in a vision of the world in which the marginalized are brought to the center and the poor are raised up. Christians are beckoned to shape a "new community" oriented toward God's future and to negotiate the terms of a unity in which diversity is prized. Moreover, these traditions authorize contemporary efforts to articulate and secure those rights each person may claim as a valued member of God's inclusive community. The fact that Christian ethics seems so "alien" to the nationalistic ethos of nation-state politics may not signal its irrelevance so much as, precisely, its relevance.

While the sentiments in America seem to be moving in a more restrictionist direction, the thrust of a Christian perspective is toward greater inclusiveness. There are contextual factors as well as specifically normative considerations that support a societal openness to migrants. First, the United States has been formed from the historical experience of immigration. The United States is an immigrant nation.

By most accounts, this is a highly valued national characteristic, whatever persons may think of future directions. Second, the United States is an exceptionally affluent nation. It is also a country with sufficient dynamism that many persons still believe in the United States as a land of freedom and opportunity. The United States can afford to sustain the costs, such as they are, to continue its lively experiment with re-creating itself through encounters with migrants.

In any event, the current arguments about U.S. migration policy turn less on a calculation of costs and benefits than on the perspective we bring to bear on the questions. This is precisely where ethics becomes germane. I am suggesting that a Christian perspective does not begin with considerations about national interest but with the relational encounter between migrant and resident. We begin with the concrete appeals of migrants and the enfleshed stories they bring into our presence. We see and respond to them as persons valued and loved by God, as persons with whom we are related in the inclusive family of God.

Migrants may remind us of our own vulnerability and dependency, of how fragile our own security systems are and how important it is to create social structures that make provision for those who must rely on the community. They remind us that we were liberated from the inhospitality of enslavement by the astonishing hospitality of God. They remind us that it is often through migrants that God communicates news that settled folk need to hear. It is always possible that the migrant is Christ incognito. It is no wonder that hospitality to strangers is so important in the narrative faith of Christians. In the encounter with migrants, Christians are disposed to hear their cries, listen to their appeals, learn from their experience, and extend hospitality.

This relational point of departure is concrete and personal. The question is not centrally what the government's responsibility is, or even which universal human right is applicable. The question is what is *our* responsibility as we encounter the reality of the migrant's personhood. From this beginning point, we are confronted with the reasons why people seek to enter the United States. From a relational perspective some reasons are more compelling than others. Migration policy is a way to struggle as a national community with which reasons, which claims, are most compelling as the United States decides whom and how many to admit.

This is not merely a concession to human selfishness, though that is always a factor, but a recognition of human finitude. Even when there is a powerful disposition to love the migrant, there are finite capacities for extending hospitality. Communities also have finite capacities for receiving and incorporating newcomers. The claim of each migrant is not equally compelling, even as each is valued and loved as a member of God's inclusive community.

It seems from both a Christian perspective of inclusive human community and a liberal democratic philosophy of individual freedom that national borders should be open to immigrants as well as refugees. But these conclusions may not sufficiently acknowledge the difficulties of forming and sustaining particular human communities. The incorporation of newcomers in settled communities is a challenge to the residents as well as to the migrants.

The task of re-creating community is a marvelous human undertaking. But it is not easy. And the number of newcomers to incorporate does make a difference. Neighborhoods and cities change. Public schools face tough challenges. The resistances to immigration should not be attributed only to narrowness and selfishness. Communities are changed by immigration. One may argue that the difficulties and challenges are the kinds that can contribute to the communities' dynamism, as I do, while also not underestimating the difficulty of re-creating community.

A relational approach does not frame the moral question primarily in terms of rights of migrants versus the rights of national communities. Instead, concrete encounters with migrants raise questions that require negotiation. There can be a strong moral force to the appeal of migrants for admission. And human rights discourse is a way to articulate what sorts of moral appeals are most compelling. But the receiving society may legitimately make its own claims, some of which also are more persuasive than others. In other words, immigration policy may be viewed dynamically as a process of negotiation between migrants and the receiving society.

The ethical theory of Joseph Allen is helpful in showing that the moral claims of special covenants like national communities have an important place in a Christian perspective. We do not live in a universal community but in bounded communities with particular histories and particular polities with specific responsibilities for *this* people rather than undifferentiated responsibilities for everyone.

Boundaries may serve valid purposes; indeed they may well be essential for human communities. If the boundaries were not national ones, they would likely be replaced by other types of boundaries. Thus it is not inherently unjust for national communities to regulate, even to restrict, the admission of newcomers.

Each particular civil community has special responsibilities for the well-being of its own members and for the specific institutions that members share. A Christian ethical perspective can embrace respectfully a multitude of diverse national societies as manifestations of the richness of God's creativity. An ethic of hospitality does not require admitting every person who wants to immigrate to the United States. It does require dealing with the moral force of immigrants' appeals and viewing them in the context of our relatedness to them in the inclusive community of God.

Another way to express this idea is a familiar one in Christian social ethics: justice requires order. Order needs to serve justice, but there cannot be justice without order. Immigration laws are necessary to ensure a reasonably orderly pattern for admitting and incorporating migrants. For this reason, even though Christiansen supports an open-border admissions policy, he recognizes the need for regulating the movement of people. Human communities require a degree of boundedness, and the boundaries must be maintained by sufficient orderliness and stability for them to function justly. Governments are responsible for establishing an order to human interaction across the boundaries, especially when migrants seek to become members of the host society rather than temporary visitors.

Yet the structures of order always need to be kept under moral criticism. National borders should foster interaction rather than seal off territories from those who are outside. Borders must be characterized by a certain permeability to be justified. For Christians, borders are viewed morally in relation to the wider communities of persons who are, no less, daughters and sons of God. Whatever steps are taken to enforce restrictions on admission should be responsive to these concerns. High walls and the use of lethal force should be repudiated. It is morally significant that the only way, seemingly, to seal off the border entirely from illegal entry is to adopt police-state mechanisms. Order that stifles the cries of the poor or that tramples on persons' basic rights is oppressive.

From a Christian perspective, the appeal of the migrant should not be discounted merely because the person is outside the national community. The moral force of the migrant's appeal for admission should be heard and felt in its concreteness. And the migrant deserves a considered response that takes seriously the moral significance of her life situation. The national policy, then, can be interpreted as the responses that the national community is making to the concrete appeals of migrants. Descriptively, the twists and turns of U.S. immigration policy can be seen in this light—responding in one era (e.g., post 1965) in a reasonably receptive way while severely limiting immigration in a different time (e.g., 1920–1965).

In this sense, also, Michael Walzer is descriptively accurate. The U.S. national society *will* determine whom it will admit to national membership. What kind of community do we choose to be and for what reasons? Like it or not, Americans will decide through the political process how open or restrictive we will be. If members view migrants merely as outsiders and threats, then U.S. policy will be restrictive. If, however, members view migrants in a more inclusive way and value the richness of the encounters between residents and newcomers, then U.S. policy will be more receptive.

In other words, U.S. policy depends a great deal on the moral character of Americans. The perceptions and values of Americans determine what we bring to the negotiation with migrants about their appeals and claims. The readiness or resistance to extend hospitality to migrants is a character trait of major importance in the determination of public policy.

To be sure, a serious problem with the "negotiation" metaphor is the huge inequalities in power between migrants and the government of the receiving society. Immigration policy may well satisfy some elements of reciprocity since the immigrant needs work and the United States benefits from her work. These considerations are a legitimate part of the dynamics of negotiation. By and large, even by a cost/benefit measurement, migrants have benefited the United States in all sorts of ways. But when it comes to decisions about migration policy, it seems all the power is with the nation-state—and very little with the migrant.

While this is certainly a realistic appraisal up to a point, it is qualified in at least three ways. First, some migrants who are shut out of the United States continue to come anyway. Those who are courageous or desperate enough to enter the United States illegally are

141

limiting the power of the U.S. government to determine its migration policy. Undocumented workers are participating in the negotiation with their feet and their work even if they are permitted little voice.

Second, U.S. citizens continue to form functional and personal relationships with migrants, including undocumented immigrants. Sometimes the relationship is exploitive, using the vulnerability of the immigrant to pay lower wages and to avoid taxes. But sometimes the relationship is one of affection, as well as utility in which persons establish bonds that are more important than national boundaries and legalistic restrictions. Residents' behavior that is in conflict with government policy often leans in the direction of greater receptivity. These "palpable"[31] ties between people across borders also qualifies the power of the nation-state.

Third, communities that believe moral considerations are germane to public policy often seek to represent the voices of the voiceless in public advocacy. That is, churches, among other voluntary associations, can bear the moral force of migrants' appeals in national debate about migration policy and thus ensure that the migrants' perspective is part of the negotiation. It makes sense, theologically and politically, that churches largely defend the cause of migrants in public discussions where their claim often counts for so little.

In summary, regulations and controls on migration are not inherently unjust. A chaotic influx of newcomers jeopardizes the well-being of both migrants and residents of the receiving society. Community does not occur automatically through good intentions alone but must be negotiated and shaped over time. A Christian perspective leads to a presumption on behalf of a generous admissions policy[32] that is limited by a low-threshold view of order. Supporters of a highly restrictive policy must bear the burden of making a compelling moral case, especially given America's immigrant history and its privileged position in a world of appalling inequalities.

Implications for U.S. Migration Policy

INTERNATIONAL JUSTICE AND HUMAN RIGHTS

The best strategy to deal with human ills is prevention. Much of what fuels the vast movements of peoples is violence, injustice, and lack of opportunity in their homelands. Alarmists raise the spectacle of poor people from southern countries flooding affluent northern countries unless something is done to slow the flow. Even realists point to the threat to international peace and stability that results from massive migrations. One response, of course, is the fortress strategy. It calls for closing the borders by building higher walls and using more sophisticated technologies of surveillance. The alternative response is effective international action to make it possible for people to remain safely and securely in their home countries.

Refugees, especially, are uprooted from their homes. Most would remain if it were safe. Encounters with refugees lead us to ask not only what we can do to provide protection, but also what we can do to change those conditions that put their lives at risk. Hospitality to refugees leads Christians to be concerned with international justice and human rights. These are not mere abstractions but are as real as the violence that compels persons to run for their lives. Even though preventive strategies seem most removed from personal responsibility, they are surely one expression of it. Compassion for the specific refugee can hardly leave one indifferent to the disorder of the world system that turns so many of our extended neighbors into refugees.

The same point needs to be made with immigrants as well. People will keep moving so long as there are vast inequalities in income and opportunities. The long-range "solution" for illegal immigration is neither tightened restrictions nor expanded admissions but justice at home. And the establishment of justice is not merely the responsibility of the governments of sending countries. Often the obstacles these countries must overcome have to do with the policies of more powerful nations. International sanctions against governments that violate their peoples' rights is certainly appropriate. But even more important are cooperative efforts between sending and receiving countries that make it possible for governments to protect and promote their peoples' rights.

ADMISSIONS POLICIES

A Christian perspective on migration policy leads more readily to open borders than to closed borders, whether one relies on narrative traditions of hospitality to strangers or on contemporary norms of human rights. Yet it is difficult to find persons who support a thoroughly open border. Generally, advocates for refugees and immigrants seem to accept the necessity of border controls, however regretfully. But little direct attention is given to which controls are ethically justified and on what basis they are defensible.

In a sense this is quite understandable. Realistically one can assume that national societies will impose controls on admission. It is more important to use one's energies in supporting the cause of migrants and in widening any windows of opportunity that are available. Many people are ready to defend the interests of the national community. The greater need is to express solidarity with migrants so that their claim will have at least some influence.

As important as this advocacy role is, I believe it is also necessary to be clear about which kinds of limitations are morally acceptable. Two questions must be faced in supporting a limited admissions policy, as difficult as they are to deal with from an ethical perspective. First, if the United States will not open its borders to all migrants, which ones will be admitted? Which priorities are of greater moral weight, and which are valued less? The second question concerns enforcement. If there are justifiable limits to migration, how will those limits be enforced? Which types of enforcement are morally acceptable and which ones are not?

First, the admission of a refugee or an immigrant should mean, as a matter of course, the admission also of close family members. Churches have long supported the principle of family unity, for very good reasons. From a Christian perspective, persons are relational beings whose family ties have a special religious and moral significance. These are bonds of intimacy, affection, and mutual responsibility, which need to be supported and nurtured. The need for family is, if anything, even stronger when one is trying to embark on a new life in a strange land. U.S. migration policy should ensure that refugees and immigrants with families are admitted as families.

The more complex questions emerge as one considers the diversity of families in varied cultures. As we well know, the nuclear family ("immediate family" members) is not the dominant pattern in many parts of the world. Extended family might well include many additional persons. Yet, if extended families are admitted, then this limits the number of additional persons who can enter the United States. This policy would work on behalf of the "lucky few" at the expense of many others with an equally powerful appeal. For this reason, the priority of "close family" members is morally defensible even though

144

it is not fully responsive to the diversity of family relationships in other cultures.

Second, a Christian ethical perspective will give priority to migrants who are refugees. The categories we have developed for differentiating migrants is a way to sort out the kinds of reasons why people immigrate and to distinguish between the moral force of their appeals. Categories need to be tested constantly in relation to the concrete realities of migrants' lives. The distinction between refugee and immigrant may be seen in this light. The moral significance of the distinction is that the claim of the refugee is most compelling of all. Those people who are forced to move in order to be safe from persecution and possibly death have an appeal that is morally undeniable. In light of changing historical circumstances, many refugee advocates are seeking to broaden the definition of refugee to embrace people who are internally displaced or who cannot survive economically. It is appropriate that the category of refugee become more inclusive to reflect the concrete struggles of today's migrants.

The plight of refugees raises two sets of challenges to those who are reasonably secure and settled. The first challenge is protection and a homeland. The appropriate response is not necessarily admission to or resettlement in the United States. The central moral responsibility is to ensure that there is an effective international system of refugee protection. Refugees should have a safe place to go, should be able to return to their homeland as soon as it is safe, and should have a place where they can establish a new home if they are unable to return soon to their homeland. Often, the most compassionate response to refugees is to advocate vigorously for the U.S. government to provide international leadership on behalf of refugees.

A second set of challenges is to provide asylum or to resettle refugees in the United States. Those persons who are most desperate and in greatest need, and who can best be helped by entering the United States, should have the highest priority. U.S. policy needs to be clear about this, and communities of conscience should continue to hold their government to this standard. For persons geographically near the United States especially (e.g., persons from Central America and the Caribbean), the right to asylum is of critical importance. Christians have concrete opportunities to practice hospitality in ministries to resettle refugees and in public advocacy for the rights of

145

asylees. Finally, the category of refugee needs to include all those persons who are forced to leave homelands because of life-threatening violence.

The witness of the sanctuary movement is that in some circumstances to practice hospitality to refugees brings Christians into conflict with government policies. By serving God above all, Christians are accepting personal and communal responsibility to protect the basic human rights of endangered persons when their government fails to do so.[33] Christians should also seek to foster a national moral ethos of hospitality for refugees. It seems that refugees are admitted grudgingly, at best, rather than with appreciation for their courage and hope. The gifts that refugees bring and the readiness of residents to extend hospitality are exactly the sorts of qualities that a national community needs for its health and vitality.

It is not unreasonable to expect that national political leadership can be stronger in its advocacy for refugees. For example, when many Haitians were seeking asylum in the United States from terribly dangerous circumstances at home, President Clinton could have made a statement something like this:

> We have a responsibility under international law to protect the rights of refugees. Right now, Haiti is a very dangerous place for too many of its people. The United States will receive valid refugees, that is, those who genuinely fear for their lives. I invite the American people to take on the challenge of welcoming these neighbors from our hemisphere. I shall work with governors and mayors of selected areas of the United States along with representatives of Haitian communities in the United States. Together we shall create a way to do this that can work for the Haitian refugees and for our communities. There are some challenges that we should not evade. When lives of persons near our own land are in serious jeopardy, we cannot turn our backs on them and refuse them protection.

Many folk in the United States have little understanding of who refugees are and what being a refugee means. Public education and public leadership could elicit a greater readiness from Americans to cooperate in undertaking the challenges in incorporating refugees.

To summarize the argument thus far, a relational encounter with migrants requires choices about which persons' needs are greatest, because capacities for hospitality and incorporation are finite. Among

146

the large numbers of migrants today, the appeals of refugees are most compelling. Few reasons would justify the national exclusion of refugees, especially in a country like the United States. The Christian voice should be in alliance with the refugee, whether in support of international action or in support of protection and resettlement in the United States, or both. But, now, what shall we say about the appeals of immigrants, those persons who want to move to the United States to forge a better life for themselves and their families?

Third, U.S. immigration policy should give priority to admitting persons who are in greatest need and to ensuring cosmopolitan diversity. An ethical perspective on immigration policy focuses on the negotiation between immigrants and the receiving society, recognizing that some considerations are more compelling than others. Even though the appeals of refugees and asylees are most compelling, those immigrants whose need for work is great should be granted high priority as well. This means that so-called labor immigrants have a stronger claim than highly educated and professionally trained immigrants. As Roman Catholic social teaching emphasizes, persons have a right to seek work to support themselves and their families. In the Christians' narrative faith, God actively seeks justice for the poor and marginalized. God defends the cause of slaves, widows, orphans, and sojourners; and God judges those in power by their responsiveness to the claims of those who are most vulnerable.

At the same time, two qualifications are pertinent. The policy on Mexican migration adopted by the Presbyterian General Assemblies in 1981 stated that "justice requires opening jobs to Mexican neighbors who need and want to work, so long as there are jobs available and the poor already residing in the United States are not further disadvantaged."[34] The first qualification, then, concerns the availability of jobs in the United States. While the fact that immigrants not only take available jobs but also create jobs needs to be taken into account, it is not humane to admit workers when there is little likelihood of employment.

The second qualification is the claim of the poor already living in the United States. There is little evidence to support the view that immigrants take jobs away from poor residents. But were this the case it would be morally relevant. There is also little reason to believe that if labor immigration were shut off the opportunities for the poor would be improved, or that progress toward racial justice would take a leap forward. To be sure, in the past factory owners sought immigrants from Europe to work in the burgeoning industries to keep from employing African Americans. There are good historical reasons why many people of color are skeptical about the moral force of immigrants' appeal for admission.

In any event, advocacy for the labor immigrant should not replace or weaken the Christian commitment to seek economic and racial justice for the poor members of U.S. society. In fact, support for the cause of immigrants needs to be viewed as one element in the struggle to achieve a national society that is good for the poor and vulnerable neighbors in the United States. Steps toward a more just economy with protections for workers and dynamic employment opportunities will benefit both poor residents and poor immigrants.

In addition to the criterion of need, U.S. immigration policy should be shaped by the priority of diversity and inclusiveness. A Christian perspective is biased in favor of the cosmopolitan principle of community—a society made up of a great deal of the world's diversity. Diversity, in this perspective, should not be walled out but welcomed inside in a dynamic process of negotiating and renegotiating the terms of community. Divisions between peoples are obstacles to be overcome rather than permanent barriers. The ongoing challenge in America is to fashion a racially and culturally diverse people, mirroring the diversity of the world itself, into a society sufficiently unified to pursue the common good of its members. This is, for historical reasons and now by choice, America's opportunity and its most compelling national project.

It may well be that this is the critical element in the immigration debate. Is a multicultural America a good to be valued and adventurously pursued or a threat to community cohesion to be vigorously resisted? A Christian perspective is shaped by the promises of God's inclusive community in which differences are negotiated.[35] This fosters a strong bias in favor of cosmopolitan community whether this is realized in international organizations like the United Nations, or in national communities, or in ecumenical church relations. In 1965, the United States adopted an immigration policy that somewhat unwittingly established a cosmopolitan principle in place of a racialist principle in deciding which immigrants should be admitted. Whereas Peter Brimelow believes this is where American policy took a wrong turn,[36] I argue that this is a moral good that should be reaffirmed and advanced. Christians can make a vital contribution to public discourse on this question.

Thus far I have identified two primary criteria for evaluating and shaping U.S. policy on the admission of immigrants: the severity of the need for work and the value of multiracial and multicultural diversity. The first is responsive to the morality of imperatives. We ought to admit persons who need to work when we have work available. The second is responsive to the morality of goals. A multiracial and multicultural society is a compelling moral good for America. The two will sometimes be in conflict, in which case the priority of need is greater. But when the needs of persons are roughly the same, the cosmopolitan principle provides a morally relevant basis for choosing whom to admit.

Fourth, U.S. migration policy should give priority to persons from countries that are contextually interrelated with the United States in especially pertinent ways. In the case of refugees, especially, this would require that priority be given to persons whose vulnerability and flight have been caused directly by U.S. foreign policy, for example, Indo-Chinese and Central American refugees. With immigrants, there may also be persons whose need to migrate is linked in direct ways to U.S. politics. For example, many of the Cuban immigrants should be included here rather than as refugees. This principle has special pertinence for people who seek to migrate from countries in close proximity to the United States, such as the Caribbean, Mexico, and Central America.

In many instances patterns of migration to the United States, particularly labor migration, have been operative for generations. Labor in an international economy tends to travel across borders. Dependencies and expectations get established between peoples on both sides of the border. This pattern is intensified, of course, in relations between Mexico and the United States. The border is exceptionally long; the justice of the border alignment is highly suspect from a historical perspective; the geography and culture on each side of the border is often similar; the affluent United States has frequently turned to Mexico to find labor, and Mexicans have frequently gone north to support a family or to escape a seemingly hopeless future; the differences in wages and standards of living between Mexico and the United States are huge; and the two countries have developed

149

interdependencies that give moral claims an especially strong contextual force.

In past years, U.S. immigration policy placed fewer restrictions on persons from countries in the Western Hemisphere than on persons from countries in the Eastern Hemisphere. There are understandable historical reasons why this has changed. Still there is moral validity in giving greater weight to the appeals of migrants from nearby countries, especially when the patterns of migration are so deeply established in the recent histories of the peoples. This principle of proximity does not replace the cosmopolitan goal but functions within it to give somewhat greater priority to persons from neighboring countries.

Fifth, what about the priorities of occupational needs in the United States? It is not unusual for persons to argue that the admission of refugees and family members of immigrants is the moral aspect of U.S. migration policy, whereas the admission of immigrants with needed occupational skills is the self-interested aspect. Some want to make occupation the primary criterion for immigration admission. Usually these are occupations that require considerable education with specialized scientific or technological skills. There is no question that immigrants are making great contributions to professional fields. Currently immigrants are a quite diverse segment of the U.S. population, not only in national and cultural origin but also in occupation, income, and class.

If immigration policy is construed in terms of negotiation between migrants and receiving countries, it is not inappropriate for the receiving society to identify its own needs and interests. Reciprocity is an indispensable component of the relationship. Both parties may benefit. Moreover, the admission of educated and middle-class immigrants helps to promote more just patterns of multiracial diversity than would be the case if immigrants were almost entirely low wage workers. To relegate immigrants entirely to the lower rungs of employment and social position is to perpetuate unequal divisions between residents and immigrants. A just immigration policy will give high priority to labor immigrants because of the severity of their need for employment and income. It will give lower priority to persons with professional training and skills, giving special preference to those who are denied the opportunity to use their skills in their homelands.[37]

It is true that there is moral ambiguity in admitting skilled professionals. Specifically there are two qualifications. From the standpoint of Catholic social teaching, such persons have a strong moral obligation to contribute to the common good of their homelands, not to take their skills elsewhere. In a world of striking inequalities, the United States is in a position to lure the very leaders that developing countries most need for their own future (the "brain drain"). When compared with the needs of third- and fourth-world countries, the U.S. need for persons with certain skills is nowhere on the same scale.

It is ironic that some Americans are so anxious about the influx of unskilled workers while eagerly welcoming highly educated professionals to the United States. Yet these immigrants might be the ones who could make the greatest long-range contributions to their home countries, thus making the emigration of the many less necessary. In principle, the United States should at the least compensate countries for highly skilled immigrants, although the most appropriate form and channel of compensation is complicated indeed. Clearly, immigration should more often be a matter of negotiation between the governments of sending and receiving countries.

The second qualification is that the United States is in a position to take strong initiatives to educate and train its own residents to fill such occupations, especially members of its existing underclass who are disproportionately persons of color. If the United States needs more engineers or nurses or research scientists, then it is wrong to look abroad as a way to fill these positions cheaply at the expense of the U.S. poor, whose occupational opportunities seem depressingly closed. The United States should as a matter of policy seek to engender hope through active recruitment and education of motivated persons in historically marginalized communities. For these reasons we should keep the criterion of skilled occupational needs low on the scale of priorities.

In summary, a just and humane immigration policy gives priority to labor immigrants, with fewer openings for skilled immigrants. The policy should ensure the admission of immigrants from all parts of the world, not only allocating ceilings but also stipulating a minimum number of available admissions, especially from countries where the need to migrate for work is especially severe. Finally, the number of immigrants from countries close to the United States or greatly affected by U.S. policies should be relatively greater than from other

151

areas of the world. In other words, it is a policy that acknowledges the moral force of historical ties with neighboring peoples within a broader cosmopolitan framework. This justifies, indeed requires, specific policies that address the special relationship between Mexico and the United States.

We have yet to deal with proposals about how to enforce limitations on migration to the United States. If there is to be a system of regulation and control at all, there must also be enforcement mechanisms. Much of the debate about immigration centers on this question. While some ways to enforce immigration laws are legitimate instruments of social order, others may run the gamut from morally questionable to morally appalling. We will take up this discussion in chapter 6.

5

HOSPITALITY FOR REFUGEES: PROPOSALS FOR U.S. REFUGEE POLICY

Readiness to receive and protect refugees is a test of the moral character of a people. It is one thing if a society is weak and its people are desperately poor. Then it is morally credible for the government to say that its people simply cannot accept many newcomers. But for stable and affluent countries like the United States, the complaint that they cannot afford to admit refugees strains credulity. A moral community will make it possible to protect people whose lives are in danger. Political and religious leaders should challenge their peoples to cooperate in the necessary practical measures. The irony, of course, is that by far the greatest number of the world's refugees is located in poverty-stricken areas of the world, not in the affluent nations that seem so panicked about the possible influx of safety-seeking peoples.

In the current restrictionist climate, Christians need to make the moral case for refugee protection. The United States has never been as hospitable as its mythology would lead us to claim. Yet the mythology has carried some weight. In today's environment, however, the moral basis for a generous refugee policy has to be made all over again. We cannot presume that it is already present in the way that Americans think about refugees. A neo-nationalistic ethic of America First is gathering support. It often goes hand in hand with the sense that what American freedom means is to be able to maximize one's own affluence without being bothered by the claims of others. Refugee protection has little place in this (im)moral scenario.

In previous chapters we have made an ethical case for a generous refugee and immigration policy from a Christian perspective. I further maintain that it is important to keep the distinction between

153

refugee and immigrant. It is important, not least of all, for ethical reasons. When it is acknowledged that there are finite limits to a society's capacity to receive newcomers, then it is necessary to decide who should be given priority. Most agree the United States cannot admit everyone who wants to live in this society. Whom should we admit? I answer: Refugees should be given priority. These persons have the strongest moral claim for admission and protection. This is why we need to keep the refugee and asylum avenues open.

To take this position, however, does not settle all the issues that need to be considered in U.S. refugee policy. In this chapter we shall consider a range of differing proposals that are put forward in contemporary debates. And I shall offer my conclusions about what U.S. policy should be. To be sure, reception of refugees is not the only response to refugees that is morally required. But it is the beginning point. In our willingness to be open and hospitable to refugees, we are expressing our relatedness to others at the most fundamental level: protection of others from death and severe abuse when we have the opportunity and the capacity to render assistance. For Christians, it is the minimal requirement for neighbor relations in the inclusive community of God.

Current Proposals

In the U.S. Congress, debate centers on two aspects of refugee policy. First, some proposed legislation radically cuts the annual ceiling on refugee admissions to fifty thousand. This would be a reduction of more than 50 percent over the number of persons received in the early 1990s, and just under 50 percent of the ninety thousand that Clinton's administration proposes for fiscal year 1996. The rationale is that there are fewer genuine refugees in Southeast Asia and the former Soviet Union, where the great preponderance of refugees have come from in recent years. The president would have to get the approval of Congress to go beyond the fifty thousand limit.

Second, Congress is also focusing on asylum issues. Many people are eager to keep people who are not really refugees from using asylum as a way to enter the United States and stay. Some also want to be more restrictive about who is granted asylum. Concerns about the numbers of newcomers again lie behind these efforts. Already some new procedures have been adopted to speed up decisions about asylum claims. Now, fewer avenues of appeal are available to persons seeking asylum. An additional measure would permit officials to deny asylum quickly to persons who have fraudulent documents or who are interdicted at sea.[1] Also, in another effort to discourage asylum seekers, asylees now cannot work for the first 180 days after they have filed their application.

Critics of these proposals focus on the need to have greater flexibility in the number of refugees who may be admitted. It is simply not possible to project a meaningful number when the need for protection often emerges suddenly and involves many people. The number of refugees admitted should be kept at current levels or increased rather than cut back. Critics of trends in Congress also want to ensure that asylum remains a genuine option for persons who need and deserve protection. They maintain that efforts to streamline procedures and reduce the misuse of the asylum system may close the door to vulnerable persons who genuinely require safe haven.

Now let us proceed to recommendations about a comprehensive set of questions about refugee policy.

Definition of *Refugee*

U.S. adoption of the definition of refugee in international law (1980) was an important step, and U.S. Christians should continue to hold our government accountable to this standard. To be sure, the Convention definition is insufficient in a world where so many have to move, not because they are targeted for persecution, but because of other threats to their lives. But this does not mean that the Convention definition should be discarded. Many continue to be singled out for persecution, and they must be protected. The United States should initiate and support efforts to implement more effectively international responsibilities regarding refugees.

Should Christians and churches seek an expanded definition of refugee in international law? As we have seen, some refugee advocates favor working for a new United Nations Convention on refugees that would better reflect the realities of our time. I agree that the Convention definition needs to be more inclusive. I support the expanded definition proposed by Zolberg, Suhrke, and Aguayo that refugees be

155

regarded as those persons who are seeking to escape life-threatening violence, whether or not it is targeted at them specifically.[2] I would go further to include also those millions of persons who are internally displaced. These persons, too, have to leave their homes and seek a place of safety. Their governments will not or cannot protect their rights to protection and security. They should be able also to turn to their neighbors for assistance—neighbors in the region and neighbors in the broader international community.

But for practical reasons the attempt to change the Convention definition in international law is not a particularly promising strategy to pursue at this time. It is more important to work for national, regional, and international agreements that respond to the varied circumstances of people whose lives are threatened. Thus I shall advocate that an expanded definition inform U.S. refugee policy. And, as another example, Francis Deng proposes that the international community enter into an evolutionary process of institutional and legal responses to internally displaced persons that would result eventually in a specific convention; but he does not advocate that the displaced be incorporated into the definition of refugee in international law.[3]

Moreover, governments have fallen far short of implementing current standards of refugee protection. It is not likely that they would agree to a change in the definition that would double the number of persons covered by international refugee law. In fact, in the course of debating a new Convention, governments might seek to adopt a more restrictive definition.[4] The challenge is how best to respond to the matter of refugees. Clearly, there is much to be done internationally as well as at levels of national policy. There is much to be done in public education to help people understand the varied forces that create refugees today. However, to seek a new United Nations Convention that redefines refugee is not the most promising strategy in the current international situation.

United States Policy: Criteria of Selection

Which policies should Christians support or oppose in seeking to contribute to a compassionate and just response to refugees? I suggest we need to consider both (a) U.S. policies regarding asylum and resettlement of refugees in the United States, and (b) U.S. refugee policies in international relations. I am not arguing that receiving refugees into the United States is the best option for all refugees. It certainly may be for *some* refugees, but most refugees would prefer to stay close to their homeland and return as quickly as possible. Yet U.S. admission policy is the way American people are most personally related to refugees. It is the mechanism through which Americans can express their personal and political responsibility for refugees. At best, the experience of receiving and welcoming refugees inside the United States is a bridge to stronger international leadership by the United States in addressing the immense worldwide challenge.

In this section I am asking, Which criteria should govern U.S. refugee admissions? In the past, the overriding criterion was those persons who would best serve the anti-Communist agenda of U.S. foreign policy. By definition, people who wanted to leave Communist countries were escaping persecution. So, often they did not have to satisfy the stringent requirements of proving persecution that other refugees were required to meet. Now, with the exceptions of a small number of countries, the anti-Communist criterion is moot; and the context of the Cold War is gone. Which criterion or criteria will take its place?

What is not moot is the continuing tension between the criteria of need for protection and U.S. foreign policy interests. In the latest set of priorities, the Clinton administration maintains that "those in greatest need" have first claim and "groups of special concern to the U.S." come second.[5] This is a welcome change, because during the past year *both* criteria were incorporated in the first priority. Without this change and the consistent implementation of this change, foreign policy priorities continue to dominate decisions. Senator Alan Simpson, chair of the Subcommittee on Immigration and Refugee Affairs and longtime Senate leader on migration policy, maintains that many persons admitted as refugees were in fact "State Department refugees."

> Thousands of people are admitted each year as refugees, with all the special privileges and immunities of that unique and cherished status, even though their claims of political persecution are questionable, at best. Claims of persecution made by persons from certain countries are judged by different standards, with the result that many are granted a

status not possibly available to others who come from elsewhere. I call
them State Department refugees.[6]

Simpson's blunt critique reinforces the witness of the sanctuary
movement in the 1980s that the U.S. government has undermined
the integrity of U.S. refugee admission policy. The United States
should adopt uniform standards of refugee admission that are applied
fairly across the board. If, for reasons of foreign policy, the president
wants to make the case for admitting groups of people who would not
meet the refugee standards applied to others, he or she should be
required to seek their admission on other grounds: for example,
broadened definition of refugee, or special class of immigrant. Refugee admission should not be used as an alternative channel for
immigration.

The *first priority* should be the refugees whose need for protection
is most urgent and who can best be assisted by admission to the United
States. Urgency can be defined in terms of both the "immediacy and
the degree of life threatening violence."[7] When all refugees are
escaping from violence, it may seem cynical to try to determine who
is most deserving of admission. Yet, the needs of refugees are not
equally urgent and desperate.

Norman and Naomi Zucker suggest that the severity of probable
danger in the home country should be given priority.[8] Mark Gibney
contends that persons who have been tortured present a more immediate claim than those who have been imprisoned but not tortured.[9]
Whether it is "degrees of desperation,"[10] or "seriousness of persecution,"[11] the point is basically the same. Some persons are at especially
severe risk of losing their lives or being tortured and are in desperate
need of protection. When resettlement is the surest way to provide a
place of safety, these persons should be admitted above all. Beyond
this, Gibney has made the important suggestion that refugee receiving countries should actively seek out those who are most endangered
rather than just wait for them to present themselves for protection.[12]

The *second priority* should be all those who need protection under
the terms of the definition of refugee in international law. Even within
this priority certain distinctions can be made. For example, too many
refugees have had to remain in camps for too many years. Although
they are protected in a sense, the longer they remain in the camp the
more compelling is their claim for resettlement in a country where

they may seek full membership and full rights.[13] U.S. policy has failed to give sufficient priority to these persons, preferring instead to bring refugees directly from their homeland (called "in-country processing").

The *third priority* should include all persons who can be regarded as refugees under an expanded definition—in other words, persons fleeing life-threatening violence. In other words, I am proposing that instead of trying to get the United Nations to adopt a new Convention on Refugees, U.S. Christians should seek to write this broadened view of refugee into U.S. refugee admission policy. Refugees, then, are not just those persons who have been targeted for persecution (second priority) but those whose lives are endangered by war, environmental collapse, natural disaster, and economic deprivation. With this definition there would have been less ambiguity about the eligibility of Haitians for asylum in the United States.

A number of persons have advocated the addition of a category for refugee that goes beyond the Convention definition. Ghosal and Crowley propose the term "political-economic migrants,"[14] and Dowty favors calling them immigrants "of special humanitarian concern."[15] Similarly, Gil Loescher challenges European governments to move beyond a narrow definition and to provide protection to new kinds of refugees. He maintains that "increasing numbers of people who apply for asylum cannot demonstrate that they are victims of persecution per se, even though their motives for leaving their homelands may have been politically generated and their circumstances may have been life-threatening."[16]

These suggestions deserve our support. The United States should adopt a new category for refugee admission, applicable for asylees as well. It might be identified as Inclusive Refugee to distinguish it from Convention Refugee. In fact, an opening for this category is the term, "humanitarian admissions," which acknowledges that refugee eligibility in the United States has been broader than the Convention designation.[17] It has long been apparent that the United States has functioned with a more flexible definition of refugees while holding to a more stringent definition in granting asylum. In other words, there is precedent for establishing a third priority. The difference in the category of Inclusive Refugee is that these are persons fleeing life-threatening violence rather than immigrants who fit the geopolitical interests of the U.S. government.

159

The specific inclusion of this category would provide a way to expand the range of persons eligible for protection in the United States without requiring a change in the international definition. Yet it encompasses the legitimate moral claims of many persons who are forced to leave their homes for reasons other than specifically directed persecution. The ethical basis for this provision is clear. Refugees must turn to others for the protection of their most basic and elemental rights: protection and subsistence. The United States has the responsibility to play a leading role in forging national and international responses to this challenge.

In summary, I am proposing three criteria in priority order: urgent and immediate need, Convention refugees, and inclusive refugees. Any person who fits these criteria would be eligible for admission either for resettlement or for temporary protection. Yet within these priorities are additional principles which are appropriate in processes of selection.

First are people who clearly have been made refugees by policies of the United States. Most of us would readily agree that the United States had an especially strong moral responsibility to admit Vietnamese refugees in the aftermath of U.S. warfare in that country. Similarly the United States should give priority to the protection of Iraqis who are in danger because of their opposition to Saddam Hussein.[18] The relation between U.S. policy and the creation of refugees needs to be clear and direct, however. It is possible to make the case that in indirect ways U.S. economic, political, and military policies have contributed to the generation of many, if not most, of the refugee movements in the post–World War II era. The global reach of U.S. power provides a contextual grounding for its moral responsibility to address refugee challenges in international affairs. But as a principle of selectivity for admissions, persons who need protection as a direct result of U.S. actions are the ones with a very strong moral claim.

Second are refugees from countries near the United States. This is the principle of proximity, which also has pertinence for U.S. immigration policy. In refugee policy, moral and practical considerations often join together. Most of the world's refugees seek protection in countries nearby. They need to escape. To cross the border or to risk a relatively short boat journey is the most ready avenue to a safe haven. But there are other reasons as well. This neighbor is close at hand and protective assistance can be more readily provided. Moreover, the

U.S. government and its people have often built strong historical ties with peoples in neighboring countries. Refugees generally want to stay in places where there is a level of cultural familiarity. It makes sense, therefore, for the United States to give priority to refugees from the Caribbean and Central America just as it makes sense for European countries to take major responsibility for protecting refugees from the former Yugoslavia. Regional strategies for refugee assistance are more and more central to an effective international response.

If these two principles of selectivity had been applied during the 1980s and 1990s, refugees from Cuba, Haiti, and Central America would have had a particularly strong claim for protection. To be sure, if the definition of "life-threatening violence" is applied, a number of Cubans received as refugees would not have been eligible. But for those who were genuine refugees, U.S. policy had a great deal to do with the dangers they experienced in their homelands, and the United States was the country that was most accessible and able to provide protection. U.S. treatment of Haitians and Central Americans, especially, was morally appalling. The protection of these peoples should have been a priority. The explicit adoption of the principles outlined here is one way to make U.S. responsibilities clearer when we face similar situations in the future.

A few additional principles are also relevant. Third, it is sometimes helpful for the United States to agree to receive refugees as part of broader international agreements. For example, while European countries are receiving most of the Bosnian refugees, the United States has agreed to admit some of these refugees to do its part in concert with other countries. International plans of action may also seek to reduce or prevent large-scale migrations by refugees. Insofar as these plans may involve agreements about resettlement, the United States is certainly justified in giving priority to the implementation of these agreements.

Fourth, it is also appropriate to give a certain priority to refugees who have close ties to constituencies in the United States that are prepared to sponsor them. This principle is not without its problems. There is a tendency already for constituency groups to compete with each other to bring their peoples to the United States. And since there are constituencies in the United States for almost every national and ethnic group across the globe, the scenarios for competitiveness become all the more divisive and chaotic. Yet Jews in the United States

161

understandably advocated admitting Jewish refugees from the former Soviet Union, and evangelical Christians pressed for admission of persecuted Christian groups.

I believe the first three principles are more weighty, but this fourth principle should also be operative when the constituencies in the United States are willing to sponsor them (i.e., provide substantially for their resettlement in the United States). In fact, current refugee law provides for the option of "private resettlement," in which constituencies cover the expenses of refugees they are authorized to bring to the United States.[19] This is an appropriate mechanism for admitting refugees in line with the fourth principle.

Number and Distribution of Refugees

With the end of the Cold War and a turn toward more restrictive migration policies, the annual ceiling on refugee admissions is a primary target. As we have seen, the Clinton administration proposes to reduce the limit from 110,000 in fiscal year 1995 to 90,000 in fiscal year 1996. Other legislation would slash it further to 50,000, with provisions for increasing the number if necessary. Part of the reasoning for such a drastic reduction is provided by Senator Simpson's contention that many persons admitted in previous years are State Department refugees, not "genuine" refugees. Yet others also argue that with the end of large numbers of refugees from the former Soviet Union and from Southeast Asia, it is time for the United States to drop the total number of admissions.

Further support for this position has come from the United Nations High Commissioner on Refugees (UNHCR), of all places. This international agency appealed for governments in 1995 to resettle a minimum of forty thousand to sixty thousand persons with priority needs, excluding Bosnian refugees. Citing this report, Charles Keeley argued recently that the United States should put more energy into refugee prevention and repatriation. In his view the value of refugee resettlement in the United States has been greatly overemphasized. Clearly he believes the number of refugee admissions can be sharply reduced without harming refugees, as long as the United States undertakes a more concerted international strategy.

Others, however, challenge the estimates of UNHCR and the arguments for reducing the number of admissions.[20] C. Richard Parkins, chief migration officer of Episcopal Migration Ministries, states that "to engage in a more restrictive policy at this time signals to the international community that we are either indifferent . . . or have retreated from the moral leadership that we imagine ourselves to express."[21] More important than setting a numerical limit to control unwarranted admissions is to reform the process by which refugees are selected.[22] In other words, the United States needs to ensure that those who are admitted are genuine refugees who meet the kinds of selection criteria set forward above, and who require resettlement.

With such reforms, the United States can and should support a generous refugee admission policy for those who can best be served by the option of resettlement. On ethical grounds, refugees have a stronger claim than immigrants. The United States should be able to admit from 150,000 to 200,000 refugees a year. These figures include Convention refugees (priorities one and two) and inclusive refugees (priority three). The policy could be stated in terms of 150,000 per year as the standard ceiling, with the flexibility of adding an additional 50,000 when emergency circumstances warrant it. But there is no requirement for as many as 150,000 to be admitted if the need for resettlement is lower than this figure. In this proposal, from 150,000 to 200,000 refugees could be admitted annually, incorporating a broadened definition of who may be regarded as a refugee.

The proposal permits the kind of flexibility that is needed in an admissions policy. Many refugee movements cannot be anticipated ahead of time. Refugees necessarily burst out of orderly procedures. The United States needs to be able to act quickly to protect refugees when emergencies occur. This proposal signifies that the United States continues to value the refugees and their gifts. It further communicates to other nations that the United States will not succumb to the fortress fever of the times. In the current political climate the likelihood that this ceiling would be adopted seems quite remote. But it remains an achievable goal. This number is in the range of the highest annual ceilings during the Cold War years. There is no convincing reason why the United States cannot continue this level of refugee admissions in a post–Cold War era.

In this policy the United States communicates its confidence in an open society that is continually re-created by the courage and hope of persons who came to the United States for refuge. This is a leavening influence that cannot be quantified solely in economic data but enriches the kind of people Americans can be. In admitting refugees, the United States not only receives persons who enhance the character of the community, but also nourishes moral qualities of hospitality and generosity in citizens. It is a policy that reflects and requires the kinds of moral virtues the national community needs for its moral health. In contrast, a fortress reaction only feeds the impulses toward selfishness, isolation, and xenophobia.

I have proposed a set of priorities and criteria for determining which refugees should be admitted to the United States. What role, if any, should geographical distribution play in this determination? Should refugees be treated on an individual case basis only, or as members of at-risk groups? Currently, the State Department each year identifies particular countries where refugees best meet its criteria for selection. But, again, the predominance of foreign policy interests outweighs considerations of which peoples are most vulnerable. Moreover, certain regions of the world are vastly underrepresented in admissions to the United States. For example, as Deffenbaugh points out, "one third of all the world's refugees are in Africa, but only six percent of refugees admitted to the United States are from Africa."[23]

Deffenbaugh suggests that U.S. policy might better focus on priorities for the types of refugees the United States would admit rather than make geographical identifications so determinative.[24] Following this suggestion, the kinds of criteria proposed above are the basis for selection, not which countries fit best into U.S. geopolitical agendas. Still, it is justifiable to identify locations in the world where needs for resettlement are particularly acute and where human rights abuses are particularly egregious. In other words, I support a consideration of not only individual cases but group membership in determining which persons are eligible for admission according to morally appropriate priorities.

Policies and Procedures in Refugee Resettlement

A number of changes are called for in light of the previous discussion. First, U.S. policy needs to provide more flexibility and timeliness in responses to refugee crises. The marked tendency of U.S. programs has been to try to manage refugee resettlement in an orderly manner—which means rigid and slow. But refugees cannot simply be put on hold. Refugee-creating situations cannot be frozen until the United States and other countries institute a cumbersome process for considering refugee claims. To try to force refugees into a managed procedure that keeps them in the very countries where their lives are in danger is inhumane and unrealistic. This is one additional reason why U.S. treatment of Haitian refugees was so appalling.

The very character of being refugees—forced to flee for safety—often defies neat, orderly, and deliberate procedures. The U.S. system should be designed as much to respond to emergencies as to implement longer-range plans. Refugee emergencies will happen. That much is certain. Refugee policy should be written with enough latitude to permit flexible and timely responses. When resettlement is urgently needed for protection, the United States should be able to move quickly. For this reason, refugee advocates are critical of the proposal by Senator Simpson to restrict the parole authority of the attorney general, which is at least one mechanism for a quick response to a crisis.

Second, the integrity of refugee determination and selection must be upheld. Refugee admission should be reserved for those who need to be protected from life-threatening violence. Need should be the overriding criterion. As Elisa Massimino of the Lawyers Committee for Human Rights put it recently, the cornerstone of a refugee admission policy "is an objective refugee determination based on the refugee criteria without special treatment for particular nationalities."[25]

Several steps are proposed by refugee advocates. For one thing, the role of the State Department needs to be curtailed. When the State Department is given the major role in deciding how refugee admissions should be allocated, it is not surprising that foreign policy agendas dominate. The Zuckers propose that a refugee authority that is independent from the State Department and the INS should assess the claims of persons seeking resettlement.[26] Others argue that the United States should rely far more on UNHCR to find out who are in the gravest need. American people should have the assurance that those who are admitted are in fact deserving of special protection. This assurance will strengthen public support for refugees, in contrast to the confusion and cynicism that U.S. abuse of the refugee system has fostered.

Third, opportunities for "private resettlement" should be strengthened and expanded. This option should be of special interest to churches. When Christians believe the government is closing its doors to needful and deserving refugees, churches may seek to bring them for private resettlement. This provides a way for churches to embody their ethic of hospitality and to make a witness to the broader society, "in effect, putting their money where their mouths are."[27] However, private resettlement should not replace societal commitments to refugees. In other words, Christians should oppose the notion, often stated in debates about welfare policy, that churches alone should take care of the needy. But private resettlement can be an important element of a comprehensive public response.

In private resettlement, nongovernmental organizations would cover the expenses of refugees' resettlement. Those who are resettled privately would still have to meet the refugee criteria in order to qualify. But it provides needed flexibility. And it draws on citizen initiative on behalf of refugees, working in tandem with the overall purposes of a national refugee policy. Yet some changes are required to make this option feasible. For example, many nongovernmental organizations simply would not be able to pay the medical coverage for refugees. Deffenbaugh suggests working it out "so that the nongovernmental organization involved would bear the full resettlement and placement costs . . . but the Office for Refugee Resettlement would offer the same refugee health coverage that regularly admitted refugees receive."[28]

Fourth, resettlement efforts need to focus on the empowerment of the refugees who are admitted to the United States. Pressures are building to cut back on public assistance to refugees as well as to immigrants. At least at this moment, refugees are exempted from legislative efforts to deny assistance to noncitizens. Even under the proposed cuts, refugees would be eligible for assistance for the first five years in the United States, and those over age seventy-five would be eligible. But since refugees receive an initial stipend when they first arrive in the United States, and since refugees as a group use public assistance more heavily than immigrants, we can expect attacks on expenditures on refugees.

166

The picture is indeed a complicated one. In New York City there is a high rate of refugee welfare dependency. Yet Herb Snedden, eastern area director for World Relief of the National Association of Evangelicals, points out that in the southeastern section of the United States, "80% of refugees are employed within six months of their arrival. . . . Welfare utilization is not a problem in the southeast."[29] Welfare dependency depends on a variety of factors, such as location in the United States and the cultural and educational background of the refugees.

Let us remember that there are good reasons why refugees need initial support. Often they come with minimal financial resources and possessions. Often they have experienced severe emotional and physical traumas. And now they are in a new place, needing to manage a difficult transition to a different culture, a different language, and maybe a different way of making a living. Many Americans assist refugees in the resettlement process through nongovernment organizations, such as churches, as well as state agencies. Refugee resettlement does cost more money than the admission of immigrants, and for justifiable reasons. Still, as with immigrants, the long-range prospect for refugees to move beyond dependency is very good.[30]

Yet a number of people who work with refugees agree that welfare dependence is a problem. Resettlement strategies need to help move refugees quickly from public assistance to employment. The problem may be located just as much with the welfare system itself as with the struggles of refugees. Loc Nam Nguyen of Catholic Charities comments, "The welfare system does not place any expectations on refugees; it proves a disincentive for refugees to work; and it is ripe for abuse." Another person involved in refugee resettlement adds that often the welfare system "turns strong, independent people—not just refugees, but everyone on welfare—into dependent people."[31] Support for resettlement must continue, but critical reflection is needed about the kinds of assistance that best contribute to the empowerment of refugees rather than the perpetuation of dependence.

Asylum Reform

The asylum system is on the front burner of current policy discussions. When the 1980 Refugee Act was passed, little attention was given to questions related to asylum. Since 1980, many of the hottest debates about refugees have focused on asylum. Cubans and Haitians risked their lives to get to the United States to apply for asylum. Central Americans struggled to reach the U.S. border to seek protection. The United States was suddenly faced with large numbers of persons seeking asylum, and for various reasons the government failed to provide protection to many who needed and deserved it. Let us remember that persons seeking asylum arrive in the United States and then present their case to remain. The purpose of the asylum system is to provide protection for people who have to leave their country to seek a safe haven and who cannot take the time or risks to file an application in their home country.

The chief criticism of asylum is that it provides a cover for many nonrefugees to get to the United States and remain. Decisions on claims can be prolonged through appeals. The backlog of cases expands. In the meantime, nonrefugees disappear into the general population and add to the number of immigrants who illegally remain in the United States. The abuses are serious, and refugee advocates need to support efforts that protect the integrity of the asylum option. At the same time, some of the proposed changes seem more concerned with making asylum difficult than remedying abuses. Ethical criticism of these measures is terribly important. Strong support for asylum protection is one of the most important aspects of Christian advocacy on behalf of refugees. Indeed, asylum protection needs to be extended beyond those who are specifically targeted for persecution to all those who are escaping life-threatening violence.

Let us now look at some of the features of asylum policy that require reflection and response.

NONREFOULEMENT

This strange-looking term has a firm place in international law. It simply means that asylees may not be involuntarily returned to the country from which they have fled. Although the United States is not required by international law to admit the asylee, the United States may not send him back either. The United States is required to keep the person in the United States or send him someplace else that is safe. Forcible return is a severe violation of the refugee's rights. Indeed, it is a violent act. The U.S. government violated this principle often with Haitian and Central American refugees by categorically denying the authenticity of claims. This principle must be the linch-pin of U.S. asylum policy.

A complicating feature of this international obligation is the situation of refugees who travel through other countries to get from their homeland to the United States. The legal obligation applies to the first safe country the asylee enters. Yet certainly a powerful moral obligation applies as well to the second or third country. Refugees should not be sent to places where their lives will be endangered. The U.S. government has recently approved a procedure that permits the attorney general to return asylum seekers to countries they traveled through on their way to the United States. Yet they cannot be sent to countries where they might be endangered or are not able to apply for asylum. Although these conditions are reassuring, refugee organizations, for understandable reasons, intend to keep this procedure under close scrutiny to make sure asylees are not abused by being returned to unsafe places.

INTERDICTION

The legality of the action of the Bush administration to interdict Haitian asylees before they landed in Florida was upheld by the U.S. Supreme Court. The same policy was adopted by President Clinton soon after he assumed office. Yet when these actions prevented the asylees from applying for asylum in the United States, they were morally wrong and, arguably, contrary to international law. It is one thing to pick up the asylees in the sea to save them from the hazards of their voyage. But it is quite another matter to use a blockading or interdicting strategy, a "floating Berlin Wall,"[32] to *prevent* them from being able to seek asylum in the United States. Under international law, people have a right to apply for asylum. They should not be discouraged from seeking protection. It is splitting legal hairs to argue that because these persons had not yet landed on the Florida coast the United States had no responsibility to hear their claims.

Once again the United States was unprepared for the large-scale flight from neighboring islands. It should not be surprising that most persons who look to the United States as a country of first asylum come from nearby. That government officials need to be better prepared for such emergencies is frustratingly self-evident. The practical problems attending the reception of large numbers of asylees who suddenly seek safe haven are challenging but not insurmountable. The

169

point is that the U.S. government can do better morally in ensuring that asylum is an option available to people who desperately need protection. Making it more difficult for them to use a system that is presumably designed for people like themselves deserves vigorous moral criticism.

TEMPORARY PROTECTED STATUS (TPS)

This category for the protection of asylees should be supported. In the years to come this provision may be the most common one. It provides a way for the United States to protect people who need a temporary refuge. In the meantime, the United States should use its influence to resolve refugee emergencies so that they can return soon to their home countries. The hope would be for these emergencies to be of relatively short duration. The primary responsibility of the United States is to provide the protection for the time that it is needed, and not to return the refugees until it is safe at home. This category provides more flexibility to countries of first asylum that are worried about making permanent commitments to asylees.

Currently, TPS is granted for a specified and limited time, and it may be renewed. Asylees protected under TPS would not be eligible for eventual citizenship. Yet, this stipulation needs to be relaxed. If the duration of TPS becomes long, and there is little chance for returning home, then the asylee's claim for residency and eventual citizenship becomes morally strong. It is not humane for persons to remain in a kind of limbo too long without the opportunity to become full members of the society in which they have established themselves over time.

WORK AUTHORIZATION

As we have seen, asylees must now wait 180 days before they may seek employment. Now, imagine that you have fled from, say, Guatemala with very little in the way of money or possessions. You apply for asylum in the United States, yet you cannot work to support yourself for five months. How are you going to live? The hardships of asylee existence are only intensified. This system encourages asylees to seek work in the underground of unregulated employment. Instead, asylees should be granted temporary work permits at the time they apply for asylum. They then would be free to work until a decision is made about their claim.

It may be that the 180-day rule functions to push the INS to make decisions in a shorter period of time. Under the new procedure, if the asylee's case is not completed in 150 days, then the person would be automatically approved for work by the 180th day. But this mechanism is an effort to expedite decisions at the expense of the most vulnerable and powerless persons, the asylees themselves. This is yet another example of a punitive approach to the challenges of asylum. Asylees not only have to escape dangerous circumstances; they also have to endure distressing struggles for subsistence once they arrive. This rule clearly privileges more affluent asylees and hits hardest those who have the least. Christians should as a first priority support an asylum system that is designed to assist genuine asylees, rather than to control abuse of asylum by making their life even more burdensome than it already is.[33]

EXPEDITING ASYLUM DECISIONS

The backlog of asylum claims, as well as the number of current cases, is indeed a major problem. As of spring, 1995, the backlog was 456,345.[34] Yet efficiency needs to serve justice, not become the over-riding norm. Procedures have already been put in place to permit asylum officers to deny an application without review in some cases. Senator Simpson favors a bill that will expand the categories to include others, such as persons who seem to be using fraudulent documents.

These procedures are morally troubling. They deny the right of appeal, a basic right in the due process of law. These procedures make it more likely that genuine refugees will be summarily returned to situations of danger. Refugees sometimes find it difficult to communicate to strangers what they have gone through. Quickness alone without the possibility for review may too readily lead to the exclusion of such persons.

Again, my objection is not over the intention to make the decision-making process more efficient and timely. The problem is the design of procedures that sacrifice fairness. Procedures that ensure both greater fairness and efficiency can be adopted. One organization that advocates a fair asylum system points out the contrasts between the number of asylum officers in the United States and in other countries:

Sweden has 800, Switzerland has 500, Germany has more than 3,000, and the United States has 150.[35] An increase in the number of officers would certainly help.

Refugee advocates also are greatly concerned that asylees could be automatically excluded because they use fraudulent documents. As Elisa Massimino says, "We must be careful to craft our laws so that we do not equate fraudulent documents with fraudulent claims for refuge."[36] The point is that, for understandable reasons, genuine refugees may use flawed or false documents to try to gain entry. They should be judged by the merits of their claim, not their desperate attempt to produce documents.

In conclusion, Christians should support a strong asylum program. Access to asylum is indispensable for persons who have to find a place of safety from danger. Procedural reforms are necessary to guard against abuse, to keep current with applications, and to ensure that decision making does not drag on too long. Yet the right of persons to seek asylum in the United States should be vigorously defended. Asylees should be welcomed rather than punished. In the current debate, the right to appeal an initial judgment should be ensured, and asylees should be granted permits to work while their claims are being considered.

International Responses

It is clear that the admission of refugees for resettlement and temporary asylum, however generous, is not a sufficient response to the huge numbers of refugees in today's world. In the short run and the long run, international strategies are required. Christians need to give strong support to U.S. foreign policies that address both root causes and ongoing crises. This wider and seemingly more remote arena is a part of Christian responsibility, too. In fact, most refugee scholars today argue that this is the most important place for changes to be instituted. Otherwise, the needs of the world's refugees will continue to outstrip the capacities of nation-states to protect them.

It is sobering indeed that the escalation of refugees reflects a deeply disordered and unjust world. And it is this same flawed world that is challenged to develop more effective and humane responses. Christians may bring the resources of hope for the in-breaking of God's justice at the same time that we face honestly the obstacles that the international (dis)order presents.

There are no quick and easy answers; no policy "fixes," only a persistence in seeking a world that produces fewer refugees and protects those who continue to be endangered. There is no substitute for the moral stamina and commitment of a people who consistently press their government to respond to the challenge. "National interest" alone will not be a sufficient basis for addressing the challenge, however serious the security and economic interests of nation-states may be affected by refugee movements.

SHARING THE BURDENS

Refugees are an international responsibility. A basic principle of international justice is that the burdens of refugee protection should be shared equitably among the nations of the world. This means that the countries with greater wealth, power, and capacity have a proportionately greater responsibility than less affluent and weaker states. Although this principle does not necessarily translate into percentages of persons admitted for resettlement, it indeed challenges affluent countries to admit a larger share when this is the best option for refugees. The notion that the United States can only afford to admit fifty thousand per year out of a total of twenty-five to fifty million refugees is preposterous.

The principle of burden sharing also means that the U.S. government has a high level of moral responsibility to provide assistance to those who are receiving and helping refugees, like UNHCR, regional organizations, and receiving countries. As we have seen, other countries, much less privileged and economically wealthy, are often bearing a disproportionately heavy burden. Most of the world's refugees are being protected in third-world countries. The United States should provide international leadership in negotiating agreements about equitable burden sharing while stating unmistakably its readiness to do its part.

ROOT CAUSES

United States foreign policy should be directed toward removing the causes of refugee flight. The massive number of refugees today is a human catastrophe. It is clear now that the distresses of refugees are

173

not a temporary crisis that can be addressed adequately by an outpouring of humanitarian aid. Policies must be preventive as well as palliative. Refugee movements are an all too permanent feature of the international situation. Only a strategy that deals with underlying causes will do as we look to the future.

Since the primary causes are political repression, civil war, and economic deprivation, then government policies should seek to remove these conditions. The promotion of human rights, peaceful resolution of conflicts, and economic justice for the poor are long-term policy commitments that address the causes of refugees. Not until peoples are able to live in their homelands in relative security will there be a reduction in the movement of refugees. In other words, the worldwide struggles for peace and justice are the most promising strategies for addressing the causes of refugee flight.

Nothing points more vividly to the interrelation of nations and peoples than the refugee challenge. Turmoil in one location has severe impacts on neighboring peoples, which then requires responses by other governments and international agencies. Remedies, too, must then be at both national and international levels. Thus the right to national self-determination must be qualified. The legitimacy of states is contingent on their readiness to protect the basic rights of their peoples. International sanctions and penalties against states that abuse their peoples and international assistance to states to enable them to fulfill their responsibilities are morally required.

Just as important, however, is vigorous criticism by U.S. Christians of our own government when its policies contribute to the creation of refugees, such as the War in Indo-China and U.S. support of vicious regimes in Central America. Correspondingly, Christians need to provide a strong public voice in support of those international policies that seek to remove the causes of refugee movements.

INTERNATIONAL RESPONSES

While long-term efforts to prevent the generation of refugees are essential, more immediate responses are also needed at the international level. The U.S. government should promote vigorously the response of repatriation of refugees. This requires political and diplomatic initiatives to make it possible for refugees to return safely and quickly to home countries.[37] Efforts should be directed at making

174

refugee protection a temporary necessity rather than a more permanent condition.

Gil Loescher rightly points as well to the need to shift from the reliance on refugee camps to greater integration of refugees in host countries. He maintains that refugees can be an economic asset and are less likely to be resented if they are permitted to make contributions to receiving communities.[38] The notion that refugees can be an economic benefit, not simply a burden, needs to be pursued. It flies in the face of a great deal of conventional thinking. But it also is more consistent with the moral valuation of refugees as gifts and challenges, not primarily as burdens reluctantly accepted or vigorously resisted.

For either repatriation or local integration to work, however, economic assistance from more affluent countries will be required. U.S. refugee policy should increase financial assistance to receiving countries and sometimes even to home countries.[39] Aid to receiving countries can make local integration more effective, and aid to home countries can sometimes make repatriation more feasible. The point is that providing emergency life-sustaining assistance to refugees is not sufficient as an international response. Policies should promote environments where refugees can become self-reliant and live fully in community. And this requires aid not only to refugees themselves but also to countries that receive them or seek to reincorporate them.

As important as a generous U.S. resettlement policy is, an activist international role on behalf of refugees is perhaps even more important. Financial assistance and international political and diplomatic leadership are the primary ways that the United States can respond to the current worldwide challenges of refugee movements. In light of the principle of sharing equitably the obligations for refugee protection, the United States is morally required to contribute a great deal more than it has.

Clearly, leadership by the United States requires support for a strong and effective United Nations. Unilateralism will not do. Cooperation among nation-states is mandatory. Again, simply to entrust the United Nations with the task of providing emergency assistance to refugees is insufficient. Mechanisms also need to be developed for the United Nations to monitor situations that might give rise to refugee flight, and even to intervene with preventive strategies. Loescher calls for the development of "guidelines for graduated responses to humanitarian crises."[40]

International interdependence puts limits on the principle of national self-determination. While we need to continue to struggle with questions about what these limits are and how the United Nations can most effectively intervene in crisis situations, a more internationalist response to prevent and to respond to refugee challenges is essential. There simply is no other way to deal with the depth and breadth of the problem. And the United Nations cannot fulfill its responsibility without greater financial support from the United States and other affluent nations.

It is distressingly evident that the international system to assist refugees, formed out of European crises at the end of two World Wars, is inadequate in the present international situation. Numbers of refugees are multiplying, not receding. It is above all an immense and appalling human tragedy. It also has powerful political, economic, and military consequences. Moral seriousness about the plight of refugees requires political lobbying to press for a more effective international approach to refugee protection, vigorous leadership from the United States in this effort, and comprehensive long-range plans to remove the causes of refugee movements.

Responsibility of Churches

I have presented a point of view about the kind of refugee policy that U.S. Christians should support. I believe that love for refugees requires criticizing and advocating refugee policy proposals. Individuals and voluntary associations alone are insufficient to meet the immensity of refugee challenges, although at best they are indispensable to the formation and implementation of good policy. As Elizabeth Ferris insists:

> NGOs [nongovernmental organizations], as we have seen, are minor actors in the international refugee game. The rules of the game are determined by governments. Unless NGOs and churches play a role in shaping those rules—in determining how refugees and other peoples will be treated by the governments that receive them—they will remain marginal to the international system in responding to uprooted people.[41]

But what then is the churches' role? First, churches are crucial in the complex tasks of resettling refugees in American communities.

This is a vital ministry which is faithful to the churches' calling. The readiness of churches to be engaged personally with refugees goes hand in hand with a generous national admissions policy. If the United States is to be a hospitable place for refugees, we need the commitments of Christians and churches to express welcome in tangible deeds. We have also emphasized the desirability of expanding the private resettlement option in U.S. refugee policy, which would open up additional opportunities for churches.

Second, churches need to advocate publicly on behalf of refugees. This involves a number of interrelated tasks. It means nurturing a public moral ethos of hospitality toward refugees in our midst and support for U.S. international leadership in responding to the plight of refugees. In the current U.S. environment, with the end of ideological anti-Communism as a compelling basis for assisting refugees, the ethical rationale for refugee protection has to be developed and articulated publicly all over again. Churches must take seriously the challenge of shaping the moral climate of our communities and our national life.

The church's public role also involves advocacy on behalf of strong national policies for protecting refugees here and abroad. Often this leads churches into coalitions with other NGOs that are working on behalf of refugees. While governments remain the most influential actors in the international arena, the role of NGOs, including churches, should not be underestimated. Organizations that promote human rights and provide concrete assistance to refugees can indeed have an impact on policies and practices of governments. The transnational character of churches gives it both a perspective and an organizational reach that links international, regional, national, and local contexts. The churches' public policy witness is an essential aspect of its moral responsibility.

Third, churches may at times be called to a more demanding witness. Churches are centered not in the authority of the nation-state but in the reality of God. Christians serve the nation best by refusing to absolutize its claims and by subjecting its demands to the universalizing love and justice of God. We have seen this witness expressed recently in the sanctuary movement in the United States, which placed the protection of Central American refugees above the authority of the federal government.

Even now, "more than 200 Protestant and Catholic churches in Germany shelter foreign refugees, even when that protection violates the law."[42] In Germany, Christians are responding to the recent tightening of the country's asylum policy. They maintain that the implementation of these restrictions is endangering the lives of persons seeking protection from the war in the former Yugoslavia.

Under these circumstances Christians are challenged to protect the refugee and to provide assistance to the refugee, even if these actions violate state policy. Whether or not the refugee is legally present is quite secondary to the church's mandate to love the neighbor. The tendency of the nation-state to be excessively restrictive will always be in tension with the inclusive commitments to hospitality that are integral to the churches' faith. Sometimes the tension will require confrontation, and Christians must be prepared to serve God rather than state when the lives of neighbors are at stake. If possible, Christians should seek to express their witness within the boundaries of law and civil authority. But when this is not possible, civil resistance or civil disobedience may not only be justified but even required.

Finally, it is vital that churches not merely advocate better public policies and more activist government initiatives on behalf of refugees. Churches are challenged by their faith to model hospitality to refugees, even when these actions are opposed by others in the national community. Churches are challenged by Elie Wiesel's vision that all persons should be prepared to act as "righteous Gentiles," willingly protecting vulnerable persons regardless of dangers or opposition.

The fact is that often churches are even more restrictive in attitudes than national policies dictate. Churches are susceptible to the dominance of nationalistic perspectives over the inclusive vision of their faith. There is tough and vital work to be done within churches themselves. Always, the ethics of Christian community addresses and critiques churches above all, calling on churches to embody in their own lives the kinds of commitments they should advocate in the public arena.

6

RE-CREATING AMERICA: PROPOSALS FOR U.S. IMMIGRATION POLICY

Substantial immigration over the past thirty years is re-creating America. But whether or not this is a good thing is being contested in many public forums. The chief political and ethical divide is between those who endorse and wish to extend this re-creative process and those who believe the changes occurring as a result of immigration are increasingly destructive and who wish to apply the brakes.

I have argued that a Christian perspective more readily and more compellingly supports a generous immigration policy. But it does not give us the blueprint for a detailed policy. Christians share with many others a commitment to justice for the poor, protection of human rights, and a justly ordered multicultural society in which democratic freedoms may flourish. These norms provide a moral basis for evaluating and shaping immigration policy in the United States. However, we cannot simply derive a just policy from these norms. We must also consider contextual factors, which necessarily complicates an ethical assessment. In this chapter I shall point to policy recommendations that seem to me to be consistent with, and in some instances even required by, Christian ethical convictions. But the complexities and ambiguities raised by immigration do not lend themselves to a self-evident list of policy recommendations.

In the current situation there are two options that are polar opposites and the least complicated in terms of details. First is an *open-borders policy*. In many ways this is the policy that is most fully responsive to ethical considerations. We may point to the human right of each person to move from one place to another to seek work, livelihood, and opportunity. We may also point to the Christian

179

obligation to share the surplus of abundance with the poor of this land and other lands. Moreover, Christians are called to remove the walls that divide national compatriots from others in the universal family of God. And, finally, Christian ethics surely invites and requires Christians to provide hospitality to immigrants who must cope with the vulnerabilities of living in a strange land.

The presumption in Christian ethics would seem to be an open-borders policy. It is more difficult, ethically, to justify restrictions on immigration. This is even more so when Christians live in an affluent and democratic society while many of the world's peoples live in poverty and fear. Any restrictions on immigration seem selfish, an unjust privileging of personal and national well-being at the expense of others whose birthplace is outside the United States. Joseph Carens's critique of border restrictions as a protection of birthplace privilege that has nothing to do with merit or desert expresses the moral presumption of open borders very well.

It is not surprising, therefore, that immigrant activists often have a difficult time stating which restrictions they support and how these should be enforced. Instead, these advocates feel morally compelled to support the rights of immigrants once they are inside the United States, documented or not, and to oppose most of the measures that are proposed for enforcing restrictions. They are inclined to find restrictions morally repugnant. While open borders create strains, stresses, and challenges, the efforts at enforcement actually end up costing (in terms of money) just as much and lead to inhumane treatment of persons. Borders are increasingly anachronistic anyway. The United States, especially, should recognize its special historical and geographical relationship with Mexico and develop open and flexible policies for regulating movement across the border.

There are also persons who, for economic reasons, believe there should be a relatively free movement of persons across borders, just as they support the movement of goods and capital. In their view, people are also subject to laws of supply and demand. When there are jobs that provide for a better life, they will come. When the availability of jobs dries up, they will stop coming. Generally, immigrants are economic assets, not liabilities. But, in fact, it is difficult to find persons who advocate explicitly and without qualification an open-borders policy. Most persons, whether on moral or on economic grounds, seem to concede that some restrictions are justifiable, even though an open-borders policy would be the ethical (and perhaps the economic) ideal. Thus we are left with the questions of which restrictions can be justified and why, and how these may appropriately be enforced.

The second option is a *moratorium on immigration.* The answer to the current situation is simply to close the borders to further immigration. The moratorium may be for a short duration or for a longer period of time. The proponents of this view believe that immigration is costing the United States too much economically and socially. The United States needs time to incorporate successfully the large numbers of immigrants who have come during the past thirty years. It is also too difficult to enforce the selective admission of smaller numbers of persons. A moratorium can easily be lifted if it becomes clear that the United States needs more immigrants to fill certain jobs.

Like the open-borders position, the moratorium option is rarely advocated in absolute terms. Generally a provision for a small number of refugees, especially those whose admission best fits with U.S. foreign policy interests, and family members of previously admitted immigrants is granted. Nonetheless, this position basically bypasses questions about how many should be admitted and which persons should be given priority consideration. It is simply time to stop immigration for a while, and to use effective means to enforce the moratorium. The ethical basis for this alternative is the right of the United States as a national society to protect itself and the well-being of its members.

It is difficult indeed to find arguments supporting a moratorium from a Christian perspective. In my view, there would only be two morally defensible ways to argue for this option. First, admission of immigrants is jeopardizing the well-being of the American poor and their prospects for economic justice in the United States. This is a tricky one, because moratorium advocates can cynically maintain that immigration makes the public unsympathetic to the poor generally. Regardless of whether or not immigrants in fact jeopardize the prospects of the existing poor, the perception or assertion that this is so presumably provides a more moral face to a moratorium. This argument is suspect if it is made by a segment of the public that is anti-immigrant anyway and has shown little inclination to favor economic justice for the poor in any case. This argument can only be made credibly when it is demonstrated that the resources and capacities of American society are not sufficient both to incorporate new-comers and to secure economic justice for the native poor.

The second basis is that admission of immigrants is a substantial threat to the well-being of the members of U.S. society and the viability of its democratic institutions.[1] If unemployment becomes critically high, the United States might be justified in cutting off immigration and giving current members greater priority. If the United States suffers a socioeconomic disaster (such as the depression of the 1930s), a moratorium could be justified in order to ensure that the basic needs of its current members would be met. But at present the admission of immigrants does not constitute such a threat to the social order, alarmists notwithstanding, nor does it seriously erode the situation of the existing poor. In the current context, a moratorium policy is supported by a fortress mentality that is morally repugnant and politically shortsighted. In an interdependent and unjust world situation, a moratorium is a morally and politically inappropriate immigration policy.

I believe the United States should have a generous, yet selective, admissions policy. Let us reiterate briefly the principles for this kind of policy. The first principle is *a just and humane order.* From a Christian perspective, justice is viewed primarily in terms of the needs and claims of the poor. Justice is in fact that order in which the good and right of the poor has priority.[2] Immigration policy must be tested above all by its impact on and implications for the poor, both inside and outside the United States. This means that the United States should make labor immigration its highest priority, admitting those who need employment and income to support themselves and their families.

Justice also requires the protection of human rights. It is crucial from a moral perspective to defend and uphold the human rights of immigrants, legal or not. This principle extends to the grounds on which immigrants seek admission and the ways immigrants are treated in the United States, from access to education, social services and health care to treatment by law officials and deportation proceedings. Human rights criteria also pertain to employment policies and practices. Immigrants working in the United States have a right to a just wage and humane working conditions. Laws to protect these rights need to be enforced more effectively.

For immigration to be just and humane, there must be an orderly structure of decision making and enforcement. It is an illusion to think that the United States will ever be able to attain absolute control over the borders. Efforts in this direction are likely to produce appalling abuses. But the United States can adopt and reasonably enforce humane immigration laws. It is better both for the United States and for immigrants that they are here legally. Immigrants are most vulnerable when they are in the United States illegally. And illegal immigration makes it exceedingly difficult for these persons to be incorporated into the new society as active participants.

The second principle is *a cosmopolitan, multiracial, and multicultural national vision*. The United States is constituted as an immigrant nation. The United States is at present a very diverse people, racially, ethnically, culturally, and in terms of national origins. This is a descriptive statement. But it needs also to be affirmed and advocated as a normative vision. That is, the United States seeks to be a nation and society composed of the diverse peoples of the world. The *oikomene* is present here in one national community. This is a good that needs to be furthered and enriched. Immigrants are a re-creative and transformative presence in American life. The ongoing struggles and negotiations between newcomers and residents are the stuff of substantive societal challenge and revitalization. Immigrants in a real sense are a major element in keeping American society open, dynamic, and oriented to a better future.

A third principle is the historical-contextual one of *proximity*. For many years, the United States had a more open immigration policy toward countries in the Western hemisphere than those in the Eastern hemisphere. The notion of neighborliness toward people in countries closer at hand had a certain normative significance. Mexico was not subject to the restrictions of the laws of the early 1920s, nor were Western Hemisphere countries initially included in the twenty thousand annual quota applied to other countries. To argue that countries on the basis of proximity should be treated differently from others is a challenge to the universalistic norm of equal numbers from each country in the world. But the history of United States/Mexico relations, as well as the lengthy land border between the two countries, provides grounds for supporting more generous ceilings for Mexican immigrants than for others.

183

Criteria of Selectivity

Many people in the world would like to emigrate to the United States. Many apply. Some seek to enter the country without documents. Which ones should the United States admit? Should the decision be based on the needs of migrants, or the extent to which they might benefit the United States? Let us look at categories and principles for selection.

REFUGEES

In this book I argue that refugees have the strongest moral claim on admission. Their lives are endangered; they must have a place of safety and livelihood. The United States needs to give highest priority to the admission and resettlement of refugees. Even as the number of refugees from Southeast Asia and the former Soviet Union declines in the next several years, the United States should look toward increasing the resettlement of refugees from other areas of the world when this is the best solution for them.

BROADENED NOTIONS OF REFUGEE

Those persons who may not fit the strict definition of refugee but whose lives are nonetheless endangered also have a strong claim on admission. This calls for a broadening of the concept of refugee. The compelling need for protection and community is the basis for the priority. A more detailed development and defense of refugee priority and broadened notions of *refugee* are included in chapters 4 and 5.

FAMILY UNITY

It is inhumane to grant admission to a person without also giving priority for admission to close family members. Christian thought, in affirming the relational character of personhood, stresses the importance of primary relationships for personal wholeness. Family members should not be relegated to the pool or queue, subject to the same kind of review process as others. They should be admitted as a matter of course.

The United States has rightly established this as a high priority. Some authors regard family unity as the "humanitarian" aspect of U.S. immigration policy. Indeed it would not be humane to make it difficult for family members to be united in the United States. But this priority also has a great deal to do with fostering the kind of social/cultural environment for immigrants that is most likely to enable a healthy transition to a new society. In other words, it has practical political outcomes in addition to preserving important human values.

Yet who constitutes the family? In some societies, the family may be understood primarily as the nuclear family. Yet in many places the normative family unit is an extended family of some sort. Several current proposals favor granting immediate admission to certain family members (spouses, children under the age of twenty-one, parents) while removing other family members (adult children, siblings, or aunts and uncles) from special consideration. I have argued that this is a defensible way to handle a complex priority. Admission of an immigrant should also mean the admission of immediate family members, but other relatives justifiably do not have a privileged claim. It is not just to grant privileged status to a relatively few large families at the expense of other needy applicants.

GEOGRAPHICAL AND NATIONAL DIVERSITY

In 1965 the United States adopted a radically new principle for the selection of immigrants. Instead of privileging immigrants from certain nations or with certain racial traits, the principle stated that each sending country would have the same ceiling. Although there does not seem to have been a great deal of awareness at the time about the normative significance of this principle, the influence of the black struggle for freedom in the United States at least made it impossible to maintain the white racist principle from the 1920s. This criterion is responsive to the principle of a cosmopolitan national vision and should be at the center of U.S. immigration policy.

OCCUPATIONAL SKILLS

Economists are especially inclined to press for giving occupational skills or investment capital greater priority in the selection of immigrants. They are concerned with direct ways that immigrants can benefit the United States. For them, categories that they regard as "humanitarian," such as the needs of immigrants or family unity, are all right for some immigrant admissions. However, except for certain international obligations regarding refugees, immigration admission

185

should be designed primarily to benefit the United States. One concrete way that immigrants can do this is to bring skills that are needed to fill jobs that current members of the United States are not filling or do not want to fill. These jobs may be highly skilled or minimally skilled, professional or manual labor.

Another way that immigrants can concretely benefit the United States is by bringing money and investing it. We have seen that this path for the wealthy is available in current immigration policy. Sometimes we even hear proposals like auctioning visas to the highest bidders. In this option, the economic value of immigrants is dominant, even exclusive. We might label this proposal as the preferential option for the rich. It is one thing to give a preference to those who bring needed occupational skills; it is quite another to permit persons to buy U.S. citizenship.

The criterion of occupation is an acknowledgment of the reciprocal relation between the aspiring immigrant and the receiving country. Based on the principle of justice for the poor, it is most compelling in the case of labor immigrants because their needs are often the most severe, and the United States often seeks their labor as well. It is considerably less weighty for persons with specialized professional training. U.S. policy should be directed, first, toward educating its own underclass to fill occupational needs and, second, toward making it possible for persons to utilize their training in their home countries.

My conclusion is that, in correlation with the principle of greatest need, labor immigration should be the highest priority. U.S. needs for persons to fill professional occupations should be a subordinate criterion, qualified by the two considerations above. It is appropriate that the determination of occupational needs be lodged with the Labor Department. This determination should be done regularly and often. When immigration threatens job opportunities for U.S. workers and the poor who are unemployed, immigration may justifiably be curtailed.

Admittedly, organized labor tends to exaggerate the threats posed by immigration. While this voice needs to be heard and its views tested, it should not be determinative. Frequently immigration is not as injurious to U.S. workers as organized labor maintains. Still, an ongoing assessment of the impact of immigration on the well-being of the poor already inside the United States, working and unemployed, is essential. When this impact is clearly a negative one, this becomes the strongest moral basis of all for the restriction of immigration.

Issue of Border Control and Illegal Immigration

It is quite possible that immigration from Mexico, legal and illegal, is the major reason for renewed controversy over immigration policy. The border between Mexico and the United States, says the famed novelist Carlos Fuentes, is "not a frontier . . . but a scar."[3] The border has been at various times both a point of bitter contestation and a matter of relative indifference. To Mexicans the border may represent the territorial larceny of the United States in an imperialist war (1848 Treaty of Guadalupe Hidalgo). Or it may be regarded as an inconvenient and arbitrary division in a land that is a geographical and cultural unity, both north and south of the "scar." In times past, migrants have often not had much difficulty traversing back and forth across the line. But they have also been subject to periodic waves of restriction when suddenly, it seems, the border matters a great deal again to the United States.

What can be done along the border between Mexico and the United States to enforce a selective admission policy? Unless one favors an entirely open-borders policy, the question of controlling admission at the border must be addressed. Borders have a huge significance in this world of nation-states. We have considered their symbolic and practical importance in the ordering of national societies. Borders not only mark boundaries of inclusion and exclusion; they also are places of interaction and interrelationship between neighboring peoples.

First, on the grounds of geographical contiguity and historical relationship, the ceiling on legal immigrants from Mexico should be raised substantially above the 25,000 per year that is applied to other countries. The same exception should be granted Canada, but at present, of course, the number of immigrants from Canada is small. The United States should make the legal route more accessible to Mexicans desiring to emigrate, rendering illegal immigration less necessary. In 1981, the General Assemblies of Presbyterian Churches advocated a Temporary Worker Visa for Mexicans, which would enable Mexicans to come to the United States to seek work for an

187

initial period of six months. If they can find employment, then they can legally remain in the United States.[4]

The United States as well as Mexico is responsible for the patterns of migration that have developed in the twentieth century. It makes sense, morally, to acknowledge this responsibility by continuing to make provisions for legal migration rather than suddenly and severely to curtail it. Most persons who are knowledgeable about the border agree that the movement across the border cannot be stopped entirely anyway, no matter how extreme the measures might be to control the migration of persons.

Second, some of the ideas for controlling the border are morally repugnant. The "fortress" symbolism of high, presumably unscalable walls (tortilla curtain) at certain points along the border must be vigorously resisted. Most of the world rejoiced when the Berlin Wall came down. There are important reasons why people hated the wall and everything that it symbolized. Such walls are terrible things. They express the sense that "the other" is an enemy who must be kept out or kept away. Mexico is not an enemy of the United States. Its peoples are not enemies of the United States.

Erecting a wall is an act of hostility against Mexico and Mexican people. It is no way for neighboring countries to construct a future of positive political and economic relationships. The ironies are obvious: building walls to keep people from moving at the same time that NAFTA is trumpeted as a mutually beneficial way to ensure the free movement of goods and capital across the border.

The same considerations apply to proposals to use military troops, or the national guard, to protect the border against undocumented workers. The image is ludicrous, but the proposal has to be taken seriously. The idea is to militarize the border to keep relatively poor Mexicans from seeking work in the United States. One would think that Mexicans were arming for battle. Sometimes, in fact, the word *invasion* is used to talk about the movement of undocumented workers. This step, as the construction of walls, is to treat the border as a war zone, with the Mexicans regarded as the enemy. Whatever may be the level of difficulties presented by illegal immigration, it hardly qualifies as a serious enough threat to warrant responses like those of a country readying itself for war. Moreover, if restrictionists are concerned about not spending so much money on immigrants, militarizing the border is certainly no way to save money.

Some other proposed measures "to control the border" are further extensions of this same siege mentality. An example is to spray the border area with a chemical that would illumine the immigrants so they could be easily identified. There seems to be no end to imaginative schemes for keeping Mexicans inside Mexico. One could only wish that these fantasizers would imagine ways to help welcome and incorporate immigrants into American communities. Proposals to militarize or blockade the border represent exaggerations of the seriousness of illegal immigration, and foster division, alienation, and hostility between neighbors. These are approaches that Christians should vigorously oppose.

Third, instead of the warlike measures listed above, immigration law should be enforced at the border by employing more agents who are professionally trained and compensated. One thing that most people agree on is that border control needs to be made more effective. Just as important, however, border enforcement must be humanized. Stories of abuse of migrants by the border patrol tumble out of the mouths of persons who work with immigrants. In the summer of 1992, Dario Miranda Valenzuela was shot twice in the back by a border patrol agent as he attempted to join his family in the United States. Dario was unarmed. The border patrol agent was acquitted twice, demonstrating to immigrant advocates the virtual immunity of the INS and border patrol from legal accountability.[5] In the words of Carlos Fuentes, "Through the bodies of workers such as Miranda, the border is bleeding again."[6] The demand of advocacy organizations for a citizen advisory panel to examine reports of abuses and to hold border officials accountable for their actions is one very important step.

Perhaps the number of border patrol agents needs to be increased, but more important is to provide them with better training, including a respect for the human rights of migrants, better compensation, and better strategies of enforcement. For example, the border patrol has been expected to provide statistics to show a high number of people it has caught trying to cross the border. Of course the statistics are misleading because the patrol may apprehend the same person over and over again. But the strategy itself is misdirected as well. Instead of trying to prevent people from crossing the border illegally, the border patrol is placed in the position of virtually encouraging migrants to cross so it can document a higher number of catches. U.S.

government preoccupation with "head counts" or "body counts" yet again works against the goals it is presumably seeking to achieve.

Fourth, a related strategy of border control is a kind of blockade recently established between El Paso and Juárez, and San Diego and Tijuana. Official reports enthusiastically tout the success of these operations in reducing the flow of illegal immigrants. Critics, however, point to the problems blockades create for the integrated economies of border cities. Many people depend on the movement of vendors and customers across the border.[7] A gathering of immigrant-rights organizations produced a working document in 1994 which argued that "the border should be a region of historical cooperation that serves the human needs of all inhabitants on both sides of the border including labor, services, consumers."[8]

A strategy of blocking the border between cities is an inappropriately restrictive action in a context of interdependence. Another quite different approach would be an experiment in cooperation between the United States and Mexico along an open border between the two countries.[9] Indeed, a policy that acknowledges and responds to the reality of the interdependence of peoples and communities on both sides of the border and that permits flexible patterns of movement back and forth has more promise than efforts to rigidly restrict entry.

The U.S. Commission on Immigrant Reform has proposed a border-crossing card to facilitate "trade, tourism, family visits and consumer" spending along with bilateral agreements between the United States and Mexico to govern border policies.[10] Although the commission does not favor including any kind of work authorization in this plan, it would be desirable on moral as well as economic grounds to include the possibility of permits to vendors and other day workers whose home remains in Mexico but whose livelihood has for some time depended on crossing the border daily. This is a way to respect the relational networks that already tie Mexicans and Americans together along the border.

In conclusion, I am arguing for a policy that increases the number of legal Mexican immigrants and reduces the number of illegal immigrants. Reduction of illegal immigration is most justly accomplished by more effective enforcement at the border. This requires a more professionalized border patrol that is trained to enforce U.S. immigration law with respect for the personhood of Mexican migrants and subject to review by a citizen advisory panel. This needs to

190

be reiterated. By far, most Mexicans cross the border to seek work. They are not criminals or enemies. Illegal immigrants who are found guilty of criminal activity should indeed be deported quickly, consistent with the requirements of due process of law. At the same time, the U.S. government should seek to work out agreements with Mexico about policies along the border, especially at locations where cities on both sides are closely joined. The dynamic character of interaction across the border should be permitted and encouraged, by something like a border passing card, rather than severely inhibited.

Temporary or Guest Workers

In the temporary worker program (Replenishment Agricultural Worker, or RAW), the U.S. government permits certain businesses in the United States to contract with a limited number of foreign workers to labor inside the United States for a specified period of time. These workers, though legally present in the United States, are not eligible to become resident aliens and naturalized citizens. They have to go home after the work is done. Often they have not been permitted to bring family members with them during the work season. Catholic Charities opposes these programs and advocates that they be phased out.[11] Drew Christiansen, however, does not think this option should be ruled out on the grounds of justice. However ambiguous this option is, he nonetheless believes it may provide some income for needy workers and their families.[12] Other supporters argue that RAW fills the need for seasonal farm workers who will work for a low wage; and it does not lead to permanent immigration.

Few features of immigration policy have received more blunt ethical criticism than these programs. James Nickel argues that to bring persons into the United States for temporary work but not to grant them access to naturalization and social welfare services is a serious violation of their human rights.[13] Michael Walzer maintains that those who live and work inside the United States should be treated as citizens or potential citizens. Anything less would freeze the temporary workers in an unequal status with citizens and would subject them to what amounts to tyranny. Political justice requires that such workers be able to participate fully and equally in the democratic processes of self-government of the national community.[14]

191

A government-appointed bipartisan commission has also favored terminating the temporary worker program.[15] The commission argues that there are enough farm workers inside the United States; no additional workers are needed. Moreover, this commission favored an active role by the Labor Department to assist farm workers to become employed more consistently throughout the year. These workers should have the same rights as other workers: for example, unemployment insurance; unionization and collective bargaining; and access to health, education, and day care for their children. For these various reasons, the temporary worker program should be phased out as quickly as possible and not resuscitated. If the United States needs the labor of immigrants, these immigrants should be permitted to live with their families in the United States with the same rights as other immigrants.

The Temporary Worker Visa (TWV) for Mexican migrants advocated by Presbyterian churches in 1981 does not fit exactly the temporary worker category we have been discussing here, but, without protections, it could be subject to some of the same abuses. In this proposal, a Mexican with a TWV could come to the United States to look for work. If she finds work within six months, she may legally remain. If she is employed and wants to remain, she should be eligible for permanent residency status and eventual naturalization. Otherwise, she is treated unjustly. The use of a TWV may be a helpful way to think about increasing the number of legal Mexican immigrants while keeping the number in proportion to available jobs. If there is work, she can remain as an immigrant. If there is not work, then she is required to return to Mexico.

Worker Authorization System

In the 1986 Immigration Act, Congress tried to deal with illegal immigration by adopting an employer sanctions strategy. That is, employers were required by law to check the documents of workers to make sure that they were legally eligible to work. It was also hoped that the law would prevent the kinds of exploitation of undocumented workers that were all too prevalent among employers. Most observers agree this has not worked very well. Political and moral objections are voiced as well. To some it is wrong to expect employers to enforce national immigration policy. Employers should not be expected to do the work of the INS.

Numerous churches have also called for the repeal of employer sanctions.[16] When this provision is taken seriously by employers, it has too often been applied in a discriminatory way to U.S. citizens who look foreign. In other words, Hispanic Americans who are legal residents or citizens have to produce documents while whites do not. Employers become leery of hiring any foreign-appearing person for fear of running afoul of the law. In addition, when employers reject the work application of persons without documents, these persons are driven underground and experience severe hardship trying to eke out a living.

Employer sanctions has not prevented immigrants from seeking work nor has it ended unscrupulous practices by employers. The U.S. Catholic Conference has been particularly clear in opposing efforts to block the access of undocumented workers to employment. The U.S. government is not morally justified in violating persons' right to seek work as a means to control its borders.[17]

Critics of employer sanctions also contend that enforcement has been half-hearted at best, so abuses continue. In their view, energy would be better spent in enforcing existing labor laws that protect all workers than by trying to prevent undocumented immigrants from working. Then there would be less opportunity for employers to take advantage of people who are desperate for work. For some years now, a controversial proposal to enforce immigration policy through the use of a worker authorization card has been debated. In today's situation the idea is gathering support. Various proposals have been put forward, from a national identification card for everyone to the use of the Social Security card, which persons normally carry with them anyway. The U.S. Commission on Immigrant Reform regards this element as the linchpin of any effort to enforce immigration policy.[18] Each person alike would be expected to produce a Social Security number, which could be verified through a computerized registry. Advocates maintain this is different from a national identification card because no information about persons is gathered. The only thing that could be checked is the authenticity of the Social Security number and, thereby, the eligibility of the person for employment. The Social Security number could also be the way to ensure eligibility for social services and welfare benefits.

The U.S. Commission on Immigrant Reform recognizes the fears of many that this step could lead to government invasions of the right of privacy and to discrimination against nonwhites who appear to employers as likely immigrants. In response to these objections, the commission proposes a pilot program in selected states to test its impact on civil rights and civil liberties. The commission also wants to determine if this system can function efficiently with a minimum of fraud. To advocates this mechanism seems the least cumbersome and morally objectionable way to ensure a person's eligibility for employment and benefits. Employers would not have to function as agents of INS and try to figure out if documents of applicants are legal. High walls and intensive surveillance do not have to be instituted along the border. Just call a number in, like a credit card system, and quickly determine eligibility. No other questions need to be asked if the number checks out.

Opponents of this proposal raise three primary objections. The first rests on concerns about civil liberties. It is dangerous to institute this system because it would be a large step toward a centralized system of personal identification and data gathering under the control of the federal government. An immigrant advocacy organization argues that this system threatens the individual's right of privacy: "This would mean that the federal government as well as your employer might well be able to access sensitive personal information regarding your health, your financial situation, and your family."[19]

Second, critics believe this system would be discriminatory in practice, even if not by intention. Although in principle everyone would be expected to produce Social Security numbers for the limited purpose of employment, in actual fact Hispanic- and Asian-looking people, whether legal residents or not, would be required more frequently to prove eligibility to work. "White" Americans look like legal Americans and so would rarely be required to provide proof. In fact, as churches have insisted, racial and ethnic discrimination is a major problem with the current system of employer sanctions.

Third, skeptics express doubt about the practicality of the proposal. They point to how expensive it is likely to be to create and run this system. They also point to the inefficiencies currently in the INS, including what seems to be massive disorganization in maintaining files and keeping records. Is this the agency that is expected to handle a nationwide data bank of eligible workers? What if a person's number gets lost somewhere and, though she is eligible, the system fails to verify it. What is the recourse for this person? Let the critics speak again: "We're not talking about buying a car here, we're talking about the right to earn a livelihood."[20]

Indeed, the economic cost may prove exorbitant, as would the costs of blockading the border with Mexico. The costs of measures like these to stop illegal immigration might in fact be considerably higher to U.S. taxpayers than current expenditures in social services. Clearly, more work is needed to verify the feasibility of this proposal. But should the notion of a worker authorization card be ruled out entirely on moral grounds? Most immigrant advocacy organizations and religious communities oppose this plan for the first two reasons mentioned above. An exception was the Presbyterian Church General Assemblies in 1981, which supported the proposal as the most effective way to enforce a generous legal immigration policy.[21]

The U.S. Commission's proposal to set up a pilot program is worthy of support. Of course, if increasing the number of legal immigrants from Mexico and improving border enforcement prove to be effective, then this system of worker authorization may be unnecessary. But if a stronger enforcement mechanism is needed, the pilot program provides a way to assess this approach. If racial and ethnic discrimination prevents the system from working fairly, if fears regarding government intrusiveness and violation of persons' rights prove to be well founded, if it costs too much money, if fraud cannot be minimized, if major glitches render the system too inefficient, then there are good reasons to back away from the idea. Yet, if the worker authorization system satisfies the above requirements, I do not believe there are compelling moral reasons to oppose it. In my view, a selective immigration policy, so long as it is just and humane, requires some effective mechanisms of enforcement. Illegal immigration renders migrants vulnerable, and it undermines public support for legal immigration. A worker authorization system is morally preferable to the extreme measures advanced by some persons to blockade and police the border.

In summary, the Christian perspective on immigration that I am developing here supports the continuation of a generous, yet selective, immigration policy. Persons who advocate an open-borders approach or who believe the problems associated with illegal immigration are greatly exaggerated do not give much attention to the question of enforcement. Yet I have argued that order (i.e., good laws, policies, procedures, officials), can and indeed must work hand in hand with a just and humane policy. Questions of enforcement cannot be ignored.

In my view, the first priority in enforcement should be more humane and effective enforcement of immigration laws along the borders. Second is a pilot program that tests a system for verifying workers' eligibility for employment. On the other hand, I believe Christians should oppose a moratorium or a severely restrictive immigration policy. Christians should also oppose extremist proposals to block movement across the border with Mexico, to erect barriers of division and hostility, which are no way to treat a neighbor.

Social Services and Public Benefits: California Proposition 187

The recent event that galvanized debate about immigration policy more than anything else was Proposition 187 in California. This proposition aimed at cutting off social services and public benefits for undocumented persons. Children would not be able to attend public schools. Undocumented immigrants would not be eligible for any nonemergency health care. Services to protect children from abuse and neglect would be banned. Proposition 187 is an effort to ensure that taxpayers do not have to provide any support for undocumented workers. It seeks to cut them off from most public benefits of the welfare state. Governor Pete Wilson served as a lightning rod for several controversial proposals. He campaigned vigorously for Proposition 187, which was approved by a substantial percentage of voters in 1994.

Implementation of this measure is on hold, however, while its constitutionality is tested in the courts. For example, the U.S. Supreme Court in *Plyler v. Doe* (1982) ruled that the state of Texas was legally obligated to provide education for the children of undocumented persons. Although Proposition 187 will likely be tied up in litigation for some time, it nonetheless has intensified and focused the current debate. Increasingly, opponents of immigration are advocating measures that make undocumented persons ineligible for employment, education, health care, and welfare. Presumably these

196

measures would serve as a strong deterrent to illegal immigration. But even if immigrants show up, they would not be supported in any way by public funds. They would have to find some other way to manage or return home, preferably the latter.

Proposition 187 and related laws and policies have been vigorously denounced by churches and immigrant advocates—for good reason. Archbishop John R. Quinn of San Francisco, appealing to the authority of Catholic teaching, stated, "Immigrants, even the illegal and undocumented, as human persons have the right to education, employment, health care and housing worthy of the human person."[22] A similar ethical perspective is presented by the political philosopher James Nickel. He argues that international human rights are not tied to citizenship. They are grounded in territorial jurisdiction. "Presence in a territory is sufficient to generate an obligation for the government of that territory to uphold a person's human rights—whether or not that person is documented."[23] This surely applies to the right of illegal immigrants to basic economic and social conditions appropriate to their dignity as human beings.

The use of public benefits by undocumented workers is exaggerated anyway. They are ineligible for most welfare benefits and are understandably reluctant to seek assistance because they live daily with the fear of discovery and deportation. They do use public schools for their children. And they do use health care services to a certain extent, especially women with prenatal and postnatal needs. But even on grounds of expedience, is cutting off public services a good idea? The specter of uneducated children with nothing to do during the day is simply unacceptable. So also is the prevalence of untreated diseases among a segment of the population. Moreover, is it a good idea for societal well-being to discourage women from seeking reproductive health care?

Much of the criticism of Proposition 187 is explicitly moral. Who is hurt the most? It is the most vulnerable persons, especially children and women. After all, children are not responsible for their presence in the United States. It is outrageous to keep children out of school. And women are hurt in specific ways because they are childbearers. It is outrageous to deny needed assistance because they do not have documents. These measures are simply no way to treat human beings. This is a policy not of a humane society, but of a spiteful and mean-spirited people. It is a policy oriented toward long-distance officials who do not encounter undocumented persons face-to-face.

Try to imagine yourself as a public school administrator turning children away because their parents do not have documents or, even worse, turning them in to immigration authorities. Or try to imagine yourself as a nurse denying assistance to a woman having difficulty with her pregnancy, or reporting her to government authorities. Are these ways a moral person would act? Emphatically not, in my judgment. Public school staff have the responsibility to serve the community through educating children. Health care personnel serve the community through assisting persons who come to them for counsel and healing. To undertake a policing function is incompatible with their vocation of service. To sort out who is ineligible and undeserving is a Scrooge-like response to the concrete presence of another human being.

If it costs more to educate the children of undocumented persons and if it costs more to provide basic health care as well as emergency medical assistance to persons without legal papers, then this is not a burdensome price for American people to pay to treat neighbors decently. I disagree with the recommendation of the U.S. Commission on Immigrant Reform that eligibility for benefits should be denied to undocumented persons except for emergency situations. The commission believes that eligibility should be subject to verification through the same system as employment.

In my view, the right of children to education and the right to health care should not be subject to verification. Persons should be served, whoever they are. Yet, as I have argued earlier, it would be justified to test a system for verification for employment. It would also be justified to verify eligibility for income supplement programs of the social welfare system. It makes moral as well as practical sense to limit some provisions of public support to those who are resident aliens and citizens, to those who are legally admitted to participation in the national community, but not to cut off social services entirely.

By far most of the undocumented immigrants come to the United States in order to work. The possibilities for employment and the income and improved life that come with a job are the primary pull factor, not access to the welfare system. It is not cruel to enforce immigration limitations through the employment sector based on reasonable judgments about available jobs. But it is cruel to deny education to children and health care to whoever needs it. One should not have to be in danger of dying before being treated, whether one is a citizen without money or an immigrant without documents.

Churches have an important role to play also. Not only should they advocate for just and humane immigration policies, they should also provide hospitality to the undocumented immigrant. Although the government may indeed seek to enforce just immigration laws through, for example, controlling access to employment, churches are called to witness to the radical inclusiveness of God's love. Churches have no business being accomplices in the enforcement of immigration laws. They have no business in distinguishing between legal immigrants and undocumented workers. They have the responsibility within their capabilities to respond to the needs of strangers.

This ministry without distinction may indeed bring churches into conflict with government agencies called on to enforce distinctions. But it is the kind of witness to which the church is called in faithfulness to a God of all peoples, not a national god. And it is the kind of witness that can continue to renew over and over again the capacities of the wider society to treat immigrants humanely. In the current situation of backlash against immigrants, indeed all the poor, the readiness of a people to respond generously and hospitably to strangers is a witness of utmost importance. Churches are called to be communities who model a different way of treating neighbors than Proposition 187 dictates. It would be an unfaithful response indeed if churches take their cues from the national mood of stinginess rather than from Jesus' challenge to love the stranger.

Other Elements of Immigration Policy

ENCOURAGE NATURALIZATION OF RESIDENT ALIENS

One agenda of the Clinton administration is to promote naturalization among noncitizens. Resident aliens may live in the United States for years and not seek to become citizens, even though they are eligible. There are many reasons for this. Certainly complexity, the long waiting period, and the expense of naturalization procedures are inhibiting, especially if one does not speak English well. The plan for a more intentional campaign for naturalization is worthy. Although there are not actually many privileges granted to citizens that are not available to resident aliens, citizenship expresses a sense of membership in the American polity. It signals and encourages a personal investment in this society. It is a ritualized way of welcoming the contribution of this new participant in the common societal project.

Many people who participate in the process of naturalization talk about how moving it is. They remember the years of waiting and planning to come to the United States. They remember the hopes and dreams which brought them here. They remember the struggles after they arrived. And often, understandably, they have a sense of pride and accomplishment in becoming a U.S. citizen. Perhaps the ritual should be made a more public one, with a way for the larger community to symbolize its reception of persons into the role of public citizen. There is something potentially invigorating for the wider community of citizens as well to have persons from many places in the world *choose* to become members of *this* polity. Often they believe more deeply in the promise of America as an open and dynamic community than do settled citizens.

The point of a naturalization campaign is to make the process more "user-friendly." The expectation is that many resident aliens would like to be citizens if the process were more accessible and understandable. For settled citizens the advantages are not that immigrants would then be melted into the mainstream. Naturalization does not need to signify a disvaluing of diversity. Instead it signifies that the national community values the contributions that naturalized citizens can make to the wider national community. Naturalization is a way of saying, "we need and value your contribution to the American future. Welcome to active membership in this polity."

Although there is little debate about the value of a naturalization campaign, there are different interpretations of its importance. It is interesting that, unlike past eras, there is little concern today about the loyalty of immigrants to the American government. Instead, restrictionists worry that immigrants stay huddled together in isolation from American life and have little concern for the good of the whole society. Even though restrictionists believe there are too many immigrants, they would generally welcome naturalization as a decision of persons already here to identify with the national community.

I believe, however, that barriers to naturalization have not been primarily due to the desire of immigrants to remain separate, but to the numerous obstacles immigrants face in America, including negative attitudes toward their presence. If the United States values the naturalization of immigrants, then we should do what we can to encourage it, not make it more difficult.

From an ethical perspective, amnesty for undocumented persons who have lived and worked in the United States for several years or more remains a worthy policy objective. Migrants who have formed relational bonds and made contributions to the society through their labor deserve to be granted legal status and to be eligible for naturalization. Amnesty was granted to some undocumented migrants in the 1986 Act, but it needs to be extended to others as well.

The principle is an important one. Persons who are functionally part of the community ought to be considered as members. Relational ties established over time are morally more important than the legal documents. In fact, this is another avenue available to immigrants that may provide a valuable alternative to more legalistically imposed border controls. As we have seen, to enter the United States without documents is not a criminal act. Undocumented migrants have acted on their right to work by coming to the United States to seek employment. Catholic social thought also stresses the right of persons to a homeland, a place where they can belong and be participants in the life of wider community.[24] Although the United States may justifiably seek to restrict immigration, if persons establish themselves in the United States they ought not to be penalized but incorporated into the national community.

SUPPORT FOR LANGUAGE INSTRUCTION

Discussions of language policies reflect some of these same disagreements. Critics complain that immigrants will not learn English, so they need to be forced by necessity. The assumption is that a tough policy of "sink or swim" on one's own will push immigrants to learn English more quickly. Critics are especially hostile toward bilingual education programs that encourage immigrants to use their native languages as well as to learn English. They also resent the requirement that some documents and public services have to be provided in non-English languages. Again, a kind of punitive attitude is evident in these views. If immigrants want to use native languages in their communities, that is all right, but do not expect any public support for communication in any language other than English.

I maintain, on the other hand, that most immigrants want to learn English. We should have a national policy of encouraging and assisting people to learn English. Portes and Rumbaut comment that when California passed an initiative establishing English as the official language, "over forty thousand immigrant adults were being turned away from English as a second language classes" in the Los Angeles area.[25] Although there is some debate about the effectiveness of bilingual education for teaching English to non-English-speaking children, the values of bilingualism and multilingualism for the education of children and youth for today's world are self-evident. In Alamosa, Colorado, a community composed of roughly equal numbers of Hispanics and Anglos, the public schools have the goal to graduate all their youth from high school with fluency in both English and Spanish. American schools should not be "English only" schools but settings where all students are learning at least one language in addition to English.

It is also a good idea to provide translations in non-English languages for some public matters. Critics complain that immigrants do not care about the public good yet would make it hard for them to participate by insisting that everything be in English only. Bilingual or multilingual translations are not designed primarily to make it possible for people to get by without learning English. Instead, it is a way to help immigrants maneuver the difficult transition from one culture into another. This approach helps overcome immigrant isolation. It also gives a certain valuation to non-English languages, thereby reversing past practices that sought to extinguish these languages. Catholic thought appropriately calls for respecting people's right to express themselves in their native languages.[26] Instruction in English *along with* support for bilingual programs is the appropriate route, not marginalizing or stigmatizing people who speak non-English languages.

SHARING THE BENEFITS AND BURDENS

The issue of federalism is also on the front burner of immigration discussions. Representatives from states that receive large numbers of undocumented immigrants have a legitimate beef. Immigrants pay a hefty sum in taxes, but most go to the federal government. Yet the states and localities are required to pay for many of the services. Thus, even though immigration overall is an economic plus, even illegal immigration, the costs can indeed be a drain on particular states and localities. Specific proposals have once again targeted illegal immigration. The argument is that the U.S. government is responsible for enforcing immigration policy, not the states. Thus the U.S. government should reimburse states for the costs, with special focus on health, education, and incarceration of felons.

But it is not just a matter of fairness that the federal government shoulder some of the financial burdens, it is even more a matter of sharing benefits. That is, in the current system the state and local governments tend to pay the costs while the federal government receives the benefits of tax revenues. No wonder there is resentment in those places strongly affected by illegal immigration. The benefits of those tax revenues, which are, after all, greater than the financial costs, should be shared with states and localities. It is only fair that they benefit economically from the taxes paid by undocumented workers.

SOCIAL SERVICES AND PUBLIC BENEFITS FOR LEGAL IMMIGRANTS

A central feature of current congressional efforts at immigration reform is to make legal immigrants ineligible to receive public benefits. Thus the antiwelfare and anti-immigrant campaign sometimes targets not only undocumented workers but legal immigrants as well. The U.S. Commission on Immigrant Reform is against this restriction, although it advocates several measures to make it less likely that legal immigrants will resort to benefits during their first five years in the United States. It is standard in the history of immigration policy to exclude persons who are likely to become a "public charge." It is reasonable to include this restriction.

Yet those persons who are legally admitted to the United States should not be subjected to a double standard. They should not be denied the kinds of assistance that are available to citizens and longer-term residents. In other words, unequal treatment of recent legal immigrants is unjust. The problem is not immigrants but a welfare system that needs to focus more on empowerment strategies than perpetuating dependence. People for many and varied reasons may have to resort to public assistance, and a humane society will ensure that the basic needs of residents can be met. But positive change that helps persons, immigrants and nonimmigrants alike, move off welfare is the appropriate policy direction.

It is also wrong to require that immigrants pay a fee in order to enter the United States. To use the money of immigrants to help pay the costs of welfare programs is yet another wrong-headed and wrong-hearted proposal. And the immigrants would not even have access to benefits they helped pay for! If immigrants are admitted, they should be welcomed, not subjected to additional taxes or targeted for discriminatory restrictions. Once again, these proposals reflect a negative, punitive, and grudging attitude toward immigrants. To paraphrase a familiar moral tenet, so long as the United States makes provisions to admit immigrants, we should not make things more difficult for them than we are prepared to do for ourselves.

FOSTER INTERACTION BETWEEN RESIDENTS AND NEWCOMERS

This is a topic that needs book-length treatment. The Ford Foundation study on *Changing Relations* [27] emphasizes the need for communities to be more intentional about bringing residents and newcomers together. When residents and newcomers remain apart, indifference generally rules; yet specific events or conflicts of interest can suddenly produce intense antagonism. Either to expect the smooth assimilation of immigrants or to rest content with separated communities is unacceptable. We must seek to build bridges, work together on common projects, and learn to relate to each other without fear and animosity. This does not happen automatically, however. Community leaders need to work at it.

This remains a challenge of first importance. Examples and models are beginning to emerge, but we need many more. Churches can and should take the lead. In Garden City, Kansas, an alliance of church leaders provided crucial initiatives for the resettlement of Vietnamese refugees in the community. They took decisive steps to organize positive community responses before negative reactions became dominant. [28]

For Catholic churches, especially, the role of assisting newcomers and providing avenues for incorporation in the wider community is not unfamiliar. For many other churches it is a new frontier in congregational mission. In addition to advocacy on behalf of immigrants and refugees, churches can seek ways to bring residents and newcomers together. Faith in the reconciling power of God can inspire and direct church initiatives. We can also expect local governments and neighborhood organizations to foster interaction, but this challenge may well be one in which the church's witness is indispensable. The image of the table of Christ which unites diverse peoples, overcomes divisions, and creates a new and inclusive community can inspire again and again the church's efforts to be a reconciling agent in our society.

LONG-RANGE POLICY IMPERATIVES

Most people who deal with immigration agree that long-range strategies are needed to reduce the pressures of migration. In the eighteenth and nineteenth centuries, European emigration may well have benefited both the sending countries and the receiving countries. Now emigration might provide a safety valve for countries in the southern part of the world but is increasingly unwelcome in northern countries. Northern countries do not need immigrants in the way they may have in the past. Thus, although limited immigration may continue to bring economic benefits and leavening enrichment, the future of immigration appears fraught with more problems than possibilities. There simply are not many places in the world where the massive numbers of people who wish to migrate can go. Those who are able to migrate, whether as refugees or immigrants, are increasingly a privileged few out of the vast many.

It is clear that immigration cannot be the answer for the vast disparities between the privileged and the deprived. For the United States to give international leadership on behalf of human rights and human well-being for all is no longer only a moral imperative but also a political necessity. Migration pressures will only intensify if people are not able to be safe and to thrive in their homelands. Northern countries can try to keep them out, but the likely scenarios are not pleasant ones. In the long run, the dynamics of migration will have to be addressed by the international community.

Even so, to insist on the need to address root causes of migration and to develop long-range strategies is easier to enunciate in generalities than to formulate specifics. Proponents of NAFTA, for example, argue that it will reduce levels of Mexican migration over the long haul. Opponents maintain that it will increase migration. It seems reasonable to think that increasing capital investment in third-world countries would reduce the need to emigrate, yet Saskia Sassen maintains that it may in fact increase immigration.[29] A slight improvement in the lives of people may lead to new awareness of life's possibilities and a motivation to go where it is more likely these dreams can be realized.

With the contradictory trends of tightened borders and pressures to move, the United States needs to work for compliance with human rights requirements. Until governments are both capable of and committed to securing the rights of their peoples, migrants will continue to be created. Until people can survive and thrive in their homeland, they will continue to migrate. The U.S. government will need to work with international organizations and other governments to promote policies that make it possible for people to remain in their homelands. For most persons this is an aching desire. In the long run this is the only viable way to limit immigration.

CONCLUSION

At this moment in public life, the course of migration policy is uncertain. Efforts to sound an alarm and close the border with Mexico have not generated the large-scale movement that some American politicians expected. Proposition 187 in California has not yet led to a groundswell of similar measures by other states. Yet Congress is still debating whether or not to permit states to deny public education to undocumented migrants. Restrictionist pressures are stronger than they have been in a long time. Migration issues are currently a volatile component of public debates.

United States migration policy seems subject to great fluctuations between times of relative indifference and times of intense conflict. Often, although not always, opposition to immigrants goes hand in hand with hard times in the economy. When life is difficult, immigrants are convenient scapegoats. This seems to have been one of the reasons for the popularity of proposition 187 in California.

But today's debates about immigration turn less on economic analysis than on social and cultural issues. With the end of the Cold War, the peoples of the United States are contending once again about national identity, values, and priorities. These are matters for genuine contestation. The outcome is not settled or predetermined. How do newcomers fit in to what we are seeking to fashion in and for this national community? How does this national community perceive its relation to other peoples and nations?

Even the political energy given to reducing social welfare and public benefits for the poor as a way to cut the federal budget is driven less by economic considerations than by social values. What does it mean to be a member of the national community? Who is "deserving" and who is "undeserving?" How are resources to be distributed? What is the relation between rights and responsibilities? If cutting the budget were the number-one priority, still-bloated defense spending could be greatly reduced. Restrictionist attitudes toward immigrants and refugees in part reflect the societal trend toward judgmental and harsh reactions to the poor generally.

Even more, however, the debate over migration policy is about unity and diversity, cultural cohesion and pluralism. Should the American experiment with multiculturalism be affirmed and extended or should it be put on hold, or even reversed? Restrictionist attitudes reflect anxiety over the racial and ethnic composition of American society and what this portends for the American future. For them, the ways America is being re-created by thirty years of relatively receptive migration policies are more threatening than promising. So the desire is to gain greater control of the borders and reassert a kind of normative cultural uniformity in the face of multicultural challenges.

In this book I do not dismiss the complexities of these challenges, but I believe they can be addressed in ways that enrich the ongoing creation and re-creation of American society. The ethical perspective of Christians is a vital ingredient in the public formation of national responses. I am not so naive as to believe that Christians will speak with a single voice on migration issues. But I do want to emphasize how important it is for Christians to engage each other about their normative vision of community and how this contributes to national struggles over migration policy.

In Christian ethics, hospitality to strangers is one concrete expression of neighbor love. Biblical narratives portray manifestations of hospitality that call Christians to imaginative moral practices of compassionate generosity and receptivity to those who are different. Biblical narratives also point toward a future that is ritualistically enacted in the Eucharist. Human differences are no longer dominated by enmity and hostility but are incorporated and reconciled in the community of God through God's own gracious initiation. The welcoming Table is an image that calls Christians to moral practices of justice and inclusiveness. These very narratives, particular as they

208

are, can help shape the moral ethos of the wider society as well as the witness of churches.

Christians join with others in seeking to establish moral requisites of community and human well-being that cross borders and go beyond national and ethnic particularities. But in seeking more universal norms, Christians and others do not need to give up the specific moral substance of their own narratives, rituals, and symbols. The fullness of diverse religious and ethical traditions can contribute to the revitalization of public moral discourse and the moral character of societal members.

In this book I develop the position that ethical perspectives are integral to the formation of migration policies. I have shown how certain elements of a Christian perspective relate in a reasonably comprehensive way to contemporary debates about what U.S. migration policy ought to be. I believe U.S. policy should continue to admit newcomers, giving special priority to refugees, asylum seekers, and immigrants whose need is particularly urgent and compelling. While Christians should advocate vigorously for the needs and rights of migrants, they should not evade the difficult questions of justifiable limits and humane enforcement by law of these limits.

Most important, a Christian vision provides the basis and motivation for deepening rather than decrying the re-creative struggle to fashion a just multicultural national community. Migration policy is one of the primary places where this struggle is taking place.

NOTES

INTRODUCTION

1. Interview with Leonel I. Castillo, former director of the United States Immigration and Naturalization Service (INS), in Studs Terkel, *American Dreams: Lost and Found* (New York: Pantheon Books, 1980), 10.
2. Ellis Cose, *A Nation of Strangers: Prejudice, Politics and the Population of America* (New York: William Morrow and Co., 1992), 12.
3. Julian L. Simon, *The Economic Consequences of Immigration* (Cambridge, Mass.: Basil Blackwell, 1989), xxvii, xxix.
4. Vincent Harding, *There Is a River: The Black Struggle for Freedom in America* (New York: Harcourt Brace Jovanovich, 1981).
5. See Dick Kirschten, "Come In! Keep Out!" *National Journal* (19 May 1990): 1206-11.
6. However, there is some disturbing evidence that this may be changing. In recent months the "race card" is beginning to be played more explicitly again in public debate. See the book by Peter Brimelow, *Alien Nation* (New York: Random House, 1995).
7. J. Glenn Gray, *The Warriors* (New York: Harper Torchbooks, 1970), 6.
8. Quoted in David M. Reimers, *Still the Golden Door: The Third World Comes to America*, 2nd ed. (New York: Columbia University Press, 1992), 261.
9. See Cose, *A Nation of Strangers.*
10. Pastora San Juan Cafferty, Barry R. Chiswick, Andrew M. Greeley, and Teresa A. Sullivan, *The Dilemma of American Immigration: Beyond the Golden Door* (New Brunswick, N.J.: Transaction Publishers, 1983).
11. John Crewdson, *The Tarnished Door: The New Immigrants and the Transformation of America* (New York: Times Books, 1983).
12. Reimers, *Still the Golden Door.*
13. James D. Cockroft, *Outlaws in the Promised Land: Mexican Immigrant Workers and America's Future* (New York: Grove Press, 1986).
14. Norman and Naomi Flink Zucker, *The Guarded Gate: The Reality of American Refugee Policy* (San Diego: Harcourt Brace Jovanovich, 1987).
15. See an essay by John Scanlon in which he uses the metaphors of "back door" and "executive window": "Immigration Law and the Illusion of Numerical Control," *University of Miami Law Review,* 36 (September 1982), 819-64.
16. Aristide R. Zolberg, "The Next Waves: Migration Theory for a Changing World," *International Migration Review* 23, no. 3 (fall 1989): 403-30.
17. See the title to the policy on Mexican immigration adopted by the General Assemblies of the United Presbyterian Church (U.S.A.) and the Presbyterian Church (U.S.) in 1981: "Strangers Become Neighbors: Presbyterian Response to Mexican Immigration."

18. Richard Lamm, *The Immigration Time Bomb* (New York: E. P. Dutton, 1985).

1. U.S. REFUGEE POLICY: HAVEN FOR THE PERSECUTED OR PAWN OF FOREIGN POLICY PRIORITIES?

1. Elie Wiesel, "Who Is a Refugee?" *American Refugee Policy,* ed. Joseph M. Kitagawa (San Francisco: Winston Press, 1984), 17.
2. Ibid.
3. Effie Voutira, "Pontic Greeks Today: Migrants or Refugees?" *Journal of Refugee Studies* 4, no. 4 (1991): 400-20 (see also 408-9).
4. Elie Wiesel, "The Refugee," in *Sanctuary: A Resource Guide for Understanding and Participating in the Central American Refugee's Struggle,* ed. Gary MacEoin (New York: Harper & Row, 1985), 9.
5. Ibid., 13.
6. William Fullbright, quoted in Mark P. Gibney, "Foreign Policy: Ideological and Human Rights Factors," in *Refugees and the Asylum Dilemma in the West,* ed. Gil Loescher (University Park: Pennsylvania State University Press, 1992), 47-48.
7. Wiesel, "The Refugee," 12-13.
8. Nancy Gibbs, "Cry the Forsaken Country," *Time,* 1 August 1994, 33.
9. John Darnton, "U.N. Faces Refugee Crisis That Never Ends," *New York Times,* 8 August 1994, 1(A).
10. Michael Marrus, *The Unwanted: European Refugees in the Twentieth Century* (New York: Oxford University Press, 1985), 19.
11. Ibid., 18. Marrus cites a study by Bernard Porter, *The Refugee Question in Mid-Victorian Politics* (New York: Cambridge University Press, 1979).
12. Marrus, *The Unwanted,* 92.
13. Ibid., p. 22.
14. Ibid., p. 92.
15. Hannah Arendt, *The Origins of Totalitarianism,* new ed. (San Diego: Harcourt Brace and Co., 1973), 293.
16. Ibid., 297.
17. Gil Loescher and John Scanlon, *Calculated Kindness: Refugees and America's Half-Open Door, 1945 to the Present* (New York: The Free Press, 1986), xiv.
18. Ibid., 10.
19. Ibid., xviii.
20. David M. Reimers, *Still the Golden Door: The Third World Comes to America* (New York: Columbia University Press, 1992), 166.
21. *Refugee Reports* 16, no. 4 (29 April 1995): 15.
22. *Refugee Reports* 16, no. 8 (25 August 1995): 1.
23. Reimers, *Still the Golden Door,* 178.
24. Loescher and Scanlon, *Calculated Kindness,* 148.
25. Reimers, *Still the Golden Door,* 181.
26. Ibid., 182.
27. *Refugee Reports* 16, no. 8 (25 August 1995): 3. The proposed number is 25,000.
28. See Richard Lamm, "Why We Closed Our Borders: A Speech to the United Nations General Assembly by the Deputy Secretary of State, July 4, 2000," in *Megatraumas: America at the Year 2000* (Boston: Houghton Mifflin, 1985), 67-68.
29. Reimers, *Still the Golden Door,* 192.
30. Norman Zucker and Naomi Flink Zucker, *The Guarded Gate: The Reality of American Refugee Policy* (San Diego: Harcourt Brace Jovanovich, 1987), 48. Quoted from "Text of Reagan's Speech Accepting the Republican Nomination," *New York Times,* 18 July 1980, 8(A).
31. Barbara Yarnold, *Refugees Without Refuge: Formation and Failed Implementation of U.S. Political Asylum Policy in the 1980s* (Washington: University Press of America, 1990). Yarnold presents a comprehensive study to document that U.S. government officials failed to implement the 1980 Refugee Act; instead their orientation was to promote "state interest."
32. *Sanctuary: A Story of American Conscience and the Law in Collision* (New York: Weidenfeld and Nicolson, 1988), 357.

33. *Refugee Reports* 16, no. 8 (25 August 1995): 1-7.
34. Ibid., 1.
35. *Refugee Reports* 15, no. 10 (27 October 1994): 8.
36. *Refugee Reports* 16, no. 8 (25 August 1995): 3.
37. Ralston Deffenbaugh, "Resettlement as Protection: New Directions in the U.S. Refugee Program," *Refugee Reports* 16, no. 4 (29 April 1994): 10.
38. Alejandro Portes and Ruben G. Rumbaut, *Immigrant America: A Portrait* (Berkeley: University of California Press, 1990), 181.
39. United Nations, Convention Relating to the Status of Refugees, 1951.
40. Aristide R. Zolberg, Astri Suhrke, and Sergio Aguayo, *Escape from Violence: Conflict and the Refugee Crisis in the Developing World* (New York: Oxford University Press, 1989), 30.
41. Ibid., 33.
42. "People cast abroad by famine are refugees to the extent that famine is itself a form of violence, as in the case of confiscatory economic measures or extremely unequal property systems maintained by brutal force, the inability to meet subsistence needs because of unsafe conditions, or the refusal of the state to accept international assistance" (Ibid., 33).
43. See Andrew Shacknove, "Who Is a Refugee?" *Ethics* 95 (January 1985): 275-76.
44. Francis M. Deng, *Protecting the Dispossessed: A Challenge for the International Community* (Washington, D.C.: The Brookings Institution, 1993), 66.
45. *Refugee Reports* 16, no. 5 (31 May 1995): 16.
46. Ibid.
47. Shacknove, "Who Is a Refugee?" 278.
48. Deng, *Protecting the Dispossessed*, 135.
49. See Ignatius Bau, *This Ground Is Holy: Church Sanctuary and Central American Refugees* (New York: Paulist Press, 1985), 54.
50. Ibid., 50.
51. Shacknove, "Who Is a Refugee?" 276.
52. Roger Zetter, "Labelling Refugees: Forming and Transforming a Bureaucratic Identity," *Journal of Refugee Studies* 4, no. 1 (1991): 39, 60.
53. Joseph Carens, "Aliens and Citizens: The Case for Open Borders," *The Review of Politics* 49 (spring 1987): 251-73.
54. Carens draws on the views of Nozick, Rawls, and Walzer to support his argument. One may also find the open borders position argued by anti-nation-state thinkers who contest the control that the state exercises over territory and people. See Nigel Harris, *City, Class and Trade: Social and Economic Change in the Third World* (London: I. B. Tauris and Co., 1991), 152. Harris maintains that "accepting the right of the state to control immigration is accepting its right to exist, the right of the ruling class to exist as a ruling class, the right to exploit, the 'right' to a world of barbarism."
55. Joseph Carens, "States and Refugees: A Normative Analysis," in *Refugee Policy: Canada and the United States* (Toronto: York Lanes Press, 1991), 18-29.
56. See Zucker and Zucker, *The Guarded Gate*, 138-76.
57. *Refugee Reports* 16, no. 5 (31 May 1995): 10 (see also 11-13).
58. Howard Adelman, "Refuge or Asylum: A Philosophical Perspective," *Journal of Refugee Studies* 1, no. 1 (1988): 10, 18-19.
59. Zucker and Zucker, *The Guarded Gate*, 68.
60. James C. Hathaway, "Reconceiving Refugee Law as Human Rights Protection," *Journal of Refugee Studies* 4, no. 2 (1991): 113-31.
61. Jason Clay, "Ethnicity: Powerful Factor in Refugee Flows." Quoted in Elizabeth G. Ferris, *Beyond Borders: Refugees, Migrants and Human Rights in the Post–Cold War Era* (Geneva: WCC publications, 1993), 75 (see also 74-77).
62. Gil Loescher, *Beyond Charity: International Cooperation and the Global Refugee Crisis* (New York: Oxford University Press, 1993), 12.
63. Jodi Jacobson, "The Root Causes of Migration/Refugees: The Environmental Dimension," *Reformed World* 41, no. 7 (September and December 1991): 237.
64. Howard Adelman, "Immigration to Canada and the United States," *The Oxford International Review* 3, no. 1 (winter 1991): 30.
65. Loescher, *Beyond Charity*, 200-203.

66. Ibid., 149. Many analysts "are beginning to recognize that prolonged stays in closed camp environments can have extremely damaging psychological effects and are totally unsatisfactory as a long-term solution."

67. Ibid., 17.

68. See Barbara Harrell-Bond, Eftihia Voutira, and Mark Leopold, "Counting the Refugees: Gifts, Givers, Patrons and Clients," *Journal of Refugee Studies* 5, nos. 3/4 (1992): 206-7, in which they emphasize the expectation of reciprocity among many refugees. If refugees receive a gift of aid and are unable to offer anything in return, this establishes a power relation in which the refugees are in an inferior position.

69. Ibid. Also see Barbara Harrell-Bond, *Imposing Aid: Emergency Assistance to Refugees* (New York: Oxford University Press, 1986).

70. Ibid., 220, 223. A further example of assertive strategies by refugees themselves is found in "refugee-warrior communities" who organize militarily to seek their goals. See Zolberg et al., *Escape from Violence*, 275-78.

71. See my essay on "The Moral Debate Between Humanitarianism and National Interest About U.S. Refugee Policy: Theological Perspective," *Migration World Magazine* 21, no. 5 (1993): 15-18.

2. U. S. IMMIGRATION POLICY: LAND OF OPPORTUNITY OR FORTRESS AMERICA?

1. Ronald Takaki, "Reflections on Racial Patterns in America," in *From Different Shores,* ed. Ronald Takaki (New York: Oxford University Press, 1994), 26.

2. Ibid., 27.

3. Ibid.

4. Maldwyn Allen Jones, *American Immigration,* 2nd ed. (Chicago: University of Chicago Press, 1992), 79.

5. John Higham, *Strangers in the Land: Patterns of American Nativism, 1860-1925,* 2nd ed. (New Brunswick: Rutgers University Press, 1988), 4.

6. Jones, *American Immigration,* 222. (Jones quotes an unnamed source reflecting the views of the Immigration Restriction League.)

7. *Network News,* July-August 1993, 6. Publication of the National Network for Immigrant and Refugee Rights.

8. Ellis Cose, *A Nation of Strangers: Prejudice, Politics, and the Populating of America* (New York: William Morrow and Co., 1992), 10.

9. Peter Schuck, "The Emerging Political Consensus on Immigration Law," *Georgetown Immigration Law Journal* 5, no. 1 (1991): 26.

10. Doris M. Meissner, Robert D. Hormats, Antonio Garrigues Walker, and Shijuro Ogata, *International Migration Challenges in a New Era* (New York: The Trilateral Commission, 1993), 27.

11. Quoted in Cose, *A Nation of Strangers,* 10.

12. See Meissner et al., *International Migration Challenges,* 16-17; and David M. Reimers, *Still the Golden Door: The Third World Comes to America* (New York: Columbia University Press, 1992), 259.

13. Howard Adelman, "Immigration to Canada and the United States," *The Oxford International Review* 3, no. 1 (winter 1991): 28.

14. Meissner et al., *International Migration Challenges,* 26.

15. Ibid., 108-9. These authors cite the work of Rosemary Jenks, ed., *Immigration and Nationality Policies of Leading Migration Nations* (Washington, D.C.: Center for Migration Studies, 1992). They also point out that in Canada today the newcomer population is 16.1 percent of the total.

16. See Alejandro Portes and Robert L. Bach. *Latin Journey: Cuban and Mexican Immigrants in the United States* (Berkeley: University of California, 1985), 1-20.

17. Alejandro Portes and Ruben G. Rumbaut, *Immigrant America: A Portrait* (Berkeley: University of California Press, 1990), 230 (see also 223-32).

18. Gerald P. Lopez, "Undocumented Mexican Migration: In Search of Just Immigration Law and Policy," *UCLA Law Review* 28 (April 1981): 640-72.

19. L. Ling-chi Wang, "Is the U.S. Still the Golden Door?" *Migration World Magazine* 21, no. 4 (1993): 14-16.
20. Portes and Rumbaut, *Immigrant America*, 140-41. This is a central theme in this excellent study.
21. Robert Bach, *Changing Relations: Newcomers and Established Residents in U.S. Communities* (Report to the Ford Foundation by the National Board of the Changing Relations Project, 1993), 36-37. The six cities included large urban neighborhoods in Chicago, Houston, Miami, and Philadelphia; a suburban setting in Monterey Park, California; and a small-town community in Garden City, Kansas. The studies of each of these locations are included in the volume *Structured Diversity: Ethnographic Perspectives on the New Immigration*, ed. Louise Lamphere (Chicago: University of Chicago Press), 1992.
22. Portes and Rumbaut, *Immigrant America*, 180.
23. David Ronquillo, "Bilingualism Opens Doors to People and to Progress," *Rocky Mountain News*, 7 April 1994, 45(A).
24. Portes and Rumbaut, *Immigrant America*, 188-91. See the entire chapter, 180-221, for an excellent discussion of research that bears on the topic of language.
25. Portes and Bach, *Latin Journey*, 347.
26. Donald L. Huddle, "A Growing Burden," *New York Times*, 3 September 1993, 23(A).
27. Ibid.
28. George J. Borjas, *Friends or Strangers?* (New York: Basic Books, 1990), 222-23.
29. Cited in *Refugee Reports* 15, no. 4 (19 April 1994): 5.
30. For a summary of this research, see Jeffrey S. Passel and Michael Fix, "Immigrants and Social Services," *Migration World* 22, no. 4 (1994): 22-25.
31. Margaret Carlson, "Alienable Rights," *Time*, 31 October 1994, 39.
32. Denise M. Topolnicki, "Stereotypes Dead Wrong on Immigrants, Stats Say," *Denver Post*, 12 February 1995, 29(A).
33. "Immigrants Poor, but Get Rich Quickly," *Denver Post*, 23 September 1993, 11(A).
34. Julian L. Simon, *The Economic Consequences of Immigration* (Cambridge, Mass.: Basil Blackwell, 1989), 343-47.
35. "The Immigrants: How They're Helping to Revitalize the U.S. Economy," *Business Week*, 13 July 1992, 114.
36. See Rebecca L. Clark and Jeffrey S. Passel, "Studies Are Deceptive," *New York Times*, 3 September 1993, 23(A).
37. Howard Adelman, "Immigration to Canada and the United States," 28.
38. "The Immigrants: How They're Helping to Revitalize the U.S. Economy," 122.
39. Quoted from Vernon M. Briggs Jr., *Mass Immigration and the National Interest* (Armonk, N.Y.: M. E. Sharpe, 1992), 229-30.
40. Borjas, *Friends or Strangers?* 219.
41. Simon, *The Economic Consequences of Immigration*, 343-44.
42. "The Immigrants: How They're Helping to Revitalize the U.S. Economy," 118.
43. See "The Immigrants: How They're Helping to Revitalize the U.S. Economy," which tells about how Hispanic immigrants have revived a dying neighborhood in south Dallas, Texas. "There is a whole multiplier effect throughout the community," reports one analyst, 118.
44. See Portes and Rumbaut, *Immigrant America*, 238 (see also 234-39).
45. Ibid., 223. The authors report that, based on the 1980 Census, 55 percent of undocumented immigrants were born in Mexico. The remainder came from ninety-three different countries.
46. Information from "Servitude in New York," the *New York Times*, reprinted the *International Herald Tribune*, 10 June 1993, 4.
47. See the letter to the editor, "Smuggling Hysteria," by Arthur C. Helton (director of the Refugee Project of the Lawyers Committee for Human Rights), in the *New York Times*, 1 September 1993, 10(A).
48. Marilyn Hoskin, *New Immigrants and Democratic Society* (New York: Praeger, 1991), 112-18 (see also 141-49). In this work, Hoskin compared public attitudes toward immigrants in the United States, Great Britain, Germany, and Canada.

49. Richard Lamm, "Why We Closed Our Borders: A Speech to the United Nations General Assembly by the Deputy Secretary of State, July 4, 2000," *Megatraumas: America at the Year 2000* (Boston: Houghton Mifflin, 1985), 73.
50. Quoted from Takaki, "Reflections on Racial Patterns in America," 29.
51. Higham, *Strangers in the Land*, 9-11, 131-75.
52. See Peter Brimelow, *Alien Nation* (New York: Random House, 1995), 115-33, 208.
53. Lamm, "Why We Closed Our Borders," 73.
54. Higham, *Strangers in the Land*, 3-9, 175-93.
55. Roy Beck, "The Ordeal of Immigration in Wausau," *The Atlantic Monthly*, April 1994, 86.
56. Ibid., 94, 97.
57. Portes and Rumbaut, *Immigrant America*, 168-69.
58. John Higham, *Send Them to Me: Immigrants in Urban America* (Baltimore: Johns Hopkins University Press, 1984), 233-37.
59. Bach, *Changing Relations*.
60. Ibid., 48.
61. Ibid., 21.
62. Ibid.

3. THE ETHICS OF HOSPITALITY IN A WORLD OF NATION-STATES

1. Quoted in Renny Golden and Michael McConnell, *Sanctuary: The New Underground Railroad* (Maryknoll, N.Y.: Orbis, 1986), 38-39.
2. See my article, which develops this point more fully: "The Sanctuary Movement and U.S. Refugee Policy: A Paradigm for Christian Public Ethics," *Theology and Public Policy* 6, no. 2 (winter 1994): 4-18.
3. See the work of Beverly Harrison, for example, *Making Connections: Essays in Feminist Social Ethics*, ed. Carol S. Robb (Boston: Beacon Press, 1985), 75, 243-49.
4. Peter H. Schuck, "The Transformation of Immigration Law," *Columbia Law Review* 84 (January 1984): 81 (see also 50).
5. Chung Hyun Kyung, *Struggle to Be the Sun Again* (Maryknoll, N.Y.: Orbis Books, 1990), 111.
6. Patrick D. Miller Jr., "Israel As Host to Strangers," *Today's Immigrants and Refugees: A Christian Understanding* (United States Catholic Conference, 1988), 9. I am very indebted to Miller's outstanding essay for much of my interpretation in this section.
7. Ibid., 2.
8. Ibid., 3.
9. Ibid., 12.
10. Ibid., 11.
11. Ibid.
12. Ibid., 13.
13. Ibid., 15.
14. See the Presbyterian Church study of Mexican migration (1981) in which the movement from regarding the migrant as stranger to regarding her as neighbor is offered as the theological basis for the churches' response. See *Church and Society*, May/June 1982, 42-44.
15. Hauerwas has written prolifically and provocatively about the narrative character of Christian ethics. One of the clearest and most comprehensive interpretations is *The Peaceable Kingdom* (Notre Dame: University of Notre Dame, 1983).
16. Ellis Cose, *A Nation of Strangers: Prejudice, Politics, and the Populating of America* (New York: William Morrow and Co., 1992); Mark Gibney, *Strangers or Friends: Principles for a New Alien Admission Policy* (Westport, Conn.: Greenwood Press, 1986); Andre Jacques, *The Stranger Within Your Gates: Uprooted People in the World Today* (New York: World Council of Churches, 1986); Vincent N. Parrillo, *Strangers to These Shores: Race and Ethnic Relations in the United States,* 2nd ed. (New York: John Wiley and Sons, 1985).
17. Ronald Takaki, *A Different Mirror: A History of Multicultural America* (Boston: Little, Brown & Co., 1993), 24.
18. H. Richard Niebuhr, *The Purpose of the Church and Its Ministry* (New York: Harper & Row, 1956), 35.

19. Octavio Paz, *The Labyrinth of Solitude* (New York: Grove Press, 1961), 23-24.
20. Several books provide arresting insights about the importance of the stranger in the moral life, in the public arena, and in the witness of the Christian church. See Stanley Hauerwas, *The Peaceable Kingdom*; Thomas Ogletree, *Hospitality to the Stranger: Dimensions of Moral Understanding* (Minneapolis: Fortress Press, 1983); Parker Palmer, *The Company of Strangers* (New York: Crossroad, 1981).
21. Quoted in Peter Brimelow's *Alien Nation: Common Sense About America's Immigration Disaster* (New York: Random House, 1995), 270.
22. See Theodore Walker, *Empower the People: Social Ethics for the African American Church* (Maryknoll, N.Y.: Orbis Books, 1991), esp. 34-35.
23. Brimelow, *Alien Nation* 10, 264.
24. Thomas W. Ogletree, *The Use of the Bible in Christian Ethics* (Minneapolis: Fortress Press, 1983). See especially 152-206.
25. Ibid., 159.
26. Ibid., 156.
27. Ibid., 129.
28. Ibid., 158.
29. Ibid., 191.
30. Joseph H. Carens, "Aliens and Citizens: The Case for Open Borders," *The Review of Politics* 49 (spring 1987): 251.
31. Joseph H. Carens, "States and Refugees: A Normative Analysis," in *Refugee Policy: Canada and the United States* (Toronto: York Lanes Press, 1991), 23.
32. Carens, "Aliens and Citizens: The Case for Open Borders."
33. Ibid., 258.
34. Michael Walzer, *Spheres of Justice* (New York: Basic Books, 1983), 62.
35. Ibid., 51.
36. Kenneth Boulding, "Address," Geneva Conference on Church and Society, World Council of Churches, 1966, address no. 47, p. 1 (mimeographed).
37. H. Richard Niebuhr, *Radical Monotheism and Western Culture* (New York: Harper & Row, 1960), 64-77.
38. For example, see Bennett, *Foreign Policy As a Problem for Christian Ethics* (New York: Charles Scribner's Sons, 1966), 24.

4. NEGOTIATING COMMUNITY: THE QUEST FOR A JUST AND HUMANE MIGRATION POLICY

1. This contains the single most important articulation of human rights: the Universal Declaration of Human Rights (adopted by the General Assembly of the United Nations in 1948). It also includes the International Human Rights Covenants, formally adopted in 1976.
2. Jack Donnelly, *Universal Human Rights in Theory and Practice* (Ithaca, N.Y.: Cornell University Press, 1989), 5 (see also chap. 13).
3. See the important "International Convention on the Protection of the Rights of All Migrant Workers and Members of Their Families," adopted by the General Assembly of the United Nations and opened for signature, 2 May 1991.
4. For example, see David Hollenbach's excellent study of human rights in the context of recent Roman Catholic moral tradition, *Claims in Conflict* (New York: Paulist Press, 1979), 91-92.
5. Corbett, *The Sanctuary Church* (Pendle Hill pamphlet 270, 1986).
6. Max Stackhouse, *Creeds, Society, and Human Rights: A Study in Three Cultures* (Grand Rapids, Mich.: Eerdmans, 1984), 33.
7. Ibid., 104-5.
8. Ibid., 105.
9. Ibid., 128, note 63.
10. See the interpretation of the right of movement from an egalitarian ethical perspective in Alan Dowty, *The Contemporary Assault on Freedom of Movement* (New Haven, Conn.: Yale University Press, 1987).

11. See Joseph L. Allen, *Love and Conflict: A Covenant Model of Christian Ethics* (Nashville: Abingdon Press, 1984), 136-37.
12. Ibid., 265.
13. See Carens's discussion of the implications of John Rawls's theory of justice for migration policy, "Aliens and Citizens," 258-61. Carens argues that Rawls's theory leads to moral justification for open borders, qualified only by the public order principle. Only those restrictions on liberty essential to maintain public order would be justified.
14. Pontifical Council "Cor Unum" and the Pontifical Council for the Pastoral Care of Migrants and Itinerant People, "Refugees: A Challenge to Solidarity," 1992, 18.
15. Drew Christiansen, S.J., "Sacrament of Unity: Ethical Issues in Pastoral Care of Migrants and Refugees," *Today's Immigrants and Refugees: A Christian Understanding* (Office of Pastoral Care of Migrants and Refugees of the National Conference of Catholic Bishops, 1988), 85.
16. Ibid., 86.
17. Ibid., 89.
18. Ibid., 90.
19. Michael A. Evans, S.J., "An Analysis of U.N. Refugee Policy in Light of Roman Catholic Social Teaching and the Phenomena of Creating Refugees" (Ph.D. diss., Graduate Theological Union, 1991).
20. National Conference of Catholic Bishops, "Policy Statement on Employer Sanctions," United States Catholic Conference, November 1988.
21. Evans, 415.
22. Committee for Community Relations of the Catholic Bishops' Conference of England and Wales, "Towards a Statement of the Rights of Migrants and Settlers," January 1988.
23. Christiansen, "Sacrament of Unity," 91.
24. Ibid.
25. Christiansen, citing the Sacred Congregation for Bishops, *Instruction on the Pastoral Care of People Who Migrate*, 1969, in "Sacrament of Unity," 93.
26. See the argument of the moral philosopher James W. Nickel, "Human Rights and the Rights of Aliens," in *The Border That Joins: Mexican Migrants and U.S. Responsibility*, eds. Peter G. Brown and Henry Shue (Totowa, N.J.: Rowman and Littlefield, 1983), 31-43.
27. Pontifical Council for the Pastoral Care of Migrant and Itinerant Peoples, "Letter to Episcopal Conferences on the Church and People on the Move," 1978, quoted in Christiansen, "Sacrament of Unity," 93.
28. Christiansen, "Sacrament of Unity," 106 (see also 92-93).
29. National Conference of Catholic Bishops, "Policy Statement on Employer Sanctions."
30. Catholic Charities USA, "In Celebration of Our Nation's Ethnic and Racial Diversity," 25-26 September 1993.
31. Peter Schuck's wonderful word for human contact, more "real" than divisions between nations. "The Transformation of Immigration Law," *Columbia Law Review* 84 (January 1984): 81.
32. See Philip Wogaman's insightful interpretation of Christian ethics in which the notion of presumption is central. This is a way to affirm the normative force of Christian perspectives while acknowledging the ambiguities and complexities in formulating specific public policies, *A Christian Method of Moral Judgment*, 2nd ed. (Louisville: Westminster/John Knox, 1989).
33. See Jim Corbett, *The Sanctuary Church*.
34. "Mexican Migration to the United States: Challenge to Christian Witness and National Policy," *Church and Society* (May/June 1982), 45.
35. See Ogletree's discussion of Paul's insight about negotiating new forms of community that value the diversity of members, in chapter 3.
36. Peter Brimelow, *Alien Nation: Common Sense About America's Immigration Disaster* (New York: Random House, 1995), 1-22, 58-91, 202-21.
37. Animesh Ghosal and Thomas M. Crowley, "Refugees and Immigrants: A Human Rights Dilemma," in *Human Rights in the World Community*, eds. Richard Pierre Claude and Burns H. Weston (Philadelphia: University of Pennsylvania Press, 1989), 95-102.

5. HOSPITALITY FOR REFUGEES: PROPOSALS FOR U.S. REFUGEE POLICY

1. *Refugee Reports* 16, no. 3 (31 March 1995): 6; also *Refugee Reports* 16, no. 4 (29 April 1995): 4-5.
2. Aristide R. Zolberg, Astri Suhrke, and Sergio Aguayo, *Escape from Violence: Conflict and the Refugee Crisis in the Developing World* (New York: Oxford University Press, 1989), 30.
3. Francis M. Deng, *Protecting the Dispossessed: A Challenge for the International Community* (Washington, D.C.: The Brookings Institution, 1993), 135.
4. Elizabeth G. Ferris, *Beyond Borders: Refugees, Migrants and Human Rights in the Post–Cold War Era* (Geneva: WCC Publications, 1993), 288.
5. *Refugee Reports* 16, no. 8 (25 August 1995): 3.
6. *Refugee Reports* 16, no. 3 (31 March 1995): 2.
7. Zolberg, Suhrke, and Aguayo, *Escape from Violence,* 270.
8. Norman Zucker and Naomi Flink Zucker, *The Guarded Gate: Refugee Law and Policy* (San Diego: Harcourt Brace Jovanovich, 1987), 272.
9. Mark Gibney, "A Critique of Norway's Refugee/Asylum Policy and Proposals for Change," (Norwegian Institute of Human Rights, 1990), 22.
10. Elizabeth Hull, *Without Justice for All* (Westport, Conn.: Greenwood Press, 1985), 145.
11. Gibney, "A Critique of Norway's Refugee/Asylum Policy and Proposals for Change," 22.
12. Ibid., 25.
13. Zolberg et al., *Escape from Violence,* 275.
14. Animesh Ghosal and Thomas M. Crowley, "Refugees and Immigrants: A Human Rights Dilemma," in *Human Rights in the World Community,* eds. Richard Pierre Claude and Burns H. Weston (Philadelphia: University of Pennsylvania Press, 1989), 95-102.
15. Alan Dowty, *Closed Borders: The Contemporary Assault on Freedom of Movement* (New Haven, Conn.: Yale University Press, 1987), 235-38.
16. Gil Loescher, *Beyond Charity: International Cooperation and the Global Refugee Crisis* (New York: Oxford University Press, 1993), 163.
17. See *Refugee Reports* 16, no. 8 (25 August 1995): 2. An immigration bill currently being considered by the U.S. House of Representatives establishes "humanitarian admissions" as a new category that sets the ceiling at 10,000 per year.
18. See Ralston Deffenbaugh, "Resettlement as Protection: New Directions in the U.S. Refugee Program," *Refugee Reports* 16, no. 4 (29 April 1994): 13.
19. Ibid., 15.
20. See the discussion of this question in *Refugee Reports* 16, no. 3 (31 March 1995): 1-11.
21. Ibid., 4.
22. Ibid. This is the position taken by the Lawyers Committee for Human Rights.
23. Deffenbaugh, "Resettlement as Protection," 10.
24. Ibid., 13.
25. *Refugee Reports* 16, no. 3 (31 March 1995): 4.
26. Zucker and Zucker, *The Guarded Gate,* 270-78.
27. Deffenbaugh, "Resettlement as Protection," 15.
28. Ibid. Deffenbaugh's proposals regarding private resettlement deserve a great deal more attention in considerations of refugee policy and Christian responsibility.
29. *Refugee Reports* 15, no. 7 (26 July 1994): 6.
30. Howard Adelman, "Immigration to Canada and the United States," *The Oxford International Review* 3, no. 1 (winter 1991): 28.
31. *Refugee Reports* 15, no. 7 (27 October 1994): 1-8, esp. 6-7. This particular issue of *Refugee Reports* focuses on issues of public assistance and resettlement and contains illuminating reflections by people who are directly involved in assisting refugees.
32. National Immigration, Refugee and Citizenship Forum, 6.
33. See discussion in *Refugee Reports* 16, no. 4 (29 April 1995): 5.
34. Ibid., 4.
35. National Immigration, Refugee and Citizenship Forum, 5.
36. Massimino represents the Lawyers Committee for Human Rights. See *Refugee Reports* 16, no. 3 (31 March 1995): 6.

37. See Keeley's testimony to hearings of the Senate Judicial Committee, as reported in *Refugee Reports* 16, no. 3 (31 March 1995): 2-3.
38. Loescher, *Beyond Charity*, 173.
39. Ibid.
40. Ibid., 187.
41. Ferris, *Beyond Borders*, 276.
42. *Migration World* 23, nos. 1/2 (1995): 5.

6. RE-CREATING AMERICA: PROPOSALS FOR U.S. IMMIGRATION POLICY

1. The Sacred Congregation of the Bishops of the Roman Catholic Church articulated this principle in 1969 in its *Instruction on the Pastoral Care of People Who Migrate:* "Public authorities unjustly deny the rights of human persons if they block or impede emigration or immigration except where grave requirements of the common good, considered objectively, demand it."
2. See the discussion by José Míguez Bonino in *Toward a Christian Political Ethics* (Philadelphia: Fortress Press, 1983), 79-86.
3. Carlos Fuentes, "Anti-Mexican Phobia Has Name, Color: It Is Racism," *Casa de Proyecto Libertad*, spring 1994, 5. [Essay is reprinted from the *New York Times*, 1993, and the *Brownsville Herald*, 13 March 1994.]
4. The United Presbyterian Church in the U.S.A. (193rd General Assembly) and Presbyterian Church in the United States (121st General Assembly), "Mexican Migration to the United States: Challenge to Christian Witness and National Policy," 1981.
5. Arnoldo Garcia, "They Shoot Mexicans, Don't They?" *Network News* 6 (January-February 1994): 2.
6. Fuentes, "Anti-Mexican Phobia Has Name, Color," 5.
7. Debbie Nathan, "Operation Blockade," and Suzan Kern, "Who Supports the Border Blockade?" in *Network News* 6 (January-February 1994): 3, 4, 11.
8. The gathering was identified as a "Border Strategy Meeting," *Network News* 6 (January-February 1994): 5.
9. See Gerald Lopez, "Undocumented Mexican Migration: In Search of Just Immigration Law and Policy," *UCLA Law Review* 28 (April 1981): 617.
10. See U.S. Commission on Immigrant Reform, *U.S. Immigration Policy: Restoring Credibility* (an interim report to Congress), 8-9.
11. Catholic Charities USA, "Legislative Program for the 101st Congress," 1989.
12. Drew Christiansen, S.J., "Sacrament of Unity: Ethical Issues in Pastoral Care of Migrants and Refugees," *Today's Immigrants and Refugees: A Christian Understanding* (Office of Pastoral Care of Migrants and Refugees of the National Conference of Catholic Bishops, 1988), 95.
13. James W. Nickel, "Human Rights and the Rights of Aliens," in *The Border That Joins: Mexican Migrants and U.S. Responsibility*, eds. Peter G. Brown and Henry Shue (Totowa, N.J.: Rowman and Littlefield, 1983), 31-43.
14. Michael Walzer, *Spheres of Justice* (New York: Basic Books, 1983), 56-61.
15. Peter T. Kilborn, "Law Fails to Stem Abuse of Migrants, U.S. Panel Reports," *New York Times*, 22 October 1992, 1(A), 10(A), reporting on recommendations of the Commission on Agricultural Workers, Henry J. Voss, chairman.
16. See the statement of the National Conference of Catholic Bishops, November, 1988; and similar policy positions by the General Assembly of the Presbyterian Church USA (1990); the Council of Bishops, The United Methodist Church; and the American Friends Service Committee (working paper, November, 1988).
17. United States Catholic Conference, "Policy Statement on Employer Sanctions."
18. U.S. Commission on Immigration Reform (interim report), 12-21.
19. National Immigration, Refugee and Citizenship Forum, "U.S. Immigration Policy: Rational, Regulated, and Beneficial," 1 July 1993, 8.
20. Ibid.
21. "Mexican Migration to the United States: Challenge to Christian Witness and National Policy" (1981).

22. "Religious Leaders Urge Immigrant Rights in California," Catholic News Service (Friday, 8 October 1993).
23. Nickel, "Human Rights and the Rights of Aliens," 42 (see also 31-43).
24. Christiansen, "Sacrament of Unity," 94.
25. Alejandro Portes and Ruben G. Rumbaut, *Immigrant America: A Portrait* (Berkeley: University of California Press, 1990), 202.
26. See Christiansen, "Sacrament of Unity," 93.
27. Robert Bach, *Changing Relations: Newcomers and Established Residents in U.S. Communities* (New York: Ford Foundation, 1993); see also the volume of essays that provided the basis for the report, *Structuring Diversity: Ethnographic Perspectives on the New Immigration*, ed. Louise Lamphere (Chicago: University of Chicago Press, 1992).
28. Bach, *Changing Relations*, 55.
29. Saskia Sassen, "America's Immigration 'Problem,' " *World Policy Journal* 6 (fall 1989): 811-32.

BIBLIOGRAPHY

Allen, Joseph L. *Love and Conflict: A Covenant Model of Christian Ethics*. Nashville: Abingdon Press, 1984.

Arendt, Hannah. *The Origins of Totalitarianism*. New ed. San Diego: Harcourt Brace and Co., 1973.

Bach, Robert. *Changing Relations: Newcomers and Established Residents in U.S. Communities*. New York: Report to the Ford Foundation by the National Board of the Changing Relations Project, 1993.

Bau, Ignatius. *This Ground is Holy: Christian Sanctuary and Central American Refugees*. New York: Paulist Press, 1985.

Borjas, George J. *Friends or Strangers?* New York: Basic Books, 1990.

Briggs, Vernon M., Jr. *Mass Immigration and the National Interest*. Armonk, N.Y.: M. E. Sharpe, 1992.

Brimelow, Peter. *Alien Nation*. New York: Random House, 1995.

Brown, Peter G., and Henry Shue, eds. *The Border That Joins: Mexican Migrants and U.S. Responsibility*. Totowa, N.J.: Rowman and Littlefield, 1983.

Brown, Peter G., and Henry Shue, eds. *Boundaries: National Autonomy and Its Limits*. Totowa, N.J.: Rowman and Littlefield, 1981.

Cafferty, Pastora San Juan, Barry R. Chiswick, Andrew M. Greeley, and Teresa A. Sullivan. *The Dilemma of American Immigration: Beyond the Golden Door*. New Brunswick, N.J.: Transaction Publishers, 1983.

Carens, Joseph H. "Aliens and Citizens: The Case for Open Borders." *The Review of Politics* 49 (spring 1987): 251-73.

―――. "States and Refugees: A Normative Analysis." In *Refugee Policy: Canada and the United States*, edited by Howard Adelman, 18-27. Toronto: York Lanes Press, 1991.

Claude, Richard Pierre, and Burns H. Weston, eds. *Human Rights in the World Community*. Philadelphia: University of Pennsylvania Press, 1989.

Christiansen, Drew, S.J. "Sacrament of Unity: Ethical Issues in Pastoral Care of Migrants and Refugees," 81-114. In *Today Immigrants and Refugees: A Christian Understanding*. Office of Pastoral Care of Migrants and Refugees of the National Conference of Catholic Bishops, 1988.

Chung Hyun Kyung, *Struggle to Be the Sun Again*. Maryknoll, N.Y.: Orbis Books, 1990.

Cogswell, James A. *No Place Left Called Home*. New York: Friendship Press, 1983.

Corbett, Jim. *The Sanctuary Church*. Wallingford, Pa.: Pendle Hill Pamphlet #270, 1986.

Crittenden, Ann. *Sanctuary: A Story of American Conscience and the Population of America*. New York: William Morrow and Co., 1992.

Cose, Ellis. *A Nation of Strangers: Prejudice, Politics and the Population of America.* New York: William Morrow and Co., 1992.

Deffenbaugh, Ralston. "Resettlement As Protection: New Directions in the U.S. Refugee Program." *Refugee Reports* 16, no. 4 (29 April 1994): 10-15.

Deng, Francis. *Protecting the Dispossessed: A Challenge for the International Community.* Washington, D.C.: The Brookings Institution, 1993.

Donnelly, Jack. *Universal Human Rights in Theory and Practice.* Ithaca, N.Y.: Cornell University Press, 1989.

Dowty, Alan. *The Contemporary Assault on Freedom of Movement.* New Haven: Yale University Press, 1987.

Ethics, Migration, and Global Stewardship (special issue). *International Migration Review* 30 (spring 1996), published by the Center for Migration Studies, Staten Island, New York.

Evans, Michael A., S.J. "An Analysis of U.N. Refugee Policy in Light of Roman Catholic Social Teaching and the Phenomena of Creating Refugees." Ph.D. dissertation, Graduate Theological Union, 1991.

Ferris, Elizabeth G. *Beyond Borders: Refugees, Migrants and Human Rights in the Post Cold War Era.* Geneva: WCC Publications, 1993.

Gibney, Mark. *A Critique of Norway's Refugee/Asylum Policy and Proposals for Change.* Norwegian Institute of Human Rights, 1990.

———. *Strangers or Friends: Principles for a New Alien Admission Policy.* Westport, Conn.: Greenwood Press, 1986.

Gibney, Mark, ed. *Open Borders? Closed Societies? The Ethical and Political Issues.* Westport, Conn.: Greenwood Press, 1988.

Golden, Renny, and Michael McConnell. *Sanctuary: The New Underground Railroad.* Maryknoll, N.Y.: Orbis, 1986.

Harding, Vincent. *Hope and History.* Maryknoll, N.Y.: Orbis Books, 1990.

———. *There Is A River: The Black Struggle for Freedom in America.* New York: Harcourt Brace Jovanovich, 1981.

Harrell-Bond, Barbara E. *Imposing Aid: Emergency Assistance to Refugees.* New York: Oxford University Press, 1986.

Harrison, Beverly. *Making the Connections: Essays in Feminist Social Ethics.* Edited by Carol S. Robb. Boston: Beacon Press, 1985.

———. *Our Right to Choose.* Boston: Beacon Press, 1983.

Hauerwas, Stanley. *A Community of Character.* Notre Dame: University of Notre Dame Press, 1981.

———. *The Peaceable Kingdom.* Notre Dame: University of Notre Dame Press, 1983.

Higham, John. *Send Them to Me: Immigrants in Urban America.* Baltimore: Johns Hopkins University Press, 1984.

———. *Strangers in the Land: Patterns of American Nativism, 1860–1925.* 2nd ed. New Brunswick: Rutgers University Press, 1988.

Hollenbach, David. *Claims in Conflict.* New York: Paulist Press, 1979.

Hoskin, Marilyn. *New Immigrants and Democratic Society.* New York: Praeger, 1991.

Hull, Elizabeth. *Without Justice for All.* Westport, Conn.: Greenwood Press, 1985.

Isasi-Díaz, Ada María. *En La Lucha: In the Struggle.* Minneapolis: Fortress Press, 1993.

Jacques, Andre. *The Stranger Within Your Gates: Uprooted People in the World Today.* New York: World Council of Churches, 1986.

Jones, Maldwyn Allen. *American Immigration.* 2nd ed. Chicago: University of Chicago Press, 1992.

Keely, Charles. *Global Refugee Policy: The Case for a Development-Oriented Strategy.* New York: Population Council, 1981.

King, Martin Luther, Jr. *The Essential Writings and Speeches of Martin Luther King, Jr.* Edited by James M. Washington. New York: HarperCollins, 1991.

Kitagawa, Joseph, ed. *American Refugee Policy.* San Francisco: Winston Press, 1984.

Lamm, Richard. *The Immigration Time Bomb.* New York: E. P. Dutton, 1985.

———. *Megatraumas: America at the Year 2000.* Boston: Houghton Mifflin, 1985.

Lamphere, Louise, ed. *Structuring Diversity: Ethnographic Perspectives on the New Immigration*. Chicago: University of Chicago Press, 1992.
Loescher, Gil. *Beyond Charity: International Cooperation and the Global Refugee Crisis*. New York: Oxford University Press, 1993.
Loescher, Gil, ed. *Refugees and the Asylum Dilemma in the West*. University Park: Pennsylvania State University Press, 1992.
Loescher, Gil, and John Scanlon. *Calculated Kindness: Refugees and Amerifa's Half-Open Door, 1945 to the Present*. New York: The Free Press, 1986.
Lopez, Gerald. "Undocumented Mexican Migration: In Search of Just Immigration Law and Policy." *UCLA Law Review* 28 (April 1981): 615-714.
MacEoin, Gary, ed. *Sanctuary: A Resource Guide for Understanding and participating in the Central American Refugees' Struggle*. San Francisco: Harper & Row, 1985.
Marrus, Michael. *The Unwanted: European Refugees in the Twentieth Century*. New York: Oxford University Press, 1985.
Meissner, Doris M., Robert D. Hormats, Antonio Garrigues Walker, and Shijuro Ogata. *International Migration Challenges in a New Era*. New York: The Trilateral Commission, 1993.
Míguez Bonino, José. *Toward a Christian Political Ethics*. Philadelphia: Fortress Press, 1983.
Miller, Patrick D., Jr. "Israel As Host to Strangers." In *Today's Immigrants and Refugees: A Christian Understanding*, 1-19. United States Catholic Conference, 1988.
Nichols, J. Bruce, and Gil Loescher, eds. *The Moral Nation: Humanitarianism and U.S. Foreign Policy Today*. Notre Dame: University of Notre Dame Press, 1989.
Nichols, J. Bruce. *The Uneasy Alliance: Religion, Refugee Work and U.S. Foreign Policy*. New York: Oxford University Press, 1988.
Nickel, James W. "Human Rights and the Rights of Aliens," 31-43. In *The Border That Joins: Mexican Migrants and U.S. Responsibility*, edited by Peter G. Brown and Henry Shue. Totowa, N.J.: Rowman and Littlefield, 1983.
Niebuhr, H. Richard. *The Purpose of the Church and Its Ministry*. New York; Harper and Row, 1956.
———. *Radical Monotheism and Western Culture*. New York: Harper and Row, 1960.
Ogletree, Thomas W. *Hospitality to the Stranger: Dimensions of Moral Understanding*. Minneapolis: Fortress Press, 1985.
———. *The Use of the Bible in Christian Ethics*. Minneapolis: Fortress Press, 1983.
Palmer, Parker. *The Company of Strangers*. New York: Crossroad, 1981.
Paz, Octavio. *The Labyrinth of Solitude*. New York: Grove Press, 1961.
Pontifical Council for the Pastoral Care of Migrants and Itinerant People. "Refugees: A Challenge to Solidarity." Vatican City, 1992.
Portes, Alejandro, and Robert L. Bach. *Latin Journey: Cuban and Mexican Immigrants in the United States*. Berkeley: University of California Press, 1985.
Portes, Alejandro, and Ruben G. Rumbaut. *Immigrant America: A Portrait*. Berkeley: University of California Press, 1990.
Reimers, David M. *Still the Golden Door: The Third World Comes to America*. 2nd ed. New York: Columbia University Press, 1992.
Schuck, Peter. "The Emerging Political Consensus on Immigration Law," *Georgetown Immigration Law Journal* 5, no. 1 (1991): 1-33.
———. "The Transformation of Immigration Law." *Columbia Law Review* 84 (January 1984): 1-90.
Shacknove, Andrew E. "Who Is a Refugee?" *Ethics* 95 (January 1985): 274-84.
Simon, Julian L. *The Economic Consequences of Immigration*. Oxford: Basil Blackwell, 1989.
Stackhouse, Max. *Creeds, Society and Human Rights: A Study in Three Cultures*. Grand Rapids, Mich.: Eerdmans, 1984.
———. *Public Theology and Political Economy*. Grand Rapids, Mich.: Eerdmans, 1987.
Takaki, Ronald, ed. *From Different Shores*. New York: Oxford University Press, 1994.

Thomas, Maria H., ed. *Sanctuary: Challenge to the Churches.* Washington, D.C.: Institute on Religion and Democracy, 1986.

Today's Immigrants and Refugees: A Christian Understanding. Office of Pastoral Care of Migrants and Refugees of the National Conference of Catholic Bishops, 1988.

United Methodist Church Committee on Relief/General Board of Global Ministries and General Board of Church and Society, "To Love the Sojourner: A United Methodist Response to the United States Immigration Reform and Control Act of 1986," 1988.

United Presbyterian Church in the USA (193rd General Assembly) and Presbyterian Church in the United States (121st General Assembly), "Mexican Migration to the United States: Challenge to Christian Witness and National Policy," 1981.

United States Commission on Immigrant Reform, *U.S. Immigration Policy: Restoring Credibility.* An interim report to Congress, 1994.

Walker, Theodore. *Empower the People: Social Ethics for the African American Church.* Maryknoll, N.Y.: Orbis Books, 1991.

Walzer, Michael. *Spheres of Justice.* New York: Basic Books, 1983.

Wilbanks, Dana W. "The Moral Debate Between Humanitarianism and National Interest About U.S. Refugee Policy: Theological Perspective." *Migration World Magazine* 21, no. 5 (1993): 15-18.

———. "The Sanctuary Movement and U.S. Refugee Policy: A Paradigm for Christian Public Ethics." *Theology and Public Policy* 6, no. 2 (winter 1994): 4-18.

Wogaman, Philip. *A Christian Method of Moral Judgment.* 2nd ed. Louisville: Westminster/John Knox Press, 1989.

World Council of Churches. *In a Strange Land.* Geneva: World Council of Churches, 1961.

World Council of Churches. *Refugees Today and Tomorrow.* Report and recommendations of consultation in Miami, Florida, September 15-19, 1986.

Yarnold, Barbara. *Refugees Without Refuge: Formation and Failed Implementation of U.S. Political Asylum Policy in the 1980s.* Washington, D.C.: University Press of America, 1990.

Zolberg, Aristide R., Astri Suhrke, and Sergio Aguayo. *Escape from Violence: Conflict and the Refugee Crisis in the Developing World.* New York: Oxford University Press, 1989.

Zucker, Norman, and Naomi Flink. *The Guarded Gate: The Reality of American Refugee Policy.* San Diego: Harcourt Brace Jovanovich, 1987.

INDEX

SCRIPTURE INDEX